History: What and Why?

History: What and Why? is a highly accessible introductory survey of historians' views about the nature and purpose of their subject providing historical perspective and a clear guide to contemporary debates. After a discussion of the traditional model of history as an account of the past 'as it was', it assesses important challenges to orthodox views, and examines the impact of Marxism, feminism, and post-colonialism. *History: What and Why?* proposes a positive role for historical study in the postmodern era.

This second edition has been updated to reflect the continuing, and still increasing, debate surrounding these issues. In particular it discusses:

- Historians' fear of postmodernism
- Holocaust denial and the Irving/Lipstadt libel trial
- The future of the past in the light of postmodern challenges.

Beverley Southgate is Reader Emeritus in the History of Ideas at the University of Hertfordshire. He is author of *Why bother with History?* (Longman, 2000).

History: What and Why?

Ancient, modern, and postmodern perspectives

2nd Edition

Beverley Southgate

London and New York

First published 1996
by Routledge
11 New Fetter Lane, London EC4P 4EE

Simultaneously published in the USA and Canada
by Routledge
29 West 35th Street, New York, NY 10001

Reprinted 1997, 1998, 1999

Second edition first published 2001

Routledge is an imprint of the Taylor & Francis Group

Typeset in Times by J&L Composition Ltd, Filey, North Yorkshire
Printed and bound in Great Britain by
TJ International Ltd, Padstow, Cornwall

British Library Cataloguing in Publication Data
A catalogue record for this book is available from the British Library

Library of Congress Cataloging in Publication Data
A catalog record for this book is available from the Library of Congress

ISBN 0–415–25657–7 (hbk)
ISBN 0–415–25658–5 (pbk)

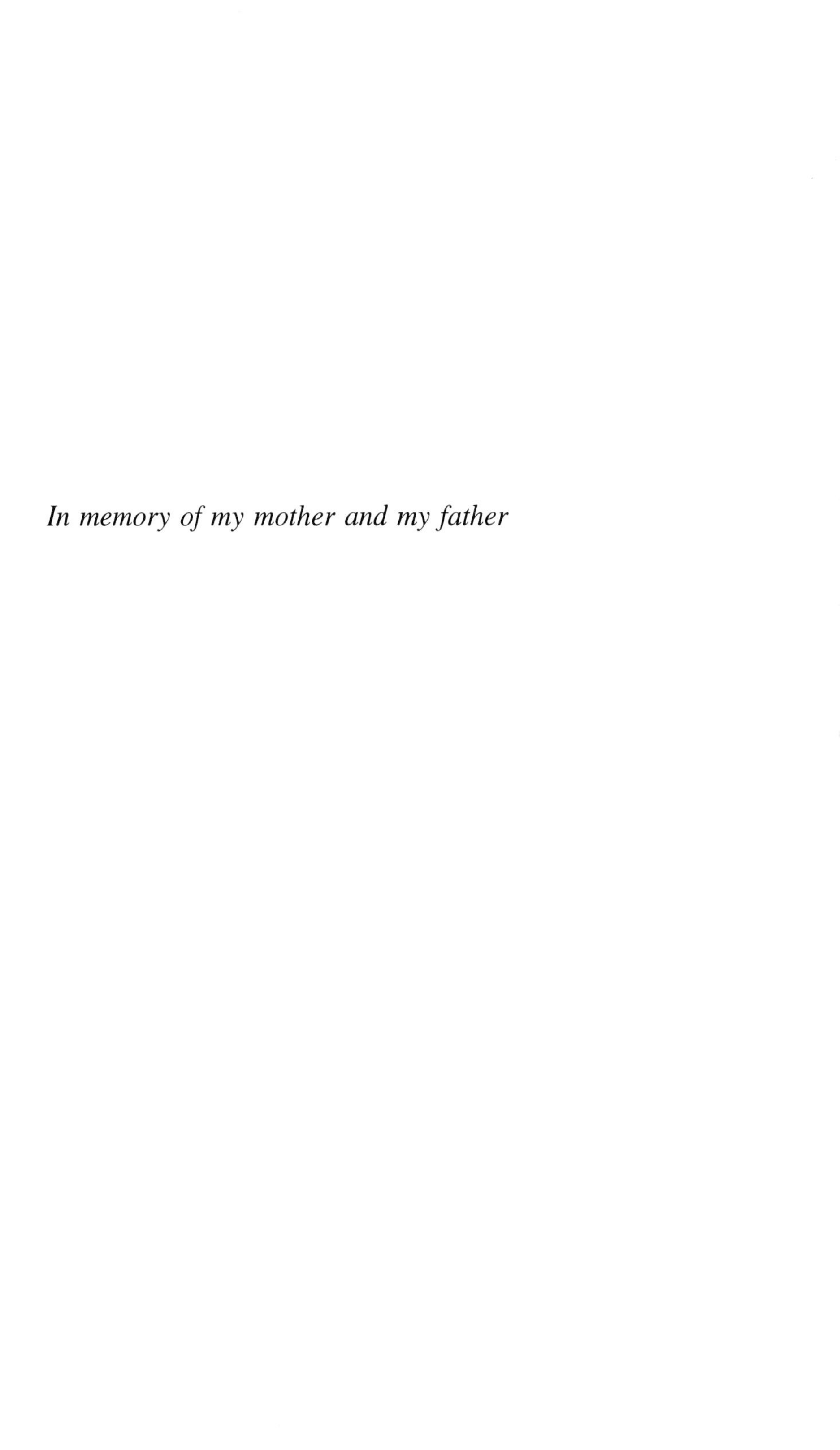

In memory of my mother and my father

Contents

Preface to the Second Edition ix
Preface xi
Acknowledgements xiv

1 Introduction: history, philosophy, and historiography 1

1 Introduction 1
2 Theory and the challenge of postmodernism 4
3 Postmodernism and historical study 8
4 Agenda 10

2 What was history? The past as it was 13

1 Introduction 13
2 History and poetry 15
3 History and science 19
4 Conclusion: the past as it was 27

3 Why history? Past answers 30

1 Introduction 30
2 Interest and entertainment 30
3 Moral teaching 32
4 Religious teaching 42
5 Politics and ideology 50
6 Conclusion: chance, change, and empowerment 57

4 External challenges to the old model: some interdisciplinary perspectives 62

1 Introduction 62

2 Psychology: problems of perception 63

3 Linguistics: problems of language 74

4 Philosophy: the problem of scepticism 82

5 Conclusion 90

5 Internal challenges to the old model: some major forces 91

1 Introduction 91

2 Marxism 93

3 Feminism 99

4 Post-colonialism 107

5 Conclusion 113

6 What and why? The future of history 115

1 The postmodern predicament 115

2 History as hypothesis 131

3 The point as 'empowerment': affecting and effecting the future 140

Postscript 148

1 Pomophobia: the fear of postmodernism 148

2 Holocaust-denial 153

3 The future of the past 158

Notes 160

Further reading 179

Bibliography 184

Index 194

Preface to the second edition

Since this book was originally published in 1996, 'History' seems rarely to have been out of the news, and often in ways that have served to enhance a general awareness of historiographical problems – of problems related to the composition and conveyance of narratives concerning 'the past'. Books, plays, films, television programmes, newspaper articles, have all raised questions about the evident partiality of any claimed knowledge of the past. Previously accepted accounts, of the second world war for example, have been challenged, and revised, adapted or amplified, in the light of new evidence. Historically orientated films have been accused of nationalistic bias, whether American, Australian, Scottish, or Irish. Alternative or 'secret' histories have revealed new aspects of events and personalities that had earlier been inadvertently missed or deliberately concealed. Newly opened museums and memorials have been criticised for misrepresentation through omission, and for demeaning the past. And above all, continuing debates about historical 'revisionism' and Holocaust denial, culminating (though not concluded) in the Irving/Lipstadt libel trial, have highlighted such crucial matters as the validity of oral testimony, the interpretation of documentary evidence, the effects of ideological commitments, and the personal integrity of historians themselves.

All these matters are now more than ever, the subject of open public debate, and together they inevitably provoke further questions about the very nature and purpose of 'History' as a discipline: just what is it that we do when we do history? and, if it's subject to so many problems, why should we bother with it anyway? Those, precisely, were the central concerns of this book when it was originally published.

Any amendments and additions to this second edition have by no means changed that focus, but have simply tried to take some account both of readers' critiques and suggestions, and of intervening events and intellectual developments. Thus, there has been some amplification of the sections on the 'old model' of history (focusing on Geoffrey Elton as exemplar), on language (and particularly Focault), on feminism (with some references to 'masculinity'), on postcolonialism, and on postmodernism (focusing on Hayden White as pioneering spokesman); and, most importantly perhaps, a postscript has been included on 'Pomophobia, Holocaust-denial, and the Future of the Past'. My own changing attitude to postmodernism and history is indicated by the replacement of the '*crisis*' of postmodernism with its '*challenge*'; and finally, the bibliography has been updated, with a list of recommended reading, to facilitate further study and discussion of these enormously important issues.

Beverley Southgate
2001

Preface

What is history? and why study it anyway? These two interrelated questions stand at the centre of a debate that is currently dividing historians into two opposed and sometimes aggressively hostile camps, and it is a debate that has far-reaching implications.

The division within the discipline of history is part of a wider intellectual upheaval which confronts any thoughtful person at the end of the twentieth century. It has to do not only with academic or theoretical questions concerning such matters as the nature of truth, but also with very practical questions of where as humans we are going; and in both respects historical study is deeply involved.

As far as the philosophical issue of truth is concerned, the debate has been running since antiquity, and is essentially between those who see it as an *absolute*, fixed once and for all and independent of any observer, and those for whom it is *relative*, with its meaning, like that of everything else, dependent upon perceptions of individuals at different times and places. For historians claiming to seek and even find the truth about the past, this theoretical debate has obvious importance.

The immediately practical concerns relate to human life itself in the late twentieth century – to politics and education, and to our very future. Here some lines of debate, in relation to historical studies, are equally well drawn. There are those who continue to argue that academic study should be engaged in simply 'for its own sake', while others insist that a multitude of pressing practical questions concerning the future now await our answers and that it is on these that all education should be focused.

The discipline of history is not always perceived as being concerned with philosophy or with the practical or with the future, but it is argued in this book that it should be. So while an attempt is made to understand the significance of an ongoing intellectual revolution in the subject, that theoretical discussion is motivated by very practical concerns.

The central questions to be addressed, then, relate to what history *is* and *why* we do it. Answers, according to the traditional picture of the subject, have seemed straightforward enough. Quite simply, history is a study of the past – a study that results ideally in a representation of that past 'as it was'. And such a study has an obvious point: it is not only inherently enjoyable, but also morally worthwhile in teaching useful lessons. Such history has, again, traditionally been validated by its appropriation of 'scientific' methods: by retaining 'objectivity', it has been claimed, we can ascertain the 'facts', and so report the 'truth'.

The problem now is that that idealised model of the subject has been undermined. The status of even the great intellectual exemplar, science itself, has undergone revision, with challenges directed at its very foundations, and even such seemingly basic concepts as 'facts', 'reality', and 'objectivity', no longer seeming as unproblematic as they sometimes did. In late twentieth-century science it seems that relativism rules.

And similarly in historical study. Some old-fashioned 'ancients' may continue trying to underpin their subject with the rubble of science's outmoded structure, but others have more fashionably conceded defeat, and have surrendered any hope of reaching 'truth'. Charged then with self-indulgently re-inventing the past in the light of nothing more authoritative than their own prejudices, historians roam freely over the past, mingling 'fact' with 'fiction', and notoriously denying 'realities' that others well remember.

So it is time to take stock, and as a contribution to that stock-taking, this book offers an account of what history has been and of what it might become. An introductory chapter deals with the sometimes vexed relationship of history with philosophy. It argues that, since any historical writing presupposes some underlying philosophy, an awareness of that underpinning is essential; and it maintains that historians can no longer afford to avoid confronting the challenges from 'theory' that currently affect all academic disciplines. Chapter 2 outlines the traditional model of history, as a subject that is clearly differentiated from such imaginative pursuits as poetry, and that has often been aligned rather with the sciences in the hope of providing an ideal representation of the past 'as it was'; and in Chapter 3 an examination follows of why that sort of history has been studied, with motivations ranging from pure entertainment to the more didactic purposes of would-be moral, religious, and political leaders.

That old model of history has been undermined from numerous directions, and Chapter 4 indicates some interdisciplinary connections. Challenges are shown to have derived in particular from psychological studies of perception, from linguistic questions concerning the nature and function of language, and from philosophical theories of scepticism. Those challenges themselves have their historical roots in antiquity, and some account is given of their origins and subsequent development. They have been compounded by more recent attacks from within the historical profession itself – attacks directed against the old model by representatives of some major intellectual forces, of which three are considered in Chapter 5: Marxism, feminism, and post-colonialism.

The combined impact of such assaults has no doubt been dramatic, but it is argued in Chapter 6 that reports of history's demise are premature. Admittedly, the status of its subject-matter may have changed: just as in science, the earlier certainties of 'knowledge' have been replaced by something much more tentative and more provisional. However, that is not to say that the new status of history 'as hypothesis' in any way undermines its importance. On the contrary, by encouraging awareness of our own motivations and requirements, it opens up new possibilities in a very practical subject that must affect our future.

This book, then, is not a guide to the 'how?' of history, of how it is researched and written; nor is it intended as a comprehensive history of historiography. Rather, by taking a thematic approach, its intention is to put contemporary debates about the 'what?' and 'why?' of history into a wider chronological and disciplinary perspective. It should therefore appeal to any student who is interested in historical study – whether as a specialist historian, or as one who approaches the subject from related areas such as philosophy, literature, linguistics, psychology, or the sciences. It aims at a critical moment for the discipline: (1) to encourage readers to assess history from an interdisciplinary perspective; (2) to provoke discussion about the nature and purpose of historical study; and (3) to provide some historical context for that discussion.

Acknowledgements

I should like to acknowledge my indebtedness to students over the years who have provoked me to ponder the issues discussed in this book, and I am grateful to my colleagues at the University of Hertfordshire who have furthered such discussions. In particular, for their encouragement and advice, I should like to thank Dr Susan Tegel, Dr Alan Thomson, and Professor Dennis Brown, and, for their unfailingly friendly and efficient service, the librarians at the Watford Campus including especially Neil Allen.

For helpful comments on earlier drafts, I thank John Ibbett and Susannah Southgate; and I am particularly grateful to anonymous Routledge readers who have variously provided provocation, constructive criticism, and encouragement.

The author and publisher wish to thank the copyright holders for permission to reproduce illustrations. Illustrations on pages 37, 47 and 55, British Library shelfmark 9006ccc18, C38i10, 9005g1 respectively, by permission of the British Library; *Absurdistan* on page 53 copyright © BBC; on page 100 Catherine Macaulay's head photo: Albert Hartley, by kind permission of Cheshire County Council.

Chapter 1

Introduction: history, philosophy, and historiography

> If philosophers are not always historians, it were at least to be wished that all historians were philosophers. (Edward Gibbon)[1]

1 INTRODUCTION

'The life which is unexamined is not worth living.'[2] So Plato insists; and it is arguable that 'unexamined history' similarly is not worth doing. In our daily routine, we may succeed in living in a semi-conscious, semi-automated way – getting up in the morning, washing, dressing, having our breakfast, and going to work; and we may, to all appearances, comfortably survive in an un-thinking but socially acceptable state until we die. But that, in Plato's account, is to live like pigs, and not as human beings for whom some self-awareness is required. And similarly with history: we may study the subject, and write about it, without ever questioning what it is that we are doing, or why; and we may be all the happier for declining to confront philosophical challenges that might serve to unsettle our emotional and professional equilibrium. But one starting-point for this book is that such *unexamined* history is equally unsatisfactory – that we need, as historians no less than as human beings, some self-awareness, some understanding of what it is that we are trying to do, and of why we are trying to do it. Otherwise we may end up professionally as Tolstoy's Ivan Ilyich ended up personally – finally, and too late, wondering as he dies what the basis of his life had been.

This, then, implies a need for some injection of 'philosophy' into historical study – some examination of the nature of the subject itself, of its aims and objectives, of its central concepts, and of the validity of claims that might be made by its practitioners. It implies, in other words, some study of historiography – of what it is that historians have thought, and do think, they are doing, and of what we ourselves think that we should be doing.

Such concerns, in our self-reflective age, may appear as unexceptional. Over the last decade there has been a veritable deluge of articles and books on the 'what?' and 'why?' of history. Postmodern theorists have challenged the fundamental assumptions of conventional historical study, and have gone so far as to question the very point of persisting with the subject at all. Historians themselves have responded, sometimes positively, by adjusting their claims and practical approaches, sometimes more defensively, by reiterating traditional modernist principles against what they perceive as nothing less than a barbarian threat to western civilisation. And such debates are not confined to academia, but increasingly impinge on a much wider public.

Awareness of historiographical issues has been stimulated by a number of fashionable factors: for example, by so-called 'docudramas', where the borderline is blurred between 'factual' documentary and 'fictional' embellishment; by the production of films that purport to represent 'historical' people and events, while blatantly traducing the historical record; by the revelation of 'secret histories', or aspects of the past that have long been inadvertently missed or deliberately repressed; by the publicity given to politically inspired 're-writing' of the past, whether to embrace what has previously been ignored, or to efface unwelcome memories; and above all by the huge interest in the Holocaust – its memorialisation on the one hand counterbalanced by attempted refutations and outright denial on the other. All these (to some of which we'll return later) have served to enhance awareness of such historiographical issues as the nature, validity, and interpretation of evidence; the respective reliability of oral and documentary testimony; the ideological commitments, political agendas, and even moral integrity of historians themselves.

Yet despite such continuing debates that stimulate examination of history's nature(s) and purpose(s), the relationship between history and philosophy has not always been as obvious as the quotation from Edward Gibbon (heading this chapter) might seem to suggest. 'I don't believe in the philosophy of history', exclaimed one Regius Professor of Modern History at Oxford in the later nineteenth century;[3] 'nothing distorts facts so much as theory', concurred the intellectual historian Leslie Stephen, so 'a scientific historian should be on his guard against the philosopher of all men';[4] and numerous historians even in the twenty-first century might agree. The philosophy of history has for the most part been safely cordoned off as a sub-branch of philosophy, with which historians need not be greatly concerned – any more than most scientists are concerned with the philosophy of science, or practising artists with theories of aesthetics.

Admittedly, some ritual obeisance is conventionally paid to historiography during the academic training of historians, but it often seems possible to exclude from that any fundamental questioning of the actual nature of the subject, of the validity of historians' claims to know about the past, and of the inevitable intrusion of ideological considerations into their historical judgements. Any philosophical standpoint revealed in the writing of history is frequently taken as a sort of veneer, extraneous to the inner core and glued on with varying success to a solid historical carcass; and it can then be seen as something to be assessed, praised or condemned, independently of the underlying historical research itself. Thus Herbert Butterfield writes of events being 'laid out by the technical historian', for subsequent judgement, evaluation, and use by those with some ideological commitment. In this way, it is supposed, 'they can at least begin by having some common ground for the great debate that still lies open to them'.[5]

Such an assumption, of the possibility of sharply differentiating between a supposedly pristine, 'objective' historical account and any philosophical or ideological accretions, still lives on. As Mark Cousins has complained, 'It is commonplace to read praise for a historian's research coupled with a tut-tutting over the vagaries of the Hegelian or Marxist arguments in which it is inserted.'[6] Philosophy, after all, is a separate and theoretical subject, and on the whole historians, as practical people in a craft tradition, like to avoid theorising and get on with their history. Professor G. R. Elton admitted to 'a suspicion that a philosophic concern with such problems as the reality of historical knowledge or the nature of historical thought only hinders the practice of history'. Raphael Samuel has described how, 'when faced with conceptual difficulties, they [historians] instinctively reach for the "facts", and, rather than waste time in philosophical speculation, prefer to get on with the job'. In the context of actually doing history, theorists can be perceived, in Professor Arthur Marwick's words, as 'interlopers' and philosophy as nothing better than 'the route of all error', for 'the true concern of the historian is history, not historiography'.[7]

It will be argued in this book that historians can no longer afford to take this dismissive attitude towards contemporary philosophy, or towards postmodernist theories. More importantly, though, it will be urged that they do not need to. There is little doubt that the vehemence with which the debate between traditionalists and more theoretically inclined 'meta-historians' is sometimes conducted, indicates some considerable anxiety on the part of its participants. It is as if not only the discipline of history, but the very integrity of the historian is coming under threat. But the issue is above all about self-consciousness, and that can be seen both as a desirable quality for individuals, and also as a potentially positive stimulus for historical study.

2 THEORY AND THE CHALLENGE OF POSTMODERNISM

The movement, or the new world view, of postmodernism has come to affect all areas of intellectual life.[8] Raising questions, as it does, about the 'core' subject of science, it inevitably scatters collateral challenges to all those subjects in the social sciences and humanities that have for so long aped the methodologies of science. The evident successes of the so-called 'hard sciences' (especially mathematics and physics) in the seventeenth century provoked widespread imitation. From the standpoint of the Enlightenment philosophers it seemed clear that it was necessary simply to adopt the procedures of that successful science, and apply them universally to achieve more general progress. Scientists were confident that the natural world was best treated as a mechanism, made up of material particles moving in space; and that machine of nature was to be properly and finally understood by detached observers who succeeded in distancing themselves from the object of study. Their findings would then simply reveal the order and immutable laws of nature; and these should be expressed ideally by mathematics as the perfect form of clear and unambiguous language. Following that, the more 'human' sciences of biology and psychology could be similarly developed, in accordance with that new model. The human body could be treated as just another machine; and even the workings of the mind, or the supposedly mysterious psyche, could be mechanically explained in terms of the physical operations of the brain.

The new 'scientific' understanding of individual human beings, their bodies and their minds, could then be put to good use. For one thing, medical practice could be easily improved, as being essentially the straightforward diagnosis and repair of purely mechanical defects. Furthermore, the model could be further extended and applied to the individual's interactions with others, and to behaviour in society. Requisite social and political theories could then be formulated, in order to make possible the ideal environment in which people would act in an orderly way, as obedient to the social laws as atomic particles were to the laws of nature. Real progress at last would thus be possible.

Such a prospect was too good to miss: use of the so-called scientific method could surely be indefinitely extended, and it was eagerly applied to their subjects by humanists – linguisticians, philosophers, geographers, historians. As ever, these were determined to demonstrate their academic credibility through subscribing to the latest fashion; and the prospect of having a share in the projected universal progress was no doubt alluring.

It is precisely that optimism which has now been so sadly dented, and conformity is beginning to lie in another direction. The nature and above all the direction of modern science have increasingly been questioned, and with that centre itself failing to hold, a wider intellectual anarchy has loomed. The crisis has been exacerbated by developments elsewhere: some twentieth-century trends in psychology, linguistics, and philosophy were particularly significant. This book is concerned mainly with the effects on historical study, but it is worth noticing here that other subjects are affected, not least because there is much common ground between them.

It is in literary studies that the effects have so far been most obvious. As a literary theorist, Terry Eagleton has noted in particular the importance for his subject of work in linguistics and philosophy. So he has argued that 'the work of Derrida and others [has] cast grave doubt upon the classical notions of truth, reality, meaning and knowledge, all of which could be exposed as resting on a naively representational theory of language'.[9] His point here is, that what have traditionally been perceived as *philosophical* questions, concerning the nature of language, have had serious implications for our understanding of concepts such as 'truth, reality, meaning and knowledge'; and the importance of those concepts is by no means confined solely to philosophy. Such considerations have inevitably impinged on his own subject-area of literature, for the central issue, as he explains, boils down to whether language itself represents some external 'reality', or is, rather, a free-standing, self-contained structure, without any representational function. In the former case, 'truth' can be defined in terms of the correspondence between language and the objects it purports to represent; in the latter, it is only in relation to the system's own internal coherence that such concepts are defined. This fundamental debate about language is, as we shall see in Chapter 4, by no means new. But contemporary linguistic theoreticians have come to view the 'representational' standpoint as 'naive'; and the consequent re-definition of the central concepts noted by Eagleton inevitably has important implications, not only for theories of literature, but also for *all* language-based disciplines, including history.

Even the firmly grounded, seemingly earth-bound subject of geography has received some tremors. This is worth a brief examination, since the geographer's concern with space links closely with the historian's main interest of time.

The representation of space seems on the face of it a simple matter. Just draw it as it is. This corresponds exactly with the historian's task of describing what happened in the past, where again (as we shall see in the next chapter) the seemingly unproblematic aim has been, in Thomas Hobbes's words, to lay out the matter 'as it is'. But geographers have come to be suspicious of that aim's apparent simplicity.[10] Taking their most obvious means of representation, what really is a map? Maps have long been considered to be 'objective' representations of the physical world. But they now appear as something rather more complicated. Following theoretical challenges to the subject, it is conceded that they are not 'objective' or absolute in any sense: rather, they are to be viewed as relative constructions, not representing 'reality', but presenting an inevitably partial representation of space from an inevitably partial ideological position.

Now it could be argued that there is nothing new here. Historians, of all people, are well aware that past geographers drew their maps in terms of their own sometimes very limited perspectives. Ancient cartographers lacked facilities for world-wide travel, and in recognition of their own limitations openly labelled many parts as 'land unknown'. Some mediaeval maps likewise are obviously drawn from a specifically Christian perspective, and so show spaces set aside for angels, and represent the whole world centred on the religious capital of Jerusalem. In modern times, though, we have prided ourselves on achieving a greater 'objectivity', a more accurate transcription of external 'reality'; and as with the physical sciences, the proof of the geographical pudding has been seen to lie in the eating, or in our undisputed ability to fly around the world quite confidently and know where on earth we are.

That practical confidence, however, is under theoretical threat. Whereas cartography, or map-making, has been thought to be a properly 'scientific' activity, it is now, like science itself, seen to be deeply involved with other considerations. For, as with any literary description or pictorial representation of the external world, a map has to be drawn from a certain viewpoint, from a single chosen position; and the choice of that position is significant. It reveals in short what map-makers think is important, for it enables them to include and exclude, and to express relationships between places and spaces according to their own (often unstated) criteria. In a sense, then, cartographers classify, categorise, and even define, their own material; and beneath the cloak of description lies (however invisible) a whole body of judgement.

That ideological ingredient of geographical representation is revealed with particular clarity in post-colonial analyses of earlier attitudes towards other lands. Nineteenth-century reports from Africa, for example, stressed the 'otherness' of a 'dark continent' that awaited redemption from European civilisers. Africa itself was described as a land of disorder and savagery, to be contrasted with the civilisation exemplified by Europe; its indigenous peoples, as less highly evolved, were naturally inferior and rightly subject. That picture, that unthinkingly adopted Eurocentric representation, served to justify what has later been characterised as imperialistic exploitation, and we shall see in Chapter 5 how the re-thinking in geography in this context parallels post-colonial re-assessments in history.

Recognition of the ideological component of such representations, in whatever area of life or study, implies the adoption of a moral position in relation to the subject. This highlights the important point that, for all its assumed relativism and even cynicism, postmodernism does have (or can have) a positive agenda. For there is a recognition that something quite literally needs to be done. Academic subjects are to be justified, not only in terms of their intellectual interest or theoretical coherence: they are to be remoulded as vehicles for determining very practical steps for the future. The representative early-modern philosopher Francis Bacon in the seventeenth century condemned the intellectual sterility of scholastic learning – those theoretical studies that resembled intricate cobwebs but which were sadly lacking in any practical effects. Bacon's twentieth-century postmodernist counterparts are now similarly questioning the value of studies that are seemingly remote from practical concerns and whose proponents actually proclaim as a virtue the supposedly 'value-free' nature of their subject-matter. The analysis of the ideological underpinnings of literary, geographical, and historical texts is not an academic witch-hunt (or should not be), designed to root out the politically unsound. Rather, it aims at the sort of self-consciousness that has been an educational ideal since Socrates, and its moral commitment is not to one specific ideological position, but rather to a pluralism in terms of which individual contributions are valued as parts of an ever-expanding and never-completed whole.

3 POSTMODERNISM AND HISTORICAL STUDY

The impact of postmodernist ideas upon historical study has been late in coming, but is nonetheless crucial. For in the context of historiography, postmodernism implies especially a challenge to those conventional certainties – such as 'facts', 'objectivity', and 'truth' – in terms of which much history has in the past been written (and read). The sceptical approach of postmodernist theorists questions the absolute validity of such concepts; it concludes that there can never be one single privileged position from which the story of the past can finally be told; it implies an inescapable and inevitable relativism in our own positions in relation to that past; so it requires that we see any version of history as nothing more than a tentative hypothesis underpinned by a possibly unstated, but nonetheless specific purpose. Furthermore, most such historical hypotheses will be presented in linguistic form, and that provokes questions again of what the historian's language represents: whether there is assumed to be a correspondence with a past reality, or whether what is presented is just an internally consistent system constructed from and for a specific point of view. Acceptance of the latter position additionally highlights the interrelationship of any historical 'discourse' with ideology and power. For, it is argued, there will inevitably be some stated or unstated motive behind the point of view adopted, the data consequently selected, the interpretation proposed, and what by implication is ignored or denied (as in the case of the Holocaust, to be considered in our Postscript).[11]

There are important implications here for the role which historical study has and might in future have in education. For while the traditional model of the subject might often seem to favour an intellectual *acceptance* of existing structures, a postmodern approach should provoke *questions* about those structures' very foundations. Thus, the 'old model' of history, as it will be outlined in Chapter 2, essentially presupposes the existence of an 'objective' historical truth that can, at least in principle, be finally uncovered to reveal the past 'as it was'. That truth in its entirety may not have been revealed, but each piece of individual research can make some contribution to the final edifice, and each will be recognised and valued accordingly. Historians can then be seen as working positively together towards a high ideal, and their profession can be duly applauded as having some importance.

But the role of the history student is not, in such circumstances, to question the direction of the team or to rock the boat by raising fundamental challenges to the subject's aims and methods. Rather, individual contributions must be seen to fit within a coherently elaborated whole, anomalies will tend to be avoided or ignored, and any analysis of 'objectivity' itself will be discouraged. Some danger then may follow that students of history will be taught not so much to question as to conform to existing dogma; and fears on that account are only increased by the determined rejection by some historians of any philosophical and theoretical consideration of their subject.

Within a postmodern context, the educational role of historical study changes, for here one starting-point must be some recognition of the limitations of the subject itself. The removal of 'objective truth' as a meaningful goal is counterbalanced by a perceived need for many different accounts of the past – none claiming any special privilege, but each providing some illumination from its own perspective. From that, in turn, there follow two practical benefits. First, humility results from the recognition of one's own limitations and of the equal validity of contributions from others who may be quite different from oneself; and the avoidance of dogmatic assertion may come to be one of the history student's hallmarks. Second, a high degree of awareness is implied, of both oneself and others – an awareness of what is being done and of where that might be leading; and that is another characteristic to which students of history might properly aspire.

The application of such theoretical analysis to historiography thus has results that are far from being necessarily negative. On the contrary, it may positively encourage 'empowerment'. For not only does it show how history has in the past been used to underpin ideals or ideologies – whether moral or religious, social or political – but it also indicates how our own history may similarly serve as a validating foundation for any future programme. And that, again, implies above all a need for self-awareness. We may legitimately construct our own histories, so long as we remain aware of, and openly acknowledge, the bases upon which we are constructing them. It is impossible to write any history without *some* standpoint – and that means some philosophical or ideological standpoint. The only questions are whether or not we acknowledge that standpoint, and whether or not our choices have been *consciously* made. If postmodernism denies the possibility of attaining any absolutes, then, as Keith Jenkins has argued, 'The only choice is between a history that is aware of what it is doing and a history that is not.'[12] And it is again, as Plato implied, only the former – the 'aware' or the 'examined' – that can really be worth doing.

4 AGENDA

So we need to be concerned with what the nature of our subject is – with what historically it has been, and with what it has more recently become. The old question 'What is history?' still needs to be addressed, and a transition in definitions traced. That is to say, some historical explanation is required for the radical change that has recently been witnessed in the assumed status of historical accounts. For an apparently confident belief in the attainability of certain historical knowledge, or truth about the past, has been largely replaced by far more circumspect claims to have provided nothing more solid or definitive than one possible version, or a tentative hypothesis that is subject to continual revisions. Some properly tentative historical account, then, of this revolutionary intellectual change will be attempted, by outlining traditional ideas of history and its role, and then assessing the various challenges which have resulted in the present need for re-definitions.

In Chapter 2, therefore, the old ideal of aspiring to historical truth, to an account of the past 'as it was', will be presented. This will be followed in Chapter 3 by various past answers to the question of why such history should be studied. Challenges to the traditional model of the subject will be examined in Chapters 4 and 5. First, consideration will be given to those that have derived from three 'external' sources: from psychological studies of perception, which have emphasised the active role of any perceiver; from recent re-assessments of the nature and functions of language; and from the long-standing tradition of philosophical scepticism. Then attention will shift to the 'internal' crises provoked by Marxist, feminist, and post-colonial historians themselves. Chapter 6 will be concerned with attempted re-definitions in the light of what has preceded – re-definitions both of what history *is* and of *why* it should still be studied.

That last is of particular importance for all engaged in education, whether as students or teachers, for it raises the problematic issue of 'relevance'. It sometimes seems that few still care about what happened yesterday – let alone what happened last week, or last year, or (getting worse) last century; or (worst of all) what happened in times and places altogether different from our own. In our self-assertively confident age in which 'the end of history' has been proclaimed, and whole degree courses are mounted in which only 'contemporary history' is confronted, the past has truly become 'another country' where things were differently, and therefore irrelevantly, done; and the further removed from us that past is seen to be, the more different and more irrelevant and more dispensable it is often adjudged.

In such an anti-historical context, it may be salutary to consider some past historians' varied motivations. Comprehensive coverage is clearly impracticable, and particular attention will be paid to ancient and early-modern sources. That emphasis derives partly from personal interest, but is offered also as a deliberate antidote to current trends. It is, after all, in classical antiquity that one finds the roots of historical study and also of theorising about that study, so that many of the issues still debated by historians were discussed by the Greeks and the Romans. Some knowledge of that earlier period, then, serves at the very least to put our own theoretical debates into some wider historical perspective, and so promotes perhaps a salutary irony about our own achievements. And the early-modern renewal of interest in antiquity, its retrieval and re-working of ancient thought, provided the foundations for the 'modernism' that has persisted to our own time. We are still very much the heirs of early-modern thinkers, even though we may now be belatedly questioning the value of our inheritance.

So there are gaps, and in particular historical writing of the mediaeval period is grievously under-represented; one cannot do it all. But it is hoped that, by considering some historical foundations of those ideas and attitudes by which we are still affected, we may better understand current challenges, and may be better positioned to formulate arguments for deployment in contemporary debates.

This is, then, a historical examination of the 'what?' and 'why?' of history. What is it that people who have written history have thought that they were doing; and how have they done it; and why have they done it in the ways that they have? Have they been justified in their aims and in their methods, and have they been successful; or have they suffered from shortcomings to which we are happily immune? Through some such enquiry, we may be led in particular to question received notions of what is historically important, and we must be provoked to re-consider what we think that *we* are doing and why. At the very least, as embryonic historians we should have become, as Gibbon wished, to some extent 'philosophical' and thereby more self-aware. Admittedly, we may continue to wander in confusion, and find it hard to identify, or to articulate, any one acceptable model for ourselves. But some consolation may derive from Plato's presumed approval of the fact that our academic lives will not have remained entirely 'unexamined'.

Chapter 2

What was history? The past as it was

Laying out the matter as it is. (Lucian of Samosata)[1]

1 INTRODUCTION

Everyone knows, of course, what history was and is: quite simply, the study of the past.[2] While other subjects, like philosophy, or physics, or geography, may include some consideration of the past – of earlier philosophers like Plato, of Newtonian mechanics, of the chronological development of land-forms – history is differentiated by its nature of having the past as its exclusive subject-matter. All historians have to do, therefore, is to find out what happened in that past, and then accurately record it – simply, in the words of Lucian in the second century AD, 'laying out the matter as it is', or was.

Underlying such a view is a belief that there is a past reality or truth, waiting to be discovered and described. The historian just has to clear away the darkness and confusion, behind which that past sometimes regrettably takes refuge, so that it can be seen in all its proper light and clarity. Admittedly, there may be complications, and certain precautions have to be taken: data must be approached without prejudices; facts must be clearly differentiated from opinions; evidence must be accepted only from impartial witnesses, and duly subjected to critical analysis; objectivity must be maintained, with any personal prejudices properly suppressed; and the record subsequently written must be scrupulously accurate. But given a properly professional approach, it should be possible to learn and then convey the truth of what is out there waiting to be discovered as the past.

This optimistic view of history's nature has itself had a long history, and is exemplified in the second century AD by the Greek writer Lucian, who proposed that the historian should 'bring a mind like a mirror, clear, gleaming-bright, accurately centred, displaying the shape of things just as he receives them, free from distortion, false colouring, and mis-representation'. With that achieved, the historian could reasonably expect to leave to posterity nothing less than a 'true account of what happened'.[3]

That historiographical ideal has subsequently persisted even up to our own time. As one twentieth-century example, J. H. Plumb still aspired to a history which was able to 'create for us a new past as true, as exact, as we can make it'.[4] And, referring to that sort of account, John Slater (HM Staff Inspector for History, 1974–1987) has even more recently written of 'the bluff and widely held commonsense view that there is an objective view of the past waiting to be seized and communicated, and an acceptable truth acceptable to all historians'.[5]

It is noteworthy that even in the early twenty-first century that still largely prevails as a popular conception of the subject. Indeed, it is such a view that has often been seen to make historical study respectable, describable even as a 'science' – the model to which, for the last three hundred years, all academic disciplines have ideally tended to aspire. The scientist, it is assumed, strives towards a direct perception and understanding of natural phenomena. There is an external natural reality, which is the subject-matter of science, and the truth of which may be grasped with the use of appropriate techniques. An account of that truth, free from any personal bias, can then be presented, and it can be assumed that there will be general agreement about that truth, at least by experts working in the field. And similarly with history and its own subject-matter of the past.

History, then, has often been described in relation to science and even modelled upon it, and the scientistic aspirations of some historians will be considered in section 3 below. But first some additional clarification about the nature of the subject may emerge from briefly noting its relationship with another subject with which it has traditionally been associated: writing in the fourth century BC, the Greek philosopher and literary theorist Aristotle clarified his views on history by contrasting it specifically with poetry, and it is in its relation to that seemingly disparate subject that history since has often been (and, as we shall see in Chapter 6, section 1.3, still sometimes is) considered.

2 HISTORY AND POETRY

2.1 Ancient origins

History and poetry were first linked, long even before Aristotle's time, in the eighth century BC, when in his poetic *Iliad* Homer recounted the history of the Trojan War that had taken place hundreds of years before. Basing his work on a much earlier oral tradition, Homer describes how the Greek armies under their king Agamemnon finally, after a ten-year siege, managed to defeat their Trojan enemies. As a poet, he made no claims to what we would think of as historical accuracy, but having left a record of much earlier times, he was later recognised as being himself an important historical source. Owing to a lack of alternative evidence, he was necessarily taken as such by the great Greek historian Thucydides. Writing in the fifth century BC, Thucydides used the Homeric record for his introductory material on 'pre-historic' Greece, but at the same time he expresses some reservations about his predecessor's reliability, and he himself clearly distinguishes the two roles of poet and historian. Homer, he realises, may well have been guilty of inaccuracies and exaggerations, for as a poet his priority would have been to 'charm for the moment' rather than to present a less romantic but more enduring work in the manner appropriate to a historian.[6]

This distinction between the two respective roles was powerfully perpetuated by Aristotle (384–322 BC). Best known as a natural philosopher whose views on what we now call 'science' persisted with various modifications for some two thousand years, Aristotle was also enormously influential in the context of literature, and here he draws a sharp distinction between history on the one hand and poetry on the other. He suggests, first, that the two are clearly distinguished by one obvious thing: 'that the one [history] relates *what has been*, the other [poetry] *what might be*'. He thus makes a seemingly unremarkable demarcation of their chronological concerns, with the past assigned to history, and poetry allotted some hypothetical present and future. But, second, Aristotle claims that 'poetry is chiefly conversant about *general* truth, history about *particular*' – a point that has more serious implications, not only for their respective methodologies, but also for their relative status, since, because of its greater generality, poetry is to be accounted 'a more philosophical and a more excellent thing'.[7]

Aristotle's definition of history as being concerned with particulars rather than with universals or generalities, implies that it is a simple record of particular past events; and for the enumeration of those past events only crude sense-perceptions are required. No attempt is to be made by historians to subsume those events under more general laws, so that their task becomes purely mechanical, a straightforward gathering of empirically identifiable data. Aristotle describes elsewhere his belief that those who investigate *causes* of phenomena, and try to formulate general principles about them, are superior to those who simply accept appearances as data, as literally 'given', without wondering or questioning further. Wisdom, he asserts, is not evidenced by a knowledge of specific details, for that is simply a matter of sense-perception of which anyone is capable; but it has to do with a more generalised knowledge of underlying principles – a far more difficult attainment, because further removed from the senses.[8]

Aristotle himself, then, sees poetry as the superior discipline, because it is concerned not, like history, with particular events, but rather with universal truths. Although a Sophoclean tragedy, for example, may tell a particular story, the telling of that particular story is, in a sense, unimportant – not least because everyone knows the outcome already. What is important about it, is the way that it is made to exemplify a general truth – a truth that is not specific to one character, but that is relevant to the human condition of us all. It is then to that portrayal of the human condition in tragedy that, as humans, we all make some emotional response. In other words, while poetry necessarily makes use of particular names in particular stories, its real concern is with general principles of human character and conduct; but history by its very nature characteristically remains embedded in the particular. So in the actual example Aristotle cites in his *Poetics*, it is concerned with recording one man's specific actions and experiences, with 'what Alcibiades did, or what happened to him – [which] is particular truth'.

Aristotle thus proposes here a view of history, in terms of which it is identified with a mechanical procedure of recording particular data, without any need for that imaginative understanding and interpretative flair which enable one to generalise from such particulars. That superior function is now reserved for poetry.

2.2 Early-modern and modern continuities

However unfair to Herodotus and Thucydides, the two great historians who preceded him, Aristotle's views on the respective roles of history and poetry have proved highly influential. In the context of literary theory especially, his ideas on historiography frequently reappear from the time of the Renaissance on. In the sixteenth century, one Giraldo Cintho, for example, observes that, 'Whereas the historian ought to write only the facts and actions *as they are*, the poet shows not things as they are, but *as they ought to be*'.[9] Again the distinction is made between what is and what ought to be, and again the poet alone is assigned some imaginative function. And following the same Aristotelian tradition, the Englishman Sir Philip Sidney makes a similar comparison of the two subjects, favouring poetry not least because the poor historian once more is so limited, 'tyed, not to what shoulde bee, but to what is; to the particular truth of things, and not to the general reason of things'.[10]

This Aristotelian distinction between history and poetry has in our own time been subject to postmodern challenges to be considered in Chapter 6, section 1.3, but not before the demarcations between the two subjects had become even more rigidly drawn. In his own influential treatment of how learning might be advanced in the early seventeenth century, Francis Bacon, although a determined intellectual revolutionary and self-professed anti-Aristotelian, discussed the relative characteristics of history and poetry in such a way as to confirm the old Aristotelian distinctions. Poetry, he concluded, is actually misleading: with its imaginative emphasis, it is effectively a pretence, or 'feigned history'. Far from being a vehicle for universal truths, poetry has been used to compensate for deficiencies inherent in the real world, and so has diverted its readers from reality. Thus, first, poets have been guilty of exaggeration, imagining and describing 'acts and events greater and more heroical' than those that have actually occurred. Second, poets have been able to impose a more moral order on their subjects than is actually apparent in historical events: 'because true history propoundeth the successes and issues of actions not so agreeable to the merits of virtue and vice, therefore poesy feigns them more just in retribution, and more according to revealed providence'. And the third deficiency of real life that requires poetic remedy, is that actions can all appear as rather ordinary and mundane: so poetry 'endueth them with more rareness, and more unexpected and alternative variations'.[11]

With this ability to improve on life, by modifying descriptions of reality by reference to what one wants, or 'submitting the shows of things to the desires of the mind', it is small wonder that poetry has proved popular, especially in times and places where life is hard. History can offer no such advantage. Lacking any imaginative input, it is properly governed by reason, which 'doth buckle and bow the mind unto the nature of things'. That is, it is constrained by what has actually happened, and if that makes it unappealing and generally less popular, it can at least be seen to be a more seriously important study. History's supposedly simple recording of what has happened in the past is duly confirmed as a virtue, even if that virtuous reputation has, like that of so many, been bought at the price of any poetic or imaginative input.

That Baconian view of history proved enduring. Renowned for his own challenge to the long-lived philosophical dictatorship of Aristotle, Bacon himself became something of a philosophical dictator, and by the middle decades of the century his views had become largely established as politically correct. Evidence of his influence is not hard to find in the writings of what one modern scholar has called the 'Bacon-faced generation',[12] and acceptance of his revised evaluation of the distinction between history and poetry is well illustrated by Walter Charleton. A writer on natural philosophy and theology, Charleton published in 1669 an essay on what he terms 'the different wits of men'. Again he distinguishes between history and poetry, this time in the context of an examination of various 'Vertues of the Mind'. So he suggests that we all possess, in different proportions, the two characteristics corresponding to 'reason' and 'imagination', or what Charleton himself and many others refer to as 'Judgment' and 'Phansie'. These characteristics are to be variously applied in the case of the two subjects under review. Poets, on the one hand, require both, but the more imaginative 'fancy' needs to predominate since it is this that provides originality: 'Phansie ought to have the upper hand, because all Poems of what sort soever, please chiefly by Novelty.' In historians, on the other hand, the frivolities of fancy must be subdued by something rather more serious:

> *Judgment* ought to have the Chair; because the vertue of History consisteth in Method, Truth, and Election of things worthy Narration; nor is there need of more Phansie, than what may serve to adorn the stile with elegant Language.

The historian, then, like the Baconian inductive scientist, is to investigate data 'with an observant but empty mind'. For such practitioners imagination might mislead, so that that unruly faculty is to be downgraded, and used only to provide some ornamental icing on a cake whose ingredients are to be rationally selected in conformity with truth and moral worth.[13]

Such suspicion of imagination has characterised much subsequent thought in relation to both history and science, and the Baconian style has been characterised by an obsessive recording of 'facts', coupled with a professed disinclination to indulge in imaginative speculations. In both science and historiography, there is evidence for this emphasis by the end of the seventeenth century. Samuel Parker describes imagination as 'climbing up into the bed of reason . . . [to] defile it by unchaste and illegitimate embraces';[14] Isaac Newton's self-conscious refusal to indulge in publicly hypothesising is well known;[15] and that a similar self-denying ordinance prevailed among historians is suggested by Bernard de Fontenelle's complaint about his contemporaries' mechanical approach: 'To amass in the head fact upon fact . . . that is what is called doing history.'[16]

The long continuation of that tradition right into the twentieth century, is indicated by J. B. Bury's characteristic contention in 1902, that 'It is . . . of supreme moment that the history which is taught should be true; and that can be attained only through the discovery, collection, classification, and interpretation of facts.'[17] Bury's assumption that a straight, non-judgemental description of 'the truth' about the past constitutes the historian's attainable objective, shows how Aristotle's differentiation of history from *poetry* is paralleled by its attempted alignment with a simplistic view of *science*.

3 HISTORY AND SCIENCE

3.1 Ancient origins

That alignment of history with science can be seen as early as the fifth century BC, when Thucydides specifically distanced himself, not only as we have seen from poets, but also from previous chroniclers who were not, like him, concerned with 'telling the truth'.[18] Refusing to compromise by emulating more seductively romantic writers, he modelled his own approach on the medical pioneers of the Hippocratic school. These emphasised the need for careful observation, and for the maintenance of regular records which would then facilitate accurate prognoses, or predictions about the future: by building up a reliable set of data, one could hope to establish patterns in the course of diseases, and the effects of various prescriptions; and such knowledge of past processes could then serve to inform decisions in the future.

As a historian, Thucydides saw clear parallels in their respective approaches, and duly applied the scientific methods of the Hippocratic writers to his own treatment of the past. Like the medical theorists, he was well aware of problems of bias and of deficient evidence, and he noted the need thoroughly to check the reports of witnesses who may be partial or suffer from imperfect memories. But in the end he was reasonably confident that, having subjected all his data to critical scrutiny, he could distinguish truth from falsehood and produce a valid and reliable historical account. And as in the case of medicine, that account should prove of lasting value, in that it facilitated prediction of what might happen in the future. Precise observation of human behaviour made possible the formulation of those psychological laws which would continue always to determine people's actions. So he believed that his history, as being based upon a scientifically derived model of human nature which remained essentially the same, would prove a valuable 'possession for all time'.

Reading Thucydides' work today, one might feel tempted to agree. His account of the great plague in Athens is particularly instructive, and highlights his emulation of the contemporary Hippocratic medical writers. A 'scientific' model is adopted from the start, inasmuch as he recounts some theories of why and where the plague originated, but he himself declines to speculate. His purpose is simply to give a detailed description of what actually happened – something which he feels competent to do as not only having observed other sufferers, but as also having personally experienced the disease. The symptoms, then, are carefully described for each day – first, the physical symptoms as a doctor might record them, and then the ensuing moral and psychological breakdown. People's hopelessness and despair in the face of a disease which struck at random and for which there seemed to be no cure, lowered their powers of resistance. And among those who did for the moment survive, there seemed no point in any moral restraint. The plague struck all – both good and bad – quite indiscriminately, so any faith in laws or gods or providence was lost, and there followed a period of anarchic self-indulgence and 'unprecedented lawlessness'.

It is these descriptions of human behaviour in times of crisis – during the plague, or at various turning-points in the war – that best exemplify Thucydides' determined attempt to convey to posterity an account of how things were. His detailed descriptions and analysis, his refusal to speculate, his careful evaluation of evidence and witnesses, and his belief in universal laws of human behaviour, all derived from the model of contemporary science which he self-consciously adopted. It was the application of a scientific approach that gave him the confidence to aspire to historical truth.

3.2 Early-modern and modern continuities

Thucydides' belief in the attainability of historical truth continued to be largely taken for granted through the middle ages and into the early-modern period. Just as philosophers expected to penetrate to the actual truths of nature, reading the signs that had been written there by God, so historians presupposed a past reality, similarly written by God, and the truth of which could be reached and recorded. So in the sixteenth century the English scholar Roger Ascham defines the first requirement of the historian as simply being to 'wryte nothing false'.[19] There is an assumption here, simply taken for granted, that this is an attainable objective, and that assumption is apparently shared by many others. The historian Thomas Blundevill, for example, in his own theoretical treatment of historical writing, again draws the distinction between historians and poets, with the former characterised specifically by their desire 'to tell things *as they were done*, without either augmenting or diminishing them, or swarving one jote from the truth'.[20] And this same tradition continues to be well represented by William Camden, whose self-confessed motive in writing the history of Elizabeth is simply 'the love of Truth'. He considers that to provide for his readers anything less than truth is to substitute 'a Draught of Poison' for the 'wholsome Liquor' that history properly dispenses.[21]

This approach of treating wholesome history as quite simply a true record of the past, continues to parallel scientific confidence in humans' ability to penetrate to the God-given underlying laws of nature. Both historical and scientific dogmatisms were (as we shall see in Chapter 4, section 4) theoretically challenged by the early-modern revival of sceptical philosophy, but in practice both subjects have often been marked by a refusal to take such theoretical issues on board. Pragmatism rules: science has been seen to 'work', and so too in its way has history. And the confidence of practitioners in both fields seems to have increased following the intellectual successes of the scientific revolution.

That confidence is clearly seen in the writers of the so-called 'Enlightenment' – the period of history which follows the scientific revolution and which is characterised above all by an optimistic faith in 'progress'. By the turn of the eighteenth century, the new science had finally prevailed over the old. The mystical cosmos of the middle ages had been superseded by something more recognisably modern: mechanical explanations were assumed to be applicable in principle to all phenomena, and the theoretical models so successfully applied in science could, it was believed, be indefinitely extended. Newton's *Mathematical Principles of Natural Philosophy* (*Principia*, published in 1687) may have been incomprehensible to all but a few other mathematicians; but the perception that the laws of the universe, instead of being shrouded in the mysteries of occult qualities, could be reduced to the assumed simplicities of mathematics, was itself enormously reassuring. If nature herself was so orderly, then people too, and their societies, could surely be similarly ordered. Illumination had at last been provided: the way forward was clear.

And of course the way back. In line with the assumed simplicities of science, history and its trajectory could be simply defined. So Enlightenment historical theorists are doubly confident. First, they remain assured that history can still be presented as a record of the past 'as it was'. Quite simply, in the words of a contemporary definition, it is 'a recital or description of things *as they are*, or have been; in a continued, orderly narration of the principal facts, and circumstances thereof'. Like the former mysteries of nature, earlier fabulous reports of the past can be jettisoned, and replaced by a proper historical 'account of things represented *as true*'. And second, building on the newly established science-based foundations of their subject, historians can confidently deduce from their clear vision of the past that human beings are on a progressive march forward. Standing in the light at the end of the historical tunnel, 'We contemplate the gradual progress of society, from the lowest ebb of primitive barbarism, to the full tide of modern civilisation.'[22] Traces of that earlier primitive barbarism were in fact still conveniently represented in the present, for people in recently discovered lands clearly indicated the extent of European development. They could be used as a bench-mark: by reference to them, the development of a contrasting civilisation could be judged. And it was that intervening path of progress which was revealed by history.

The account of that history was, like science, to be constructed from 'an uninterrupted chain of facts and observations'. There was no more need of guesswork or of mere 'hypothetical surmises': 'it is enough to assemble and order the *facts* and to show the useful truths that can be derived from their connections and from their totality'. And the required conclusion duly followed, that a study of the past revealed 'the picture of the march and progress of the human mind'. From that, in turn, an inference could be drawn, that such development would continue, and perfectibility itself could be envisaged. The time would no doubt come when all peoples would at last be brought up to the highest standard and when all could 'work together for [humanity's] perfection and its happiness'.[23]

Those words of the French philosopher Condorcet have their own ironic pathos, both in the short term and the longer. Only months after writing them, Condorcet himself died as a victim of a revolution designed to realise the very ideals he had proclaimed. For the longer term, he had defined for modern history its direction and its goal: as late as 1965, the eminent English historian Hugh Trevor-Roper still unrepentantly focused on history of Europe, contrasting that with 'the unrewarding gyrations of barbarous tribes in picturesque but irrelevant corners of the globe: tribes whose chief function in history, in my opinion, is to show to the present an image of the past from which, by history, it has escaped'.[24]

Condorcet thus helped to establish that meaningful narrative course, progressive and Eurocentric, which is only now being belatedly challenged; and the Enlightenment optimism exemplified by him seemed indeed to have been vindicated during the following century, when the continuing success of the sciences encouraged further belief in the wider applicability of their methods. This tendency towards *scientism* – the attempted extension of scientific methodologies to other areas – is apparent not least in history, where it is typified by Leopold von Ranke's now notorious dictum (itself derived as we have seen from earlier sources), that the historian's task is 'simply to show how it really was'. For Ranke, 'the strict presentation of the facts . . . is undoubtedly the supreme law', and such a presentation becomes a practical possibility, on the assumptions that the historian 'will have no preconceived ideas', and that 'history . . . is able to lift itself . . . to a knowledge of the objectively working relatedness'.[25] In other words, the historian must be unbiased, must work out what actually happened, and must then accurately present a factual record. And although deriving this ideal from antiquity, Ranke's very terminology indicates that he has drawn on a new authority to help validate his historical claims. The model of nineteenth-century science, in accordance with which the truth about nature will be revealed to the conscientious enquirer, is now self-consciously appropriated.

History itself, then, is to acquire that academic respectability which, in the new scientific age, can derive only from its identification as a 'science'. As Auguste Comte (1798–1857), another enthusiast for the indefinite extension of 'scientific method', expressed the matter: 'History has now been for the first time systematically considered as a whole, and has been found, like other phenomena, subject to invariable laws.'[26] The 'progress' so evident in science is thus happily seen to be paralleled by developments in historical study. Even practitioners of the humanities, instead of endlessly debating insoluble problems, could at last claim to be getting somewhere, to be solving practical problems, once those problems were seen (as they were by another contemporary) as being 'nothing but a problem of mechanics'.[27]

This scientistic approach was used to justify the establishment of historical study as a reputable academic discipline. In the context of a 'scientific' model, historians could be seen as serious contenders for an 'objective' truth, which could ultimately be reached through the application of proper procedures. Francis Bacon had taught the virtues of a scientific enterprise to which all could contribute, and history was now similarly to be seen as a collaborative construction. With a selflessly disciplined approach to their own chosen study, individuals could perfect a building-block, however small, that could be profitably utilised in the construction of a finally perfect edifice; and their personal and professional value was thereby assured.

It was Charles Darwin who, as a self-confessed Baconian, apparently provided the ideal modern model. It was he who had claimed to work on those 'true Baconian principles' that had taught him to spend years diligently acquiring data before venturing on any speculations. So historians were encouraged to follow him. As the President of the American Historical Association clarified in 1910:

> What we need is a genuinely scientific school of history which shall remorselessly examine the sources and separate the wheat from the chaff; which shall critically balance evidence; which shall dispassionately and moderately set forth results. For such a process we have the fortunate analogy of the physical sciences;

> did not Darwin spend twenty years in accumulating data, and in selecting typical phenomena before he so much as ventured a generalisation?[28]

Once again, a layperson's understanding, or misunderstanding, of the nature of science is set to determine the course of historical study. A 'remorseless' examination of sources will result in the possibility of their correct evaluation; evidence can then be 'critically' balanced; and finally, avoiding the intrusion of any personal involvement, the 'results' can be published. The historical evidence relating to Darwin's own actual, rather than professed, procedures, is overlooked; for the desirability of the ideal of his supposed detachment and 'objectivity' has become an unquestioned assumption.

That ideal has also, whether in science or in history, become a matter of faith and religious intensity. The laws both of nature and of past events derive from nothing less than the hand of God himself, and it is these that are to be revealed to the disciplined scholar in both fields. For the historian, Ranke makes the point: 'God dwells, lives, and can be known in all history. . . . Every deed attests to Him, every moment preaches his name. . . . May we, for our part, decipher this holy hieroglyph! Even so do we serve God. Even so are we priests.'[29] In the face of such conviction, of such faith in the historical enterprise as a scientific activity devoted to the acquisition of final truth, it is hardly surprising that non-conformists, doubters, and non-believers, have been treated as heretics fit only for the stake.

For they are also seen often as pessimists, questioning not only God's providential ordering, but also its secular replacement – that is, progress. One of the virtues of the Baconian endeavour was that it justified a belief that things could and would get better. That collaborative effort to which all could contribute would actually culminate in a completed task, in a 'final solution' – in scientific terms, a completed description and explanation of natural phenomena; in historical study, a definitive account of the past 'as it was'. So while Max Planck was advised in the 1870s against becoming a physicist, on the grounds that in that subject there was then little more to do, so Lord Acton some twenty years later could envisage the end of history, 'now that all information is within reach, and every problem has become capable of solution'.[30] Anyone challenging such confident optimism was – and perhaps is – hardly to be tolerated.

A confident and essentially scientistic approach towards history continued largely unabated through the twentieth century. The pattern was set at the century's beginning in the pronouncements of J. B. Bury, who announced the divorce of history from her traditional humanities partners. The subject was to confirm its allegiance elsewhere, and had 'begun to enter into closer relations with the sciences, which deal *objectively with the facts* of the universe'.[31] And that approach to the subject was effectively perpetuated by Geoffrey Elton, whose influence has persisted into the new millennium.

Elton, indeed, personally exemplifies what I have described as the 'old' (or modernist) model of history. Essentially an empiricist, he repudiated any 'philosophising' on history as not only unnecessary, but as actually threatening both to the subject and its practitioners. Thus, the very titles of his two main reflections on the nature and purpose of history are revealing: *The Practice of History* (1967) suggests his practical (as opposed to theoretical) approach; and *Return to Essentials* (1991) implies a conservative consolidation of the basics outlined some thirty years earlier. The latter was written in the face of philosophising, which might have seemed to some to challenge his earlier position, but he remained more than ever adamant that theorists could never get to the heart of what was an essentially practical matter.

The way to the heart of history remains, for Elton and his numerous followers, the empirical path to those primary sources in the archives, which stand as the tangible relics of the past, ready to reveal themselves (only) to the self-effacing historian who (alone) is competent to receive their (truthful) message concerning what actually happened. By removing, so far as possible, their own subjective selves, properly trained historians could eliminate any personal preferences, prejudices, and present concerns that might obstruct the reception of that past – a past which was, of course, to be taken in its own terms and for its own sake. The authority of the sources (paralleling 'nature' in the case of science) is paramount: they are to be allowed to speak to the researcher, without any promptings or expectations or hindsight that would pre-empt the revelation of 'the reality – yes, the truth – of the past', which inheres in the material evidence. 'There is . . . a truth to be discovered if only we can find it'; but its discovery will be made only through the realisation that the past 'must be understood for itself and in all its variety, undetermined by the predilections of the present'.[32]

History's specific concern, in short, is 'the rational reconstruction of the past'. It's that that makes it unique and an autonomous discipline, with an agenda that few may be able or willing to address. Indeed the well-meaning attempts at collaboration by 'amateurs' and intruders from other disciplines might actually prove counterproductive, for the 'work must be carried out *in a cage*', by which is presumably meant a disciplinary structure within which only properly trained and self-effacing professionals can operate.[33] That might seem a tough prospect, and is; but the reward lies (as it does for the scientist, similarly engaged in a cumulative enterprise) in awareness of a contribution (however small) made to that grand edifice which constitutes our knowledge – in the historian's case, our knowledge of the past.

4 CONCLUSION: THE PAST AS IT WAS

It is indeed something of a paradox that would-be *avant-garde* historians, such as Bury, Elton, and their followers, should still subscribe to such beliefs about the nature of science, as being to deal 'objectively with the facts', long after their renunciation as overly simplistic by leading scientists themselves. But the power of the scientific model even now persists.

A convenient link between the nineteenth and twentieth centuries in this respect is provided by John Hale's comments in 1967 upon the eminent Victorian historian Samuel Gardiner, who is described as having had typically scientistic aspirations and as having arranged his work accordingly:

> To resist any temptation that might develop in himself to stress certain aspects in his story at the expense of others, he decided to work through the material year by year, publishing as he went, so that his work should demonstrate *what actually happened*, and not his hindsight of what had happened. . . . His sacrifice of nearly every device whereby a historian writes himself into his history makes him the first English historian to write in the modern manner.[34]

What is interesting in that quotation is not only the idealised view of history ascribed to Gardiner – a view derived again from the then-contemporary simplistic model of supposed 'sciences', which reach truth by the direct apprehension of an external reality on the part of an impartial and detached observer. What is of equal interest is that Hale himself still apparently subscribes to the possibility of the totally detached historian, and his assessment of Gardiner reveals much about the continuing allure of Ranke's model. It is assumed that, by some supreme effort of 'sacrifice', the historian is enabled to repudiate everything (or almost everything) that might result in any personal intrusion into his own writing. The word 'device' suggests something slightly underhand that lesser historians might resort to, and for anyone to 'write himself into his own history' seems to imply unwarrantable self-indulgence. Indeed, it is the avoidance of such sins, and the cultivation of an ideal detachment, that is claimed by Hale to characterise the 'modern manner'.

Writing at about the same time as Hale, E. H. Carr, in his well-known and still popular (though now heavily criticised) discussion of the nature of history, is far more reticent about claiming any such possibility of acquiring 'facts', or of attaining perfect correspondences between external 'reality' and any historical account; but traces of the old model do remain. Thus, he notes numerous problems relating to so-called 'facts', to the selection and interpretation of evidence, and to historians' own social and psychological constraints. But he still rejects what he calls the 'cynical' approach of extreme relativism, and also seems at least periodically to retain an absolutist approach to the subject that seems inconsistent with his own generally more tentative stance. So he asks:

> What then do we mean when we praise a historian for being objective, or say that one historian is more objective than another? Not, it is clear, simply that he gets his facts right, but rather that he chooses the right facts, or, in other words, that he applies the right standard of significance.[35]

The implication still is, then, that there are 'right' facts (as opposed, presumably, to 'wrong' facts) and that these 'right facts' can be chosen by a historian through the application of some generally accepted 'right standard'.

This approach has been expressed yet more recently in John Tosh's *The Pursuit of History* (1984), where it is again implied that the historian can reach some essential truth in his sources; for even if those sources themselves are in some respect distortions of the truth, due allowances can be made, in relation again, presumably, to some ideal standard:

> When properly applied, the critical method enables the historian to make allowances for both deliberate distortion and the

> unthinking reflexes of the writer. . . . What historians *can* do is to ensure that within the area of the past which they find significant they are as true as they can be to the reality of the past.[36]

There is still an assumption here of some ideal 'reality of the past', to which historians, working 'properly' with their 'critical method', have due access; and it is presumably by reference to that that they both 'make allowances' for the conscious and unconscious distortions of *other* historians, and also ensure that their own accounts are 'as true as they can be'.

Such traditional confidence in historians' access to ideal criteria has increasingly come to seem somewhat over-simplified, for there have been a number of important challenges, to be considered below in Chapters 4 and 5, to the traditional conception of history as thus simply 'laying out the matter as it is'.

First, though, we should look in Chapter 3 at some past answers to the question of *why* anyway such history should have been studied.

Chapter 3

Why history? Past answers

1 INTRODUCTION

'Their's not to reason why' may seem to have been the motto of some past historians, but to avoid Plato's indictment of living an 'unexamined' life, it is necessary to be aware of *why* we do what we do. In fact, the question 'Why?' is always implicit in historical writing. That is to say, there must always be a reason for picking up our pens or opening our books, whether or not that reason is clearly articulated: the motivation for much of what we do remains unexamined, hidden even from ourselves, but that is not to deny its existence. So throughout the history of the subject itself, there have been many answers, some explicit, others implicit, to this fundamental question 'Why history?'

2 INTEREST AND ENTERTAINMENT

> What amusement, either of the senses or imagination, can be compared with it? (David Hume)[1]

The first answer to the question of why we do history – why we write about the past or study it – must be, as Hume asserts in the quotation above, that it provides incomparable 'amusement'. It is intrinsically interesting, and we want ourselves and others to be entertained by it. This is probably the earliest of motivations. An account of the Trojan War had been passed on by word of mouth long before the poet Homer committed it to writing, and both the oral and written traditions of that history were no doubt primarily intended to give 'amusement' to the listeners and readers. Other countries and cultures, too, have maintained links with their past by means of such informal 'historians', and some continue to do so. So, for example, in the main square of Marrakesh in the late twentieth century, a historian, or teller of traditional tales, still regularly entertained a circle of variously aged Moroccans; and that sight could be paralleled in many other places.

Such diversions at the very least take people's minds off contemporary troubles, and this therapeutic function of their subject has again long been recognised by historians themselves. Two examples are provided by Roman history. First, from the viewpoint of the writer, is Livy (59 BC–AD 17). Distressed by the violence and moral decline of his own lifetime, Livy wanted to encourage a return to earlier republican virtues, and he notes in the Preface to his work how, by concentrating on that idealised past, he had been enabled to take his mind off the less appealing realities of the present, and to 'withdraw mine eyes from beholding the raging wickedness of the times'.[2] (Sounding remarkably similar, a current Oxford professor, Niall Ferguson, has described how 'Studying history is a form of therapy for me, because it helps me escape the tackiness of the modern age'.)* For some, then, the writing of history can provide an escape route from present difficulties; and for the reader too, in the second place, there can – it has been claimed – be similar advantages. In the seventeenth century Pierre Le Moyne wrote of history's 'many Charms', whereby 'the Sad lose their Grief, and oftentimes the Sick their Maladies'; and he illustrated his point by citing the example of the Spanish King Alphonso. Given up by his physicians, and having emptied every chemist shop without effect, the king was reportedly soon cured of his illness by a dose of Roman history which, again, took his mind off current problems.[3]

Few twenty-first-century historians would expect their work to be prescribed in this way as an alternative medicine, but it is clear from the flourishing 'heritage industry', and from currently popular books, films, and television programmes, that people do continue to find a study of history both interesting and entertaining. History can still be justified by its sheer amusement value.

* *Sunday Telegraph Magazine*, 11 February 2001, p. 21.

3 MORAL TEACHING

> History enhanceth noble men, and depresseth wicked men and fools.
> (Ranuphus Higden)[4]

For puritanical historians, however, mere entertainment has seldom been an adequate objective, and – as the fourteenth-century author of the above quotation claims – their writings often include an element of moral teaching. Even Herodotus, who has often been accused of being just 'an agreeable story-teller, who meant to entertain, and nothing more',[5] can be seen to have had a serious moral purpose. Recounting the story of the ancient Greeks' struggles against Persia with engaging naivete, and with apparently ingenuous repetition of other people's entertaining stories, Herodotus in fact sets out to teach a lesson. In the opening lines of his work, he expresses the hope of 'preserving from decay the remembrance of what men have done, and of preventing the great and wonderful actions of the Greeks and the Barbarians from losing their due meed of glory'.[6] But why should we be encouraged to remember 'great and wonderful actions', if not for some moral purpose? Why should it matter if the Greeks or the barbarians fail any longer to receive 'their due meed of glory', unless some overarching moral order is assumed, with the maintenance of which we are ourselves to be concerned? Clearly, Herodotus believes that his story of the Greeks and barbarians actually illustrates the existence of a moral framework, in accordance with which the Greeks overcame their enemies, and good triumphed over evil. The Persians are represented by their king Xerxes, who patently displays the sin of hubris (pride): his invasion of Greece involves bridging the intervening Hellespont, and when his engineers' work is destroyed by a storm he shouts and behaves in a highly presumptuous way that is typically 'barbarian'.[7] Such sin is then shown to be inevitably followed by the nemesis (retribution) of defeat, and the validity of some moral order in the universe is duly re-affirmed.

As Herodotus's professional successor, and as one who wrote self-consciously as a historian, Thucydides deliberately and explicitly distances himself from any tradition of mere entertainment. Some writers are concerned, not so much with truth as with attracting immediate attention, but his own work, he explains, has been written '*not* as an essay which is to win the applause of the moment'. Rather, it is designed to be useful and to last, to be 'a possession for all time'.[8] It will, he believes, prove of lasting value, because it contains a *moral* lesson of universal applicability. Again there is the assumption of a moral order, of which we should be aware, and in accordance with which we should organise our lives. This had been ignored by the Athenians, who like the earlier Persians displayed hubris in their imperialistic ambitions and in their inhumane treatment of their enemies. This is clearly shown by Thucydides in his dramatised account of the diplomatic exchanges and debate between the Melians, the inhabitants of a small island who wanted to remain neutral, and the powerful Athenians who were determined to enlist them on their side. The moral arguments of the Melians are brushed aside with a terrifying cynicism by the militarily stronger power, and the scene of that hubristic denial of morality has its later resolution in another Thucydidean set-piece, showing the catastrophic defeat of the Athenians in Sicily. Their demoralisation and ultimate defeat by the Spartans then constitute their deserved retribution, nemesis, and it again reveals the continuing existence of a moral order. So Thucydides' particular history of the Peloponnesian war unfolds like a tragic drama, intended to teach its audience some general truth about the human situation.

Some two thousand years after Thucydides wrote, his seventeenth-century admirer and translator, the philosopher Thomas Hobbes, is similarly convinced of history's moral value. In the Preface to his translation of Thucydides, he writes of 'the principal and proper Work of History being to instruct, and enable Men by the knowledge of Actions Past, to bear themselves prudently in the Present, and providently towards the Future'. Again the moral dimension is clear: history is to be not only delightful, but also useful and instructive. An important function of the subject is to provide practical guidelines, by showing the past workings of a morally ordered universe in which the good are rewarded and the bad punished. Thus, in the words of one of Hobbes's contemporaries, it can be seen that history 'stirs up men to vertue, and deters from vice, whilst they read how the one is rewarded, and the other punished'.[9] In much, if not most historical writing, some such underlying moral is evident – a moral that almost inevitably emerges from any attempt to make some *sense* of the past, or to give it *meaning*. That moral is sometimes made explicit, but it may more often be implied.

3.1 'Truth'

Truth . . . is the Soul of History. (Pierre Le Moyne)[10]

While some moral lessons derive from accounts of specific actions or events, others relate to a more general search for 'truth', which has often been claimed (as in the above quotation) as the very 'Soul of History'. Indeed, a 'search for truth' has motivated many past historians, who have remained largely unaffected by any philosophical or theoretical problems provoked by that phrase.

There is thus a long tradition of historians aspiring to convey 'the truth' about the past events of which they write. This objective of reporting 'truth' often derives from an explicitly stated wish to correct what are seen as other people's misconceptions. So, for example, the first-century chronicler of the Romans' confrontation with the Jews, Flavius Josephus, had an over-riding aim, as a Jew himself, to set the record straight concerning his people's past experience. For many, he indicates, are still ignorant of what happened; historians have left distorted accounts, after using 'vain and contradictory' sources or simply false reports; or they have adopted a position of partiality, through hatred of the Jews or a desire to flatter the Romans, so that their writings 'contain sometimes accusations, and sometimes encomiums, but nowhere the accurate truth of the facts'. It is, then, to 'the accurate truth of the facts' that Josephus aspires. Unlike those who are biased in either direction, he will seek to 'prosecute the actions of both parties with accuracy'.[11]

Now, this may to the twenty-first-century ear sound an over-simplified, unrealisable goal; but what is significant is that Josephus does show himself aware of some of the difficulties that lie in the way of his achieving it. So he sets out his own credentials: he is 'by birth an Hebrew, and a priest also, and one who fought against the Romans myself, and was forced to be present at what was done afterwards'. He can therefore, he concedes, hardly qualify as a detached observer: having been so closely involved in the events which he intends to record, he recognises 'the passions I am under'.

So he is clear that he 'must be allowed to indulge some lamentations upon the miseries undergone by my own country', but on the understanding that his personal lamentations are to be kept isolated from his actual historical account. This last, he explains, has cost him 'great pains', aspiring as he does to 'the real truth of historical facts', in order 'to preserve the memory of what hath not been before recorded, and to represent the affairs of one's own time to those that come afterwards'.

Josephus realises, then, that it is not easy to keep personal interests out of his own account, but, like Thucydides, he makes a serious attempt to write a history, not for the sake of his readers' immediate amusement, but rather 'for the sake of those that love truth'. His aspiration to bear witness and to publish a true record of events in the face of uncomprehending disbelief, was paralleled in the twentieth century by survivors and reporters of some of the horrors of the Second World War. The charismatic envoy from the Polish resistance forces, Jan Karski, hoped in 1944 that through his personal account 'the free peoples all over the world will be able to form an objective opinion as to how the Polish people reacted during the years of German conquest'; and Primo Levi has recorded that he was determined to survive the Auschwitz death-camp, 'with the precise purpose of recounting the things we had witnessed and endured'.[12] The desire to record historical 'truth' in this way has survived the challenges to be considered in later chapters.

3.2 Examples

> History is philosophy teaching by examples.
>
> (Dionysius of Halicarnassus)[13]

Moral teaching, though, usually goes beyond a simple attempted presentation of 'the truth': it additionally seeks to provide good examples from the past for emulation in the present. This programme was set for the subject as early as the first century BC, when Dionysius of Halicarnassus made the often repeated claim above, that 'History is [moral] philosophy teaching by examples.' By that he meant, like Herodotus and Thucydides before him, that history gives evidence of some universal moral order, in the context of which bad people are punished and the good rewarded; so that historians actually provide *particular* and *practical* examples of those moral precepts which may be formulated in more *general* and *theoretical* terms by philosophers.

That view of history's moral function has long persisted, with Dionysius's catch-phrase often plagiarised or quoted, and the examples cited by ancient historians of Greece and Rome frequently recycled. Not surprisingly, these classical models become particularly prominent after the Renaissance, and they are constantly appealed to by early-modern historians. So it is Livy again who, together with Herodotus, Thucydides, and Tacitus, appears on the frontispiece to Richard Braithwait's *Survey of History*, published in 1638, and it is by reference to these predecessors that Braithwait sets out his own objectives.

Thus, with an obvious awareness of working within a continuing historiographical tradition, Braithwait early in his work seeks to clarify the moral point of it all. History is to record what has been done in the past, in order to inspire others towards the right direction in the present and future:

> The true use and scope of all Histories ought to tend to no other purpose, than a true Narration of what is done, or hath beene achieved either in Forraigne or Domesticke affaires; with a modest Application (for present use) to caution us in things Offensive, and excite us to the management of imployments in themselves generous, and worthy imitation.[14]

Emphasis is again put on the moral aims of the subject. Without history, we would lose our knowledge of those past models which need to be presented for the reader's imitation. For we can benefit from looking back at what happened to good people and to bad; we should naturally emulate the virtuous and successful; and we may learn from past mistakes. Such moral aims will of course affect the historian's presentation of material: the focus must be on the provision of good examples, and 'a good historian will alwayes expresse the actions of good men with an Emphasis, to solicite the reader to the affecting the like meanes, whereby he may attain the like end'.[15]

Models, then, are to be deliberately provided, so that the reader can easily see what has happened to the ambitious, the greedy, the sensual, and the slothful; and armed with such knowledge it should be possible to avoid their awful fates. Nor for Braithwait are the lessons confined (as they sometimes are for others[16]) to one specific

Figure 1 The moral purpose of history: Richard Braithwait and some ancient models. *A Survey of History*, frontispiece of 1651 edition.

social group. At one level, members of the humbler classes may be taught to curb their ambition – a characteristic that is seen to be too often accompanied by excessive servility; and at the other end of the social scale, the high-ranking might learn to moderate their natural arrogance. In short, anyone should benefit from the examples provided by the study of history; and there are, incidentally, social spin-offs, in that the subject admirably equips one for all social intercourse: 'to inable you for all Companies, no study may better accommodate, nay accomplish you, than the knowledge of History'. But the main point remains moral: even for those lacking social aspirations, history will inevitably remind everyone on a personal level of their own mortality, and so it will prepare them for death by showing 'what diversity of infirmities accompany us; how they are the Suburbs of Death: and how every yeere, nay, every Moonth bringeth some one or new malady, as a Messenger of Man's mortality'.[17]

Embedded in history, then, are exemplary lessons for everyone. But that granted, Braithwait warns that we must beware of learning only what we want to learn, of extracting from the past only what confirms our own prejudices – with ambitious people perceiving only success-stories to be emulated, and the 'voluptuous' concerned only with light love-stories in which they can fantasise about their own participation. History has to be used properly, to provide moral and educational benefit; and even historians themselves may then learn one further and important lesson: that they should avoid subservience. For history teaches not least that the historian should never be 'bought', that he should never, in view of some political or financial obligation, forsake the pursuit of truth. So Braithwait fulminates against 'all clawing Parasites that make their Pen *Mercenary*, and therefore . . . dare not unrip the vitiousnesse of times; lest by unbosoming Truth, they should incurre the offence of some person'.[18] Historians in short can learn to remain true at least to themselves.

This high moral purpose of history is similarly emphasised by Braithwait's near-contemporary, Degory Wheare, whose *Method and Order of Reading both Civil and Ecclesiastical Histories* was originally published in 1635 and frequently re-printed through the seventeenth century. Wheare is scornful about the value of mere military history, and advocates rather the study of those historical examples which will, again, re-emphasise the moral order. So we should concentrate on 'what things are famously and wisely done in relation to any vertue; what is basely and cruelly done as to vices; what event followed; how happy the ends of good Actions proved; how sad and calamitous those of leud [sic] Actions'.[19] Clearly the morality inherent in the world and in its history is never questioned. Wheare believes that what has actually happened has come about as a result of God's own providence, so that appropriate moral lessons can properly be drawn from their study. Again, though, it is desirable to concentrate attention on good people, for it is these who provide salutary examples: 'by being frequently imprinted upon our minds, [they] cause us to remember who we should be like, and who not'. Furthermore, by studying the outcome of past actions, we may expect to find guidance for the future: by the use of historical examples, we may 'foresee the Events of things, perceive their Causes, and by remembring those Evils that are past, provide Remedies against those which are coming upon us'.[20]

The moral order duly illustrated by these examples is, of course, strictly Christian, and a slight problem is revealed by Wheare in relation to the history of earlier pre-Christian periods. Early Christians themselves could maintain their approval of such Greek philosophers as Socrates and Plato, whose thought could effectively be assimilated into Christianity; but they had to concede nonetheless that something in those 'honorary' Christians must be lacking. Without the benefit of Christ, they must surely have suffered some disadvantages. And similarly in the context of historical study, some pagans could clearly be shown to have been virtuous, but (in view of Christianity's claim to be unique) they must inevitably display certain deficiencies. So, Wheare writes:

> We cannot deny but that the Stories of the Heathens propound to us very frequent and clear Examples of Justice, Fortitude and Temperance, and of all other Vertues: but if they be thoroughly examin'd and weighed in the balance of Truth, they will be found lame, imperfect and polluted, and not rightly related either to the Mercy or Justice of God.[21]

The exclusiveness of seventeenth-century Christianity precludes the possibility of a morality derived from any other source; and this has implications not least for historical interpretation and assessment.

Nevertheless, despite their sometimes pagan origins, biographies of famous people are frequently offered for moral edification. This genre originates in the first century with Plutarch's *Lives* of famous Greeks and Romans, a work which long continued to provide a rich quarry of historical examples. So they are claimed by their English translators to:

> teach us how great vices, accompanied with great abilities, may tend to the ruin of a state; . . . how Ambition attended with magnanimity, how Avarice directed by political sagacity, how Envy and Revenge armed with personal valour and popular support, will destroy the most sacred establishments, and break through every barrier of human repose and safety.[22]

It is likely that Plutarch himself originally had some such moral purpose in mind, for he carefully distinguishes his biographies or 'Lives', from 'History', indicating that his concern is not so much with comprehensive coverage (assumed to be the task of history), as with a vivid representation of an exemplary individual character, who can then be compared and contrasted with another 'parallel'.[23]

Plutarch's popular model is certainly imitated in the Renaissance and early-modern period, when the writing of biographies again becomes fashionable. Giorgio Vasari, in his *Lives of the Most Eminent Painters, Sculptors, and Architects*, was similarly concerned to give examples for future edification. In fact he declines to write of anything 'that is not good and worthy of praise', so that his 'words shall serve as a spur, moving each [artist] to continue labouring worthily, and to seek to advance himself perpetually from good to better'. His ultimate purpose here, though, is not political, but cultural: looking back over the history of art, he sees a cyclical process, in the sense that from a high point in antiquity, the arts had fallen into a decay from which they were just recovering; and he hopes that his own recorded examples will serve to prevent any future decline – that they 'may avail to keep those arts in life, or may at least serve as an incentive to exalted minds to provide them with more efficient aids and support'.[24]

As biographies become increasingly popular through the seventeenth century, their provision of moral edification remains an important motivation. Izaak Walton published his account of George Herbert, as a 'great example of holiness', written, he explains, 'not without some respect to posterity'.[25] And in the same didactic vein, William Wotton, in his *History of Rome*, included accounts of pairs of lives – one adjudged good, the other bad. They could, he suggested, constitute 'the properest Instances to set Virtue and Vice, and the Consequences of them both, in a clear and full Light'. The relevance of this was not only for the individual, but for society at large and politics, for a ruler not least could be shown 'how much more Glorious and Safe it is, and Happier both for Himself and for his People, to govern well than ill'.[26]

The use of biography for such moral instruction reached its apogee in the nineteenth century. 'Heroes' formed the very basis of Thomas Carlyle's approach to historical writing, when he actually defined his own meaning of 'universal history' as 'the History of the Great Men who have worked here'.[27] And the selection of such 'great' models then provided the starting-point for that later eminent Victorian Samuel Smiles, whose lives and biographical sketches were specifically designed to furnish exemplary 'lessons of industry, perseverance, and self-culture', in the hope that these would 'be found useful and instructive, as well as generally interesting'.[28] The fashionable virtues of thrift and self-help, application and perseverance, energy and courage, and all those characteristics that defined 'the true gentleman', were illustrated by Smiles in a varied range of paragons, embracing engineers and inventors, potters and painters, businessmen, and even biographers. His examples included George Stephenson and Joshua Reynolds, Wedgwood, Livingstone, and Stonewall Jackson; and their very diversity contributed to the establishment of his single main historical point, that 'the chief use of biography consists in the *noble models of character* in which it abounds'.[29]

That Victorian emphasis on study of the 'heroic' may in the longer term have had negative effects, inasmuch as there has arguably continued to be an excessive emphasis on those perceived as 'major' figures, to the exclusion of a host of lesser-known mortals who may, from a different perspective, be of no less importance. This is an issue that will be pursued in Chapter 6, section 1.2; but the point here remains that historians have often used biography as one clear way of teaching moral lessons through examples.

4 RELIGIOUS TEACHING

4.1 Christianity and Providence

> History . . . as a play written by God. (R. G. Collingwood)[30]

Moral examples in the European tradition have usually been given within a Christian context, and a specifically Christian morality has often been imposed upon the past. On a personal level, the events of one's life could be explained by reference to 'Providence', or the direct intervention of God in the affairs of everyday human life. Such divine interest ensured that any morally bad behaviour was immediately punished. In a seventeenth-century tract ominously entitled *God's Judgements upon Drunkards, Swearers and Sabbath-Breakers*, the case of John Bone, a coachman, provides one typical example. Already notorious for swearing and drinking, Mr Bone became so drunk one Sunday, when he should have been at church, that he fell off his coach and was trampled to death by his horses. This story was then sanctimoniously recorded as being one more 'doleful example of God's immediate hand'.[31]

More generally, history as a whole is seen as the unfolding of God's pre-ordained plan or, in R. G. Collingwood's analogy, as the performance of 'a play written by God'. Whereas classical and Jewish historians had assumed a cyclical pattern, in which the same old things came round time after time and there was 'no new thing under the sun',[32] Christians could more optimistically claim a linear progression. In God's play, the central act is the coming of Christianity itself, when Christ's birth marks the author's own entrance on to the historical stage, and gives notice that the final scene (already written) will be a Day of Judgement. Any previous pagan history, then, has to be relegated to a comparatively minor role: it constitutes merely a sort of introduction – a means to an end, in a process that is to reach its culmination only later; and pagan thought – philosophy and science – can be relegated to the dismissive category of (unacceptable) 'heresy'.[33] Augustine writes of earlier 'false doctrine [which] runs round in a circular maze': that is to be replaced by a belief that whatever happens constitutes the straightforward and progressive unfolding of God's providential plan for humanity.[34]

The fashion for this sort of 'providential' history reached its climax during the middle ages. This is not surprising, since the mediaeval period is generally characterised as an age of faith, or of belief in Christianity, and indeed, in terms of conventional periodisation, it is by that very religious emphasis that the middle ages are distinguished from secular modernity. Naturally, therefore, historical writing of the time manifests some obvious characteristics of Christian belief.

As one example of this, we may take the man often decribed as 'the father of English history' – the Venerable Bede, whose *Ecclesiastical History of the English Nation*, completed some four years before his death in AD 735, soon gained a European reputation and remains by far the best known historical work dating from this period. From a historiographical point of view, this work is particularly interesting, since Bede makes it quite clear that he is very aware of what, as a historian, he is trying to do, and why. As we might have expected, his motivation is the standard one of providing moral guidance: the history of good men should provoke imitation, while an account of the wicked should deter people from evil and again lead to actions more worthy of their God. More interestingly, though, Bede clarifies in his Preface how he has set about his work. So, like any reputable historian, he duly cites his sources. The earliest part of his history, he explains, has been derived from the writings of his predecessors, but for more recent times his principal authority has been the 'learned and reverend' Abbot Albinus, a man of impeccable credentials, having been educated at Canterbury and so at the centre of Christian activity in the country. His intermediary, one Nothelm, had reported on all written records and oral traditions, and had even gone to Rome to consult the archives there. Contacts in other parts of England had sent information on the development of Christianity in their own areas; monks had been consulted; letters had been studied; reports had been received from 'persons of good credit'; and use had been made of 'the faithful testimony of innumerable witnesses, who might know or remember'. Overall, then, it is clear that Bede had taken his responsibility as a historian very seriously, and had 'laboured sincerely to commit to writing such things as I could gather from common report, for the instruction of posterity'.

In view of such protestations, which would do credit to a twenty-first-century historian, it may seem all the more surprising to find that Bede's interpretation of events sounds in many ways strangely alien to our own time (though our surprise derives of course from anachronistic expectations). In particular, God's hand is seen as constantly intervening to further the cause of Christianity in England: what we read in Bede's history is nothing less than the unfolding story of 'a play written by God'.

This providential interpretation of events is clear from the account of the country's first martyrdom, which took place during the great persecution of Christians by the Roman emperor Diocletian in AD 305 – over four hundred years before Bede was actually writing. Alban, while still a pagan, was entertaining in his house a clergyman who was in flight from his persecutors. Through the intervention of 'Divine grace', he was suddenly converted to Christianity, and when soldiers came to arrest the clergyman, he gave himself up instead to the authorities. Having confessed to his new faith and having bravely refused to worship the pagan gods, Alban was tortured and taken away for execution, and it was then that miraculous events supposedly occurred. First, the waters of a river parted to enable him to pass on his way – a miracle which prompted the executioner to throw down his sword and offer himself in Alban's place. Next, having climbed a hill and prayed for water, Alban immediately saw a spring appear at his feet – the water having evidently been diverted from the dried-up river, which then, 'having performed the holy service, returned to its natural course'. Alban's actual execution, too, resulted in the providential punishment of the man who performed the wicked deed: he never saw the results of his work for 'his eyes dropped upon the ground together with the blessed martyr's head'. These various miracles so astonished the judge that he ordered a stop to the persecution, and Bede reports that up to his own time sick people continue to be cured and wonders to be worked at the shrine of St Alban.[35]

Other miraculous events are recorded throughout Bede's history. Ships are saved from storms; the blind have their eyesight restored, and withered limbs grow healthy; fires are quenched, and Christian armies triumph with divine assistance. Particularly good people are surrounded by miraculous events. The most Christian king, Oswald, for example, was killed by pagans, but where he fell, sick people and animals were regularly cured; earth from that same spot possessed miraculous properties; and from the king's bones themselves emanated a pillar of light. Not surprisingly, his tomb became a shrine widely renowned for its miraculous properties, and through all these wonderful events the presence of divine ordering on earth was clear.

The life of St Cuthbert similarly exemplifies for Bede the ever-present power of Providence. His treatment of this important Christian figure is particularly interesting.[36] Indeed, he devotes a whole separate work to an account of his life and miracles, and again in his Preface insists that he has 'taken care to commit to writing what I clearly ascertain to be the truth'. Bede wants to clarify that his writing derives from 'minute investigation' and 'the most accurate examination of credible witnesses', some of whom have actually been named, 'to establish the truth of my narrative'; and after his draft had been further corrected and amended by other authorities, he himself claims to be confident that, following God's assistance, his work was finally 'perfect'. And the point of that work, again, was to provide an example of an ideal Christian life – a historical example of a man whose whole life revealed the presence and unfolding of God's providential plan. So Cuthbert is shown as not only responsible for miracles during his lifetime. Manifestations of his saintliness continued even after death: having been buried for eleven years, his body was found to be 'whole, as if it had been alive . . . more like one asleep than a dead person'; and numerous miracles were recorded at his tomb. The point of Bede's account, then, was to provide one more piece of evidence for the truth and power of Christianity. His history duly demonstrates the unfolding of that truth.

Following the Reformation and the split between Protestant and Catholic branches of the Christian church, some historians' theology becomes more partisan, with God seen to favour one side or the other. In Protestant England, John Foxe's *Book of Martyrs* was designed to highlight the evils of the Catholic church and to show how reformed Protestantism by contrast had been instituted by God himself. The power of God had been manifested throughout history, being evidenced in particular by numerous Christian martyrs, but finally by the death of the Catholic Queen Mary. No fewer than 284 had been martyred during her reign, so it was small wonder that her end had been divinely authorised: 'It so pleased the heavenly majesty of Almighty God, when no other remedy would serve, by death to cut her off', leaving the way open for Elizabeth's accession as the fulfilment of his plan.[37]

This belief in providential ordering, and in the direct intervention of God into the actual subject-matter of history is further illustrated on the very threshold of the modern age. Sir Walter Raleigh, in his *History of the World* (1614), is sometimes seen as introducing into historical writing a more secular concentration on secondary causation. But the frontispiece still shows the eye of Providence overlooking that world, the history of which is about to be written; and the religious, or more specifically Christian perspective is thereby directly acknowledged. On either side are 'Good' and 'Bad' reputation, ready presumably for instant identification in terms of that all-seeing eye. And the great figure of 'History' herself is shown ready, with the help of 'Experience' and 'Truth', to trample on 'Death' and 'Oblivion'. For those who fail to read the pictorial message, a verse alongside reads (in part):

> From Death and darke Oblivion (neere the same)
> The Mistresse of Mans life, grave Historie,
> Raising the World to good or evill Fame,
> Doth vindicate it to Eternitie.

For Raleigh, then, history is once more justified by the way it serves to demonstrate the exemplary morality of God's all-seeing Providence in the affairs of human beings.

A more modern example of this sort of belief may be taken from the editorial gloss on a point introduced by Josephus in his preface. Where the Jewish historian mentions the misfortunes of the Jews as being the greatest ever suffered, his more favoured Christian commentator adds the note:

> That these calamities of the Jews, who were our Saviour's murderers, were to be the greatest that had ever been since the beginning of the world, our Saviour had directly foretold, Matt. xxiv. 21, Mark xiii. 19, Luke xxi. 23, 24; and that they proved to be such accordingly, Josephus is here a most authentic witness.[38]

History, then, had simply unfolded in accordance with God's plan and in a way that had, on divine authority, been foretold. The Bible can accordingly be presented to provide corroborative evidence for Josephus's claim, and at the same time morally to justify the infliction of misfortune. For Christians, the whole episode had been providentially ordered, and served to illustrate once more the

Figure 2 Providential history defies death and oblivion: Walter Raleigh, *History of the World*, 1614.

dramatic interactions of good and evil in 'a [morality] play written by God'.

In that unfolding play, it has always been convenient to have God on one's own side, and ambitious individuals and nations have seldom shown reticence in claiming identification as God's chosen instruments. Early in the eighteenth century, the American Cotton Mather, having fled from 'the depravations of Europe', claims his new land as a newly regained Eden in which salvation can be found.[39] America's 'manifest destiny' would later justify expansion westwards, as well as military intervention both in the civil war and World War I. Nineteenth-century European imperialists similarly claimed providential backing for their mission in Europeanising and so 'civilising' the colonies. Indeed, as late as 1948, the Afrikaaners in South Africa confirmed the traditional position that 'History must be taught in the light of revelation, and must be seen as the accomplishment of God's will for the world and humanity'.[40] And in their opposing trenches in the First World War, both English and German soldiers were assured (if not reassured) that God was on their side. The followers of twenty-first-century fundamentalist sects seem no less confident that they are acting out a history pre-ordained by their respective gods; and in 1984 readers of English popular newspapers were advised that a fire in York Minster, following the ordination there of a controversial bishop, could well have been 'an act of God'. Even in a supposedly secular society, a belief in the providential ordering of history still runs deep.

4.2 Secularisation

> Let us leave . . . the *divine* part in the hands of those with whom it is deposited, and confine ourselves solely to that which is *historical*.
>
> (Voltaire)[41]

While Christian historians have often written God into their work, others have taken no less care to exclude him, and an attempted 'secularisation' of history is evident even before the Christian era. In his account of early Rome, Livy describes how previous historians have often introduced supernatural explanations, mingling the divine with the human in order to add dignity to the city's origins. But he himself is concerned only with explanations in terms of human beings, with 'the lives and manners of this *people*';[42] so in his account 'gods' are deliberately excluded.

That classical approach started its recovery at the Renaissance, when historians focused again on Greek and Roman rather than Christian models, and, with a political rather than theological emphasis, identified history's crucial point as not so much the Incarnation as the decline of the Roman Empire. But, as we would expect, it is from the eighteenth century that attempts have increasingly been made to minimise or even eliminate supernatural explanations from history. The intellectual movement of the 'Enlightenment' is characterised not least by its tendency towards secularisation. Even if the world had been initially created by God, it nonetheless awaited its completion by human beings. Man himself, in Kant's words, is 'to bring forth everything out of himself . . . entirely as his own work',[43] so history becomes an account of what human beings specifically do. There can then be the rigid distinction, envisaged by Voltaire in the quotation heading this section: a clear distinction between history on the one hand and theology on the other.

Voltaire's proposal for such disciplinary apartheid derives from a concern that distortions in history can result from theologically induced prejudices. In this he may well have been influenced by his friend Henry St John, Lord Bolingbroke, whose work he greatly admired and whose historical writings he publicly defended. Bolingbroke expressed his own disgust at what he called the 'abuse of history' by religions, and at the way religious leaders had blatantly used history for their own purposes. He became extremely cynical about the historical account supposedly recorded in the Bible, and criticised the scriptures as being no more authoritative than mere 'holy romances'. So reflecting the new critical spirit towards such texts, he asks rhetorically: 'What are they? and how came they to us?' And he goes on to assert that they have, at times and by persons unknown, been changed, modified, and adapted; and – what is even worse – they have been deliberately misused, for the purpose of bolstering religious authority:

> Deliberate systematical *lying* has been practised and encouraged from age to age; and among all the *pious frauds* that have been employed to maintain a reverence and zeal for their religion in the minds of men, this *abuse of history* has been one of the principal and most successful.

Historical terminology itself, he claims, gives a clue to this abuse, and he instances particularly the Crusades, which 'those wretched Christians . . . so *improperly* called the holy wars'.[44]

It was small wonder, then, that Bolingbroke's *Letters on History* were widely condemned by Christian apologists, and in such circles the historian's posthumous reputation was little enhanced by any defence provided by the no less notorious Voltaire. But in the face of continuing opposition, the secular emphasis of both these men in relation to the subject of historical writing has generally persisted.

Taken in its wider sense, however, some 'religious' dimension to history remains difficult to avoid, inasmuch as 'secularisation' itself implies the adoption of an attitude towards that subject. It becomes in effect a replacement criterion equivalent to 'progress' – which is itself virtually another theological standpoint, from which to view the course of history and to determine what should or should not be included. By trying, like Livy and his successors, totally to exclude the 'divine' or religious, historians must stand in danger of excluding a whole range of human experience; and where secularisation is taken as a goal, the development of secularisation itself becomes the organising principle or 'direction' in terms of which history is made to seem meaningful. Simplicity is thus again bought at the price of open-mindedness, and secular historians can be seen to be just as guilty of distortion as their religious counterparts, similarly 'abusing' history by interpreting the past in their own exclusive terms.

5 POLITICS AND IDEOLOGY

> History is never only history *of*; it is always history *for*.
>
> (Lévi-Strauss)[45]

The ideological component of historical accounts has long been recognised: even Homer's seemingly naive account *of* the Trojan War was long ago criticised as having been politically motivated, as having been written *for* a particular political purpose. In the first century AD, the Greek orator Dion Chrysostom questioned the whole truth of Homer's account. Notoriously unreliable, he asserted, the poet had not simply exaggerated, but had gone 'so far as to represent the opposite of what actually occurred'. So, for example, the beautiful Helen, whose abduction was supposed to have provoked the war, had in fact been very pleased to marry Paris in a match that had been fully approved by her family. And as for the war's alleged dramatic ending, with the famous story of the wooden-horse by means of which Greek soldiers finally penetrated the Trojan defences, it was ludicrous to think that soldiers could have been concealed in that way without being noticed. The whole story could only be poetic fiction, and the truth was that, far from winning the war, the Greeks had actually lost it.

In support of that contention, Dion Chrysostom indicated an even earlier precedent for such ideologically based historical distortion: the Persians, he explained, had similarly claimed for political reasons to have won their war with the Greeks. That was quite clearly 'a false account; but, since it was the natural thing to do, it is quite possible that the king ordered this story to be spread among the inland tribes in order to keep them quiet'.[46] In both these cases, then, Dion Chrysostom insists that historical truth took second place to political propaganda.

Whatever the validity of those early examples, adaptations to historical data have constantly and deliberately been made for political and ideological purposes; and in particular, nationalistic emphases of the sort ascribed to the Persians and the Greeks have been noticed by more sceptical commentators. So Juan Luis Vives in the mid-sixteenth century criticised the patriotic priorities of various nationalistic European historians:

> The Frenchmen write of France; the Italians of Italy; the Spaniards of Spain; the Germans of Germany; the English of England, and others likewise, *for the sake of some specific nation.* The author of these things thinks that the only charge which he has undertaken is to inflate that people as much as he is able, and does not turn his eye to truth but to the reputation of that nation. This, they think, is how a history is written: to emphasise, dilate, embellish, and extol if that nation has done anything outstanding; and if it has acted ignominiously or basely, to conceal, to elevate, to extenuate, to defend, and to excuse.[47]

Such political emphases within history became particularly obvious and well-publicised in the twentieth century, when ideologically motivated re-writing of history became commonplace. Well aware of the power of the subject, Adolf Hitler insisted in *Mein Kampf* that 'History should not be learned as a list; it should inspire.' Any pretence of 'objective presentation', therefore, should be discarded in favour of an approach supportive of 'the more urgent goal of inspiring national pride'. History should be shown as a continual struggle, against the conspiracies of inferior peoples, to maintain racial purity; and the contribution of German heroes should especially be studied. The ideal of a distinctive and unified great nation could thus be shown to have developed from Roman times, through such heroic figures as Charlemagne, Luther, and Bismarck, to Hitler himself, in whom that glorious history reached its culmination. Meanwhile, the importance of events outside Germany could be minimised, so that, for example, the French Revolution was effectively removed as a subject of historical study – partly because Luther's revolution anyway came first, and partly because there must be no temptation to engage with any of the associated philosophical debates on political theory. The German student of the 1930s was to be protected from any 'danger of becoming a democrat, or anything of that sort'.[48]

For a post-war generation of Germans, similarly deliberate attempts have been made to re-write history, on the grounds of psychic health, and an important debate has ensued on the question of 'coming to terms with the past'. Some historians have tried to deny or to minimise the horrors of the Nazi period, effectively imposing a 'thought ban' on that time, and advocating what has been described as a 'stubbornly maintained rejection of memories'. Others by contrast have argued the need to confront and examine what happened, 'to keep alive . . . the memory of the sufferings of those who were murdered by German hands'; for, it is maintained, only by doing that can self-respect and the respect of others be gained. Only by contriving to 'break the nightmarish grip of the past over Germany's present', can a 'positive self-image . . . be created' for the future.[49]

That debate between German historians on 'the public use of history' has its parallels elsewhere, of course, and ideologically motivated history became notorious in the former USSR. 'The elimination of Trotsky from the official history of the 1917 Revolution, [and] the prominence given in it to Stalin', was noted by Pieter Geyl in 1955.[50] Since then, Stalin's role in Russian history has again been re-assessed, to the accompaniment of falling statues and the re-vision of history textbooks from which he has been virtually eliminated.[51] President Khrushchev himself noted in 1956 that 'historians are dangerous, and capable of turning everything topsy-turvy'; and in the politically inspired history utilised by leaders like him, individuals, as Marc Ferro concludes, 'come and go at the whim of those who succeed them', and historians have had to learn the 'art of double-writing, such that their work can be taken in both one sense and, if need be, its opposite'.[52]

In Britain likewise, similar adjustments continue to be made. 'Bomber' Harris's effigy, erected in London in 1992, stands as a late counterbalance to decades of neglect, during which Bomber Command in the Second World War was effectively written out of English history. Conversely, Winston Churchill, long acclaimed as the heroic war-time leader, has been dismissed in just 14 seconds of

Figure 3 History re-written: Stalin leaves Prague.

a 24-minute Government-backed video on the fiftieth anniversary of VE Day.[53] It is not clear how that changed historical perspective consists with the recent re-emphasis on the patriotic purpose of school history, in accordance with which the Secretary of State for Education in 1988 indicated that pupils should learn about 'the spread of Britain's influence for good throughout the world. . . . We should not be ashamed of our history, our pride in our past gives us our confidence to stand tall in the world today'.[54] But what is clear is that there is an explicitly accepted ideological dimension to at least some aspects of history-teaching in Britain.

In the United States there has, perhaps, for longer been a more sophisticated understanding (or more conscious and openly admitted recognition) of the inevitability of history's ideological freighting. The issue here was brought to the surface in the 1960s, not just by some trendy theoretical import from continental Europe, but by very practical domestic politics. In the context of increasingly acrimonious debates about military involvement in Vietnam, those contemporary historians known as newsreporters were forced consciously to confront their own methodologies and ideological presuppositions. Accused by politicians and by their own editors of failing to report 'objectively', they concluded, in the words of one, that 'what my editors were telling me was that objectivity meant that I should write within *their* definition of, within their unquestioned assumptions about, reality'.[55] In other words, as Peter Novick concludes in his study of 'objectivity' in history, 'what was most often at issue was their failure to accept official versions of the actions and fortunes of American troops in Vietnam . . .'[56]

Recognition of the practical impossibility of ever reporting anything (especially anything as inherently controversial as war) without adopting *some* standpoint, soon led to wider questions concerning history's implicit or explicit politicisation or utilisation for ideological purposes. Could the much vaunted concepts of 'balance' and 'neutrality' be maintained, even as theoretical objectives, in academia, when nothing less than a nation's identity – her future as well as her past – was at stake? And was such affected fence-sitting not only morally reprehensible but practically impossible, since in truth (as David Eakins perceived), 'The balancer is as committed as any ideologue, but without a real frame of reference of his own other than the prevailing mood of the moment'.[57] In other words, didn't the old historiographical ideal of 'objectivity' imply little more than ideological conformity?

American historiographical reassessments have continued more recently with such events as the 1992 celebrations of the country's 'discovery', when the achievements of Columbus were re-considered from non-Eurocentric standpoints. And in Australia, similarly, the past of the Aborigines, long conveniently considered as a 'historyless' people whose decimation should properly remain unrecorded, is undergoing re-assessment by means of their oral tradition.[58] In Africa too, John Tosh has described how, 'since independence history has been an important instrument for undermining the colonial psychology of dependence and inferiority'. In this context, he cites a significant resolution of the International Congress of African Historians passed in 1965, 'that an African philosophy of history which would serve as a liberation from the colonial experience must be a vital concern of all historians studying in Africa'.[59]

As a counterbalance to such nationalistic concerns, some historians have tried through their work self-consciously to promote more universal ideals. Writing in the mid-seventeenth century, Alexander Ross expressed views that may resonate with current aspirations.

Having in the course of his research surveyed the various doings of men over the centuries – their ambitions, their territorial aggression, their empire-building, and declines and falls – Ross comes to a radical conclusion concerning the vanity of all such earthly things; and his message is conveyed in the frontispiece to his work. This shows a triptych: in the centre, a historian; on the left, a warrior with sword and torch, and an inscription 'Nulla salus bello' ('There's no safety in war'); and on the right, a woman with an olive-branch, and 'Pax optima rerum' ('Peace is the best of all things'). Ross's own position is then clarified in the Preface:

> If you ask me to what purpose have all these stirs continually bin, and yet are stil in the World; I answer, to no other purpose, but that insatiable, covetous, and ambitious Mindes may have more of this earthly Turf to crawl and dominier upon (as if they wanted elbow-room) and some more clods of earth, whereof a little will content them, when their vast and ambitious thoughts are laid as low as their carcasses; then shall a short and narrow Coffin contain those, whom one, or more Kingdoms will not content.

LONDON, Printed for *John Clark*, and are to be sold at the Entrance into *Mercers-Chappel*, at the lower end of *Cheapside*, M. DC. LII.

Figure 4 Learning from history: the futility of war. Alexander Ross, *The History of the World*, 1652.

> . . . What madness is it then to turn the World upside-down, to cheat, oppresse, and murther one another, for more room, whereas a little will serve a contented mind.[60]

The futility of earthly ambitions in the face of mortality, thus leaves Ross firmly committed to pacifism, and this is the overall lesson that he draws from history. His knowledge of the past has given him a new and clear perspective on the present and the future, and has resulted in a distinct 'political' or 'ideological' position and answer to the question 'Why history?'.

A late twentieth-century example of the provision of historical underpinning for a more international orientation, is the new European history textbook, published in six languages, and supposedly used throughout the European Union. Written by representatives from every member nation except Luxembourg, it has been described, in its efforts not to offend any one of its potentially diverse readers, as 'rendering all countries equal', and as 're-writing the past to make a united Europe seem the continent's destiny'.[61] This approach may sound preferable to that decried by the anti-nationalistic Vives, but it is no less blatantly history *for* an ideological position.

Whether an authority's political aim is narrowly partisan, or nationalistic, or even cosmopolitan, the past can be (and has been, and is) constantly re-interpreted, and history re-written accordingly. In other words, the past is deliberately described afresh with a view to the perceived needs of the present; and this is just the situation envisaged by George Orwell in *Nineteen Eighty-Four*. His prescient totalitarian nightmare, first published in 1949, describes how the government maintained complete control of 'the past', ceaselessly re-interpreting it in accordance with the political requirements of their present. 'No written record, and no spoken word, ever made mention of any other alignment than the existing one.' So, as with the less than desirable memory of the Holocaust, which some would now write out of history, entire portions of the past had to be totally erased; while similarly, politically convenient lies could be injected into the historical record and so become 'truth'. '"Who controls the past", ran the Party slogan, "controls the future: who controls the present controls the past."' So, as the hero Winston explains:

> History has stopped. Nothing exists except an endless present in which the Party is always right. . . . [And] If the Party could thrust its hand into the past and say of this or that event, *it never happened* – that, surely, was more terrifying than mere torture and death?[62]

Political and ideological control is an essential aspect of historical study, and it is concerned not only with the sort of conscious and deliberate manipulations described above, but also with the often unconscious controls exercised in the very language or 'discourse' in which history is written. This has come increasingly under scrutiny during the last decade, and it will need to be further considered (in Chapters 4, 5, and 6), in relation to the subject's challenges and future aspirations.

6 CONCLUSION: CHANCE, CHANGE, AND EMPOWERMENT

> Chance favours only those who know how to court her.
>
> (Charles Nicolle)[63]

The most important implication of recognising history's ideological role, is that it encourages an awareness of historical contingency. In other words, it becomes evident that history could have been different, and that things could have been and could be other than what they are. Much of what has happened in the past has happened and has been interpreted quite arbitrarily, and the future course of events is no more fixed, but can still be affected. In fact, we are 'empowered' by realising that the direction of history, both as past narratives and as future events, can actually be changed.

The role of 'chance' within the development of individual lives and of national destinies is here crucial. Often 'chance' is thought of as something unavoidable, as something that inexorably *happens* without any rationale or any possibility of human control; but the force of the quotation heading this section is that one can positively *affect* matters (including historical outcomes) if one knows how to do so. The ancient Greek usage of the word 'Tyche' is here instructive: often translated as 'chance', it is a concept that related not only to what one was *allotted* (by the gods or by one's destiny), but also to what one *attained* for oneself through individual effort. The inherent ambiguity in the Greek word suggests that what befalls human beings is not always or necessarily outside their own power; and a historical awareness that things in the past might have been made to be otherwise, prompts speculation about the present possibility of affecting the way things turn out in the future. 'Chance' can come to be seen, not so much as a constraint, but more as a liberator.

So it is worth noticing that, throughout history, seemingly insignificant causes have sometimes had disproportionately significant effects. As Sir Walter Raleigh observed, 'Matters of much consequence, founded in all seeming upon substantiall reasons, have issued indeed from such pettie trifles, as no Historian would either thinke upon, or could well search out';[64] and that point about historical causation could be illustrated by numerous examples. One is pondered by the French philosopher and physicist, Pascal, who considers the form of Cleopatra's nose and concludes that, 'Had it been shorter, the whole aspect of the world would have been altered.'[65] His reasoning is that, had her nose been shorter, the Egyptian queen would have proved less attractive, first to Julius Caesar, by whom she had a son, and from whom her empire benefited; and, second to Mark Antony, with whom she subsequently established a relationship of enormous consequence to the development of the Roman empire. For Octavian (later Augustus, the first Roman emperor) was able to use his rival's association with Cleopatra for his own propaganda, and he ultimately gained control in Rome by defeating the two at the critical battle of Actium in 31 BC. At that point, Cleopatra's Egyptian kingdom was incorporated into the Roman empire, though had her nose been shorter she might even then have avoided the need for suicide, by going on in turn to attract yet a third Roman ruler.

However seemingly frivolous, this example serves to show the contingency of historical events, the role that 'chance' and factors as insignificant as the shape of a nose, may play in national and imperial history;[66] and the course of intellectual history seems no less open to such haphazard influences. With uncharacteristic levity, Galileo records how he came to acquire William Gilbert's book on magnetism. It would, he explains, 'perhaps . . . never have come into my hands, if a famous Peripatetic [Aristotelian] philosopher had not made me a present of it, I think in order to protect his library from its contagion'.[67] Whatever his actual motivation, Galileo's Peripatetic benefactor inadvertently helped to change the course of the history of science; and if he did so, why should not any other ordinary person? The lesson of 'chance's' power to change, is that that power lies within the reach of all. History can actually liberate us from our own apparent constraints, for it can demonstrate how *we* might affect its future course.

A recognition of such 'empowering' potentialities in the subject is again no new thing: it is in relation to that, for example, that the historian John Selden in the seventeenth century formulates his own objective. By the time he was writing, historians were becoming increasingly self-conscious about their activity, and sometimes even a little defensive, so they were concerned explicitly to justify what they were doing. When, therefore, Selden wrote his *Historie of Tithes*, he was quite uncompromising about professing his own aims, at least initially:

> To supply . . . the want of a full and faithfull collection of the *Historicall* part, was the *end* and *purpose* why this was compos'd, which might remaine as a furnisht Armorie for such as inquire about this Ecclesiastique Revenue, and preferring Truth before what dulling custom hath too deeply rooted in them, are not unwilling to change their old akorns for better meat.[68]

This, from a historian, sounds like fighting talk. Selden's work appears as highly scholarly, tracing in nearly five hundred pages the history of tithes right back to Abraham, and providing a detailed bibliography of 'ancient Records, and other Manuscripts' consulted. But its professed purpose is to furnish an 'armorie', and to provide 'truth' in place of deep-rooted traditional prejudice; and there is a strong implication of a resultant 'change' (from 'old akorns' to 'better meat') which will prove highly beneficial. It is, perhaps, no wonder that Selden incurred 'the high displeasure of the King and Bishops', and felt it expedient to present a submission, whereby 'I most humbly acknowledge my error which I have committed in publishing the history of Tithes' – especially inasmuch as he had, as a mere layman, had the effrontery to interpret the scriptures and so encroach on the preserve of professional theologians.[69]

Questioning conventional accounts has, then, long constituted a major justification for historical study, and in this respect Lord Bolingbroke is again instructive. His over-riding concern might be described as historical *self-awareness*, for he believes that it is that that brings a proper sense of *perspective*. Nationalistically based assertions of moral prejudices derive from a narrow parochialism, and a widened historical perspective should militate against such dangerously hubristic tendencies:

> There is scarce any folly or vice more epidemical among the sons of men, than that ridiculous and hurtful vanity, by which the people of each country are apt to prefer themselves to those of every other; and to make their own customs, and manners, and opinions, the standards of right and wrong, of true and false.

Whereas, then, history has often been – and continues to be – used for nationalistic, patriotic purposes, Bolingbroke offers the subject as an antidote to just such narrowness. Rather, he argues, it should serve 'to purge the mind of those national partialities and prejudices that we are apt to contract in our education'.[70]

This idealistic stance puts history at the centre of an education, which should, Bolingbroke believes, teach us not *what*, but *how*, to think; it is, as we might say, wisdom rather than knowledge that should be our concern. The subject is thus presented, not only as having a vital moral role, but as being inevitably bound up with politics. For it can, of course, be convenient for authorities to teach the virtue of submission to authority: our natural inclination to conform is then officially encouraged, and is actually confirmed by our education. So Bolingbroke explains:

> Men find it easy, and government makes it profitable, to concur in established systems of speculation and practice. . . . Much pains are taken, and time bestowed, to teach us what to think; but little or none of either, to instruct us how to think. The magazine of the memory is stored and stuffed betimes; but the conduct of the understanding is all along neglected, and the free exercise of it is, in effect, forbid in all places.[71]

Bolingbroke's recognition of the use of history to underpin existing social, economic, and political superstructures is thus balanced by his own projected use of the subject to undermine accepted and established positions. Instead of all roads being shown as duly leading to Rome, alternative routes might be signposted, so that freedom of choice might be enhanced. Instead of history appearing to run a pre-determined course, the ultimate contingency of that course might be highlighted – the fact that it could all so easily have worked out differently. And by implication, of course, the future direction of history can just as easily be changed.

Historians' offence to authority thus itself has a long history. It is not for nothing that Plato devised his Great Lie – a fictional past, a politically motivated and deliberately concocted history, with which the citizens of his ideal republic had to be indoctrinated in order to facilitate acceptance of their present situation;[72] nor is it for nothing that similarly in Orwell's *Nineteen Eighty-Four* the narrative of past history, as being an important means of establishing and maintaining power, was retained strictly within the control of the totalitarian government. An autonomous and critical history has always been a subject likely to challenge accepted views and to indicate alternative possibilities; it has thereby always been potentially subversive. This has been (and remains) an important answer to the question of why it should be studied.

Chapter 4

External challenges to the old model: some interdisciplinary perspectives

> We must consider how very little history there is; I mean real authentic history. . . . All the colouring, all the philosophy of history is conjecture.
> (Dr Johnson)[1]

> Time dissipates to shining ether the solid angularity of facts.
> (R. W. Emerson)[2]

1 INTRODUCTION

In Chapter 2, we considered the traditional and long-lived model of history as an 'objective' account of the past 'as it was' – a model that presupposed the existence of a unitary historical 'truth' which awaited the diligent historian's discovery and description; and we then saw in Chapter 3 that a number of justifications had been conventionally provided for *why* such history should be studied.

It was perhaps to that traditional model of the subject that Dr Johnson referred in the quotation above, when he wrote of 'real authentic history'. The trouble is that, as he realised, there is not much history like that. Such an account of the subject is greatly oversimplified, and soon gives way before the force of more theoretical challenges. A more conjectural 'philosophy of history' intrudes, and, in accordance with Emerson's perception, even the apparently reliable solidity of 'facts' becomes rapidly dissipated.

Challenges to the old model have come both from within the discipline of history itself and from outside, and we shall first, in this chapter, consider some aspects of the latter. Such external challenges, some with long histories of their own, have in modern times come from three main quarters, identified now as psychology, linguistics, and philosophy. Taken together, developments in these three related disciplines have demolished all possibility of viewing any historical account as a simple description of the past 'as it was'.

2 PSYCHOLOGY: PROBLEMS OF PERCEPTION

Historians are people, and history is about people, so many of the fundamental problems concerning the nature of history refer back to psychology. In order to understand what historians are doing and what they are able to do, it is necessary so far as possible to attain some understanding of human beings themselves. That requirement brings us back again to Plato's starting-point of the need for self-examination, and it takes us forward to some interdisciplinary contact with psychology.

Particularly relevant in this context is the study of perception – the study of what we perceive, and how and why;[3] for mechanisms of perception apply not only to present phenomena, but also to data relating to the past.

2.1 Data, selection, and meaning

In both present and past, we are confronted by more data, more information than we can ever hope to cope with. In everyday life, our senses are constantly assailed by a virtually infinite amount of information; so from the totality of potential experience presented to us, we select some parts and reject others. Thus, for example, we cannot hope to *see* everything that is in front of our eyes; so we *focus* on some things in what then becomes our *foreground*, and take less notice of others which are thus relegated to *background*. A lecturer in front of a large audience cannot at the same time have eye-contact with students in the front row and the back, any more than a car-driver can simultaneously focus on the speedometer immediately in front of him and on the car some hundred yards ahead. In each case, a decision has to be made about what is, at any given time, most important: a heckler in the back row of a lecture theatre may force a change of focus in the one case, just as would the sudden appearance of brake lights on the distant car in the other. The point is that we cannot concentrate on everything at once, so we *choose* what to pay particular attention to at any one time; and so we sometimes speak of people seeing or hearing only what they *want* to see or hear.

But wants may change, and so may our focus of attention. Such changes are made, sometimes consciously as in the examples above, or sometimes unconsciously, as when we suddenly realise that what we have been looking for has been all the time in front of our noses. Either way, by an adaptation of our focus, we are enabled to perceive something more clearly, but that greater clarity at one point is bought at the inevitable price of a reduction of clarity at another. The price of sunlight in one place is shadow in another, so our hypothetical car driver, through changing attention to the car one hundred yards away, may fail to take due notice of a pedestrian crossing the road just ahead.

Just as we cannot *see* everything with equal clarity at the same time, but have to choose our focus, so too with *hearing*: from the various sounds by which our ears are constantly assailed, we reject most as dispensable 'noise' and select some few to pay attention to, or hear. During the Second World War in the blitz, it was found that mothers would sleep through the noise of exploding bombs, but wake up at the crying of their babies: the noisy bombs had been filtered out of their experience as irrelevant, and so were not heard, while the babies' cries immediately impinged as being more significant. So again, consciously or unconsciously a choice had been made, and information selected for attention or rejection.

The actual *rejection* of potential information is thus a major factor in understanding our mechanisms of perception. The nineteenth-century American philosopher–essayist Ralph Waldo Emerson wrote of the world being full – full of the past as well as the present; so that 'if we saw all things that really surround us, we should be imprisoned and unable to move'.[4] And as a poet, W. H. Auden noted (what is equally true for us all) that he was 'bombarded by a stream of varied sensations which would drive him mad if he took them all in', and that it was 'impossible to guess how much energy we have to spend each day in not-seeing, not-hearing, not-smelling, not-reacting'.[5] Confronted by infinite possibilities, we feel 'spoilt for choice' and, like customers in front of overstocked supermarket shelves, suffer from agonised indecision, if not total paralysis. So what we do, as Emerson and Auden imply, is to turn a blind eye and ear to most of what surrounds us. In that way, we can at least make some sense of what remains and lead our normal lives.

But vital questions do intrude. What is the basis of our choice? What are the criteria for our selection? Why do we choose to see one thing as meaningful and important, while trivialising others? Why do we accept one thing as relevant, and discard others as irrelevant?

Why at any time do we actually perceive some things, while failing at that same time even to notice the existence of others – even though they are of course still there, awaiting our more positive perception at another time?

The answer seems to be that we make our decisions by virtue of who we are. Our own personal characteristics determine those choices and selections and meanings, and those characteristics in turn derive from genetic and environmental influences. This is not the point to introduce associated debates about the relative importance of nature and nurture, or of free-will and determinism, but it is the point to notice that our perceptions, however much they may be socially conditioned, are in the end very *personal* matters, and that they could quite easily be very different from what they are. It seems to make little sense, then, to claim that one is any more *correct* than any other: they are alternatives which we have, for the time being (consciously or unconsciously again), chosen to adopt.

Psychological studies indicate, further, that through the use of our senses from birth, we slowly build up for ourselves some meaningful interpretation of the data by which we are confronted, some 'understanding' of the nature of the external world and of our own relationship to it; and it is then in terms of that framework that we go on to make subsequent assessments. The word 'understanding' there is protected by inverted commas, since its implication might seem to be that we have grasped some 'truth' about the world as it actually is. That is an assumption which cannot initially be made. Rather, perhaps, we reach some 'accommodation' with the external world, in terms of which we can cope with it, and with ourselves within it; and the implication then is that there is available an infinite range of alternative 'accommodations' that we might have made, which would have been, or might have been, of no less ultimate validity. We might, that is, be quite different people from what we are – having different perceptions, preoccupations, and personalities; and that contingency in ourselves is shown by the very different people (people in an infinite number of respects different from ourselves) by whom we are surrounded. So we relate variously to the external world, to other people, and even to ourselves; and depending on our different standpoints in these respects, we make various judgements and evaluations, labelling some things as 'relevant', or 'noteworthy', while discarding others as their opposites.

A corollary follows, that our descriptions of what we perceive or experience can tell us more about ourselves than about the objects or phenomena that we are claiming to describe. This point has long been recognised. Leonardo da Vinci describes how one may look at a stained wall, and interpret the marks on that wall as landscapes or battle scenes, or faces; just as one can hear the rhythm of words in the sound of ringing bells. And the same insight underlies the so-called Rorschach ink-blot test, where the patient or subject is invited to describe a randomly made ink-blot, and will 'read into' what is intrinsically meaningless some interpretation that allegedly reveals his or her own preoccupations and concerns.

2.2 'Facts' and interpretations

It should already be clear that theories of perception have important implications for historians. For just as in the case of everyday perception, so too in historical study, we are faced by a potentially chaotic multiplicity of data; and we need to make some sense of that data by distinguishing identifiable particulars, by demarcating and classifying and relating them. In other words, we need to impose some structured framework on what might otherwise appear as just a jumbled mess.

First, then, we need to identify our building-blocks, our 'facts'; and, in line with theories of perception, facts may now be defined as data to which we have, consciously or unconsciously, decided to attribute some significance. A fact is something that has been chosen by us to be noticed, to be important for us. Such facts have been identified from a whole range of possibilities, an inexhaustible quarry of data relating to what has happened in the past; and, as with perception, it would be perfectly feasible to adopt an alternative standpoint, from which the data would appear quite different, and from which we might feel impelled to select quite different facts.

But having decided on significant items from the past, we need next to order them into some coherent picture, to make some general sense of what would otherwise remain as unconnected particulars. So again we cast our net over the chaos, imposing frameworks and boundaries, segmenting the past into decades or centuries, and filing people tidily into seemingly appropriate pigeon-holes. In this way, events such as revolutions can be defined and more or less accurately dated; a period of 'Renaissance' can be identified as having certain specific characteristics that emerge when the 'middle ages' end; and apparently representative writers of the seventeenth century can be classified as 'ancients' in contradistinction to some of their contemporary 'moderns'. It is within the context of such outlines or frameworks that history is written. But as in the case of perception, those outlines and frameworks, that meaning and that narrative, remain contingent. From another viewpoint, with another focus, it would all appear quite differently.

In this matter Primo Levi is instructive, as he writes about his own experience in the death-camps. For as he recounts what actually happened, he highlights the inadequacies of our rigid, mutually exclusive categorisations, and he relates his point explicitly to historiography. So he reminds us of how convenient it is to label some people as 'good' and others 'bad'. We can impose some meaning on events, or on our experience, or on our historical narrative, by identifying the 'good' Jewish (and other) prisoners who are passive victims, and by making them clearly distinguishable from the 'bad' SS guards who are cruel aggressors. That seems to make some sense of the situation. But in Levi's own perception it did not work like that. There was rather, as he describes, a merging of good and bad, of black and white, into a whole 'grey zone'. This embraced a wide spectrum of prisoners, some of whom achieved variously privileged positions in the camp hierarchy; so that on arrival, the newcomer might well experience his or her first violence at the hands, not of guards at all, but of fellow-inmates. This makes the recording and the appreciation of the history of what went on in the camps all the more difficult. Inasmuch as our normally accepted frameworks are transcended and inadequate, we actually find such untidiness difficult to cope with – difficult to comprehend, to account for and to understand. And Levi himself interestingly relates this point specifically to historical study:

> We . . . tend to simplify history; but the pattern within which events are ordered is not always identifiable in a single unequivocal fashion, and it may therefore happen that different historians understand and construe history in ways that are incompatible with one another. . . . The need to divide the field into 'we' and 'they' is so strong that this pattern, this bi-partition – friend–enemy – prevails over all others. Popular history, and also the history taught in schools, is influenced by this Manichaean tendency which shuns half-tints and complexities: it is

> prone to reduce the river of human occurrences to conflicts, and the conflicts to duels – we and they, Athenians and Spartans, Romans and Carthaginians.

In other words, this categorisation, this imposition of frameworks, makes life easier, or even possible. It enables us to live and to do history. And that must be a good thing – so long as we remember that what we are living with, what we are calling our history, is something that is imposed upon a far more complex reality than we could ever otherwise deal with, and that by accepting one history (or version of history), we are inevitably excluding many others.[6] When we recall that, in his novel *Ulysses*, James Joyce takes over one thousand pages to give his account of a single character in a single day, we must concede that historians inevitably select and simplify. But we do still need to remember that this is what is being done, for as Primo Levi continues:

> This *desire* for simplification is justified, but the same does not always apply to simplification itself. It is a working hypothesis, useful so long as it is recognised as such and not mistaken for reality; the greater part of historical and natural phenomena is not simple, or not simple with the simplicity that we would like.[7]

2.3 Re-visions

One problem that results from our personal selections and interpretations is that we are all set on self-fulfilling missions. That is, we formulate our model for coping with the world, and it is then only in terms of that model's framework that we experience the world. We accept or receive information that confirms and consolidates our model, while conversely rejecting anything that might serve to challenge or change it. We are in a sense 'imprisoned' within our own interpretations. So, for example, in personal relationships we tend to notice and record evidence that serves to corroborate previous evaluations which we have made of people; or we interpret people's actions in such a way that, on the whole, we can continue to speak of them acting 'characteristically' (i.e. in a way that we would, on the basis of past experience, expect of them); and we find prolonged 'uncharacteristic' behaviour so disturbing, that we would probably attribute it to another person's temporary drunkenness or emotional disorder, rather than to our own previous fundamental misjudgement.

Such reluctance to revise our own self-built models can again be directly related to historiography and can be illustrated with two historical examples. The first relates to the impact on Europeans of new geographical discoveries in the early-modern period. The native inhabitants of the Americas failed to fit tidily into the European intellectual framework derived from classical and Christian sources. In particular, how could they have come into existence, so far and so separate from the supposedly universal origins described in ancient texts? These anomalous intruders from the new world had somehow to be assimilated into the traditions of the old. For this reason, ancient Atlantis was commandeered. By means of that lost continent a land-bridge was provided, across which Americans' ancestors might have passed from Europe to their new home; and so their present location became explicable. With similar motivations, it has been claimed that 'scholars spent some of the best years of their lives tracing the descent of the American Indians from the lost tribes of Israel, or demonstrating that Noah had settled in Brazil'. The point is that, for Europeans at that time 'the New World had no reality except in its relation to the Old',[8] so the newly available data had somehow to be incorporated into an old framework of belief.

A more recent twentieth-century example of the difficulty of revising our perceptions, is provided again by Primo Levi. He records how the family of one Alberto, a young man he knew in Auschwitz, refused to accept the possibility of his death – refused to let the very idea into their consciousness. In fact, they refused to hear Levi's account of what had happened, because they were already convinced that they knew the truth about that: that their Alberto alone had managed to escape and find safety. A year after his first visit to the family, Levi returned, and was told that they had since received reliable information that Alberto was then in a Russian hospital suffering from a lost memory, but that he was improving and would soon return. He never did, of course. But the family were presumably consoled by their version of what had happened – by their own historical 'truth';[9] and the perceptual point is that, having once decided to view data in a certain way, nothing could persuade them to perceive it in any other way. Their minds, as we say, were made up, so anything that failed to conform with their own ideas on the subject was forbidden entrance, or not even noticed.

Periodic revisions – literally new visions or perceptions – are, though, necessary. The simple frameworks, adopted and so tenaciously maintained by early-modern European scholars and by Alberto's relatives, have to be modified in the interest of truth, of the empirical evidence that is there to see if only one's eyes are open to it. In a parallel example from the history of seventeenth-century science, Galileo insists on the need to reject the long-accepted Aristotelian framework in favour of the new; but he is no less than Primo Levi aware of the psychological issues involved. So he refers to 'the cowardice (if we may be permitted to use this term) of ordinary minds'. Such minds, he suggests, unthinkingly assent to the authorities that have earlier been presented to them: 'they refuse even to listen to, let alone examine, any new proposition or problem, even when it not only has not been refuted by their authorities, but not so much as examined or considered'. What is needed is a realisation of the numerous phenomena that still remain unexplained, for these show the inevitable limitations of any authority; and such realisation 'frees you from slavery to one particular writer or another . . . thereby slackening the reins on your reasoning and softening your stubborn defiance of your senses'.[10] It was just such a relaxing of reasoning and acceptance of newly available empirical evidence that, despite their reluctance (or 'cowardice'), was ultimately required of those coming to terms with the New World, and with Alberto's death.

Such re-interpretations, then, must from time to time be made by us all. No doubt we have our own reasons for the views we hold, and for the interpretations that we make. But these need periodically to be laid bare for scrutiny, and sometimes even changed. Australian Aborigines who had never before seen a horse-and-rider, interpreted their first perception of that phenomenon as a single entity, but were compelled to modify their interpretation when they saw the human rider dismount and detach himself from the animal. Another more personal adaptation is recorded by the American philosopher William James, who was forced to see or to interpret his experience differently after being confronted by an alternative perception of a forest clearing. The farmers who had made the clearing had been concerned only to civilise and cultivate the wilderness, whereas to James 'the forest had been destroyed; and what had "improved" it out of existence was hideous, a sort of ulcer'. But by talking with the men who had actually worked on the land, the philosopher came to realise that he 'had been losing the whole inward significance of the situation. . . . The clearing which to me was a mere ugly picture on the retina, was to them a symbol redolent with moral memories, and sang a very paean of duty, struggle and success'.[11] Our perceptions, then, are determined, not simply by external objects, but additionally by our own internal predispositions towards those objects; and they may sometimes need revision.

An enforced change of perspective of the kind experienced by the Aborigines and described by William James, may be illustrated by one further personal example. An elderly Jewish woman recently told me that she had left her native Austria in 1939. 'You were', I said unthinkingly, 'lucky to have got out'. It was of course (to defend myself) very late to have done so; but she quickly corrected me: 'Not really "lucky" to have had to leave my home and all my possessions'. And indeed her departure from Austria may be construed as 'lucky' and 'unlucky' – one, or the other, or both; for the appropriateness of each adjective must depend on one's starting-point, or on the framework within which one is thinking. In the historical context of what went on in Europe in the 1930s and 1940s, there is some logic in describing a Jew's successful flight at that time from Austria to England as being singularly 'lucky'. But from another, admittedly more 'normal' standpoint, the need for such flight seems no less 'unlucky'. At all events, my own trite response clearly needed some examination, and my own revised account of my friend's past experience, or history, will henceforth sound quite different.

In matters of perception, then, there is, as it has been said, 'more to seeing than meets the eyeball. . . . Seeing is not only the having of a visual experience; it is also the way in which the visual experience is had'.[12] In other words, what we see is determined not only by what is 'out there' in the external world, but also by the way in which we personally respond to it; and that is dependent in turn upon what we are, what we have experienced and what we have come to expect. So that our own input is an indissoluble part of the total process of perception. And similarly with our treatment of the past: the way we see that past, the 'facts' we select as significant, the way we interpret them and compose them into a coherent and meaningful whole – these historical procedures will derive from the very personal character of the individual historian.

Our own perceptions, our interpretations of experience and of history are, then, very personal, and are inevitably derived from very personal backgrounds and encounters. The main lesson of psychology for history is that any version of events, any explanation of what has happened, any perception of 'the past', is necessarily limited and contingent, and may therefore need to be revised. By taking another standpoint, by selecting other data, by adopting different criteria and imposing different definitions, that 'past' could be perceived in a light quite different from the one we have proposed; and there is no privileged standpoint from which to assess the relative validity of those different versions, no way of achieving access to any past simply 'as it was'.

2.4 Personal predilections

It is not only atomistic 'facts' that historians will choose in accordance with their own predilections and interests, but also periods and problems, and the manners of their treatment. In general, it has been noted, for example, that historians show a preference for the presentation of revolutionary flux and change, rather than of continuity and stability. That preference, however unsurprising, must itself lead to one-sidedness. As it has been argued, 'the inevitable desire of a historian to record flux may mean the omission (or at least the neglect) of a substratum of ideas shared by those of whom he writes, and this omission by exaggerating the differences, may distort the picture'.[13] The desire to record flux may not, as claimed, be 'inevitable'; but there does often seem a tendency to view past developments as dramatic and revolutionary.

One case here is the early-modern 'intellectual revolution', where a new philosophical and scientific outlook replaced an earlier scholastic model. The temptation here may be to see as a sudden 'revolution' what took a century or more to bring about, and, as with Primo Levi's example, the subtle distinctions between the 'ancient' and 'modern' positions need to be further unravelled. In fact, an ever more complex picture is emerging, with sharp black and white boundaries increasingly eroded and blurred into many shades of grey, and it may be that future studies in this field will require historians with personalities sympathetic to such subtleties.

In more specific terms, Michael Oakeshott asks: 'Why . . . did Gibbon abandon his project of writing a history of Switzerland and turn to the decline and fall of the Roman Empire, or what attracted Mommsen's attention to Imperial Rome or Ranke's to seventeenth-century England?'[14] The answer in all cases must be that it was those periods, and their associated problems, that seemed most interesting or significant or relevant to their respective historians.

Some periods resonate for us, while others seem remote; and in this respect we are all more or less subject to the *zeitgeist*, to contemporary fashion. And hems go up and down. Carr notes that mediaeval history was largely by-passed in the nineteenth century. Historians at that time, he suggests, were 'too much repelled by the superstitious beliefs of the Middle Ages, and by the barbarities which they inspired, to have any imaginative understanding' of the period;[15] and he records a similar lack of sympathetic understanding about the Soviet Union in English-speaking countries in the 1950s.[16]

It might be argued that it is one of the main points of historical study that such deficiencies be overcome, and that one of the prime tasks of the historian is precisely to extend his contemporaries' range of sympathetic understanding. That very motivation may be the predilection of those who are psychologically disposed to challenge historical orthodoxies with what has been described as a 'built-in impetus towards revisionism'. Such an impetus had already been identified by the seventeenth century: Thomas Fuller, in the context of changing interpretations of Richard III, notes parallels between historians and 'sea-pies', or 'birds . . . who cannot rise except it be by flying against the wind, as some hope to achieve their advancement by being contrary and paradoxal in judgment to all before them'.[17] And contrariness of that kind remains as an important motivator in historical research.

So we choose our subjects of study from the point at which we personally have arrived, and Ihab Hassan* has asked with good reason whether history is not 'often the secret biography of historians'. Perhaps, indeed, a whole intellectual biography might be written for each of us;[18] and in this context, incidentally, Carr does provide an answer to Oakeshott's question (to which, however, he does not refer) about Mommsen:

> Mommsen was imbued with the sense of need for a strong man to clear up the mess left by the failure of the German people to realize its political aspirations; and we shall never appreciate his history at its true value unless we realize that his well-known idealization of Caesar is the product of this yearning for the strong man to save Germany from ruin.[19]

* Ihab Hassan, quoted in Lawrence Cahoone (ed.), *From Modernism to Postmodernism: An Anthology*, Oxford, Blackwell, 1996, p. 383.

History then becomes in Burckhardt's words, 'the record of what one age finds worthy of note in another',[20] or rather the record of what individual historians find noteworthy. Try as we may, we can never attain that so-called 'objectivity', to which historians have sometimes aspired (and to which they may still be popularly believed to aspire). That is to say, we cannot remove ourselves from ourselves – neither our personal, nor our social and political selves. Lucian, as we have seen, would have had us, as historians, do just that: 'a writer of History', he maintains, 'ought in his writings to be a forraigner, without Countrey, living under his owne Lawe onely, subject to no King, nor caring what any man will like, or dislike, but laying out the matter as it is'.[21] As an ideal of impartial detachment, that sounds fine; but our human psychology, with all its problems of personal perceptions and preferences and predilections, ensures that it is in practice unattainable.

3 LINGUISTICS: PROBLEMS OF LANGUAGE

3.1 History and language

Historians use language. Not only do they study past usages of language, inasmuch as a considerable amount of their evidence for the past comes in the form of written texts; but they also commit their own thoughts and theories to writing, in order to communicate them to a wider audience. They cannot therefore stand aloof, and aspire to remain immune to the challenges presented to all language-based subjects by the comparatively new discipline of linguistics. During the last few decades, academic studies of the nature and functions of language have resulted in a so-called 'linguistic turn',[22] that has inevitably had widely ranging ramifications in the humanities and social sciences generally; and, for all their suspicion of 'theory', historians in particular cannot prove exempt.

Linguistic studies have proposed that much of what we experience as 'fact' has been actually fashioned or conditioned by language. Thus, instead of simply describing an already existing situation, language itself serves to determine the construction of that situation: it outlines the parameters within which construction can take place, it places constraints on what at any time is considered possible, it bounds our very thoughts, perceptions, interpretations and experiences. And within such a linguistically orientated framework, it has been implied that history itself could be 'reduced to a subsystem of linguistic signs constituting its object, "the past", according to the rules pertaining in the "prisonhouse of language" inhabited by the historian'.[23] This may sound like an extreme case of attempted territorial aggrandisement on the part of linguistics, and such 'word-makers who claim to be makers of reality' may properly be accused of hubris.[24] But language-games can be construed as power-games in more than one sense, and historians have suffered a major theoretical challenge to the validity of their subject. It is not enough simply to ignore that. Some adequate defence needs to be mounted, and the opportunity taken for a radical re-thinking that may have positive results.

3.2 Nature or convention?

Many of the essential problems of language were recognised in the ancient world, and were discussed by Plato in his dialogue *Cratylus*. Most important for our present context is the question of whether language is 'natural' or 'conventional' – that is, whether on the one hand language actually represents the external world, with names naturally inhering in objects and so waiting, as it were, to be properly used by us; or whether on the other hand words are only conventionally, and so arbitrarily, imposed by us on objects, and utilised in a language structure that then has no necessary connection with any external world at all. So Cratylus himself is represented as believing that 'a power more than human gave things their first names, and that the names which are thus given are necessarily their true names'.[25] That is to say, some superhuman agent is assumed to have named objects in accordance with their real natures – in the way that Adam is recorded in *Genesis* as having, with God's approval, named the newly created animals. Such a belief invests names with a peculiar power, for it indicates that a grasp of the name is tantamount to an understanding of the essence of the thing. As Cratylus is aware, his own theory implies that 'he who discovers the names discovers also the things';[26] so by a proper application of language, one can penetrate to the truth about nature.

One can also presumably assess the truth of a statement by checking the correspondence of its linguistic presentation with the actual state of affairs that it claims to be describing. But, as Plato makes clear, one main problem with Cratylus's view is that it is hard to see how one could ever be in a position to check the external state or data, without oneself resorting to a description couched in the same linguistic terms. Is one in fact ever in a privileged position from which to gain real knowledge about the external world and then to use that as a criterion by which to assess the relative reliability or truth of various descriptions of that world?

Such difficulties, long since recognised by Plato, have been confirmed and compounded by twentieth-century theories of language, which have come increasingly to question the validity of referring to some external reality outside language itself. Since the publication in 1916 of Ferdinand de Saussure's work on what was then the newly developing discipline of linguistics, the tendency has been to view language as an autonomous structure which has no necessary or god-given relationship with anything outside itself. Language is then conceived instead as actually itself determining the world as it is experienced by us. That is, our understanding of 'reality' is affected – or even effected – by the language that we use; so that if we used another language, we would perceive the world differently, or perceive it as a different world.

In this respect, attention is drawn to the various ways in which different languages discriminate, or carve up experience into discrete parts, or identify as significant (and so describable) some aspects of the totality of the world, while judiciously or inadvertently ignoring others. English people sometimes resort to French (and *vice versa*), in order to express experiences or concepts or emotions that seem to have been overlooked (and so are untranslatable) in their own language; and newly coined words that initially seem strange are sometimes soon difficult to do without. Language, then, seems in some sense to determine our very experience of the world (rather than, conversely, the world determining our language); and that language is not, as Cratylus argued, 'natural', in the sense of being inevitably as it is, but it is, rather, conventional – a product of its own space- and time-bound social and political context. And if it is thus, as it has been described, 'the medium in which the Real is constructed and apprehended',[27] it expresses as such, and duly reinforces, the dominant ideologies, the accepted ideas and values, of its day.

The debate about whether language is natural or conventional is perpetuated in disagreements about the history of etymologies or the derivations of words. On the one hand we have linguists who appeal to the supposed historical origins of a word, in order to confirm or to deny the validity of a particular contemporary usage; on the other hand, we have those who reject this historical approach as invalid, and who maintain conversely that contemporary usage is the only relevant consideration. This is a clear example of history being used in support of an ideological position, with appropriate 'roots' claimed for validation of one's own arguments; and it has recently been argued that the very citation of such roots may imply 'the belief that the earlier a meaning the better, which must depend on a diagnosis of cultural decline . . . or a faith in a lost Golden Age of lexical purity and precision'.[28] Derek Attridge's example is Muriel Spark's character Miss Jean Brodie, who is represented as informing her pupils that the Latin roots of the English word 'education' imply a meaning of 'leading out'. Whatever the supposed wider political implications, it is clear that some justification is here being sought for the teacher's own approach to teaching. Once again, then, a resort to history is being made for rhetorical purposes, with Miss Brodie assuming with Cratylus that an appeal can properly be made to a word's original and 'absolute' meaning.

This fundamental question about language is clearly analogous to that already discussed in relation to perception. The point once again is whether, in the case of perception or of language, we have some direct access to, and ultimately knowledge of, an independently existing outside world, or whether that external world is itself somehow dependent for its existence, or at least for its appearance and description, upon some perceiving or describing subject. Do we, in other words, impose our own meaning on phenomena and experience, describing it inevitably from our own personal viewpoints; or do we, after taking due care to use appropriate methods, penetrate to the already-existing truth, and simply perceive and describe it as it is?

In terms of modern linguistics, the question posed is whether language has some direct relation to a world that is external to language itself; or whether language is to be seen rather as a self-contained system of signs, the meaning of which is determined, not by any assumed correspondence with an outside 'reality', but by an agreed internal coherence and convenience. Is language simply a reflector of what is already 'out there'? Or is it a 'free-standing', autonomous entity that is imposed upon our otherwise random experience – rather like a net being thrown over a swarming group of recalcitrant wild animals? In the former case, it makes some sense to require an exact correspondence between our language and what it purports to reflect or describe; and that exact correspondence, when attained (or when it can ever be ascertained), will constitute 'truth'. In the latter case, however, the whole notion of 'truth' becomes more problematic, with our linguistic usage seeming to justify an altogether more arbitrary and relativistic concept, and also less definitive and complete. For some of that experience, or some of those hypothetical animals, which we attempt to ensnare within our linguistic net, may well elude identification and evade our capture, by burrowing around or underneath our supposedly constraining structure, or by simply being small enough to crawl right through the mesh. Nature does not necessarily play the game according to our rules.

As with the analogous psychological issues, these linguistic questions thus have some obvious implications for historical study. For historians, again, have traditionally set out to describe some assumed 'reality' – whether simple data or phenomena, or a series of events; and (as we have seen in Chapter 2) the assumption has often been that, with a careful use of language, it was possible to provide an accurate description or account of the 'facts', or situation as it was. In other words, it has been believed that our historical description of the past could be validated by its demonstrated correspondence with the assumed 'reality' of that past; and within the framework of this model, linguistic accuracy and subtlety are obviously essential historical tools. But it is precisely the validity of this model, whereby historical truth is simply dependent upon correct identification and verbal description, that the 'linguistic turn' has come to challenge.

3.3 Truth and meaning

If the whole representational model of language is rejected, and replaced with its alternative, what is left? A historical description, instead of indicating more or less accurately some external state of affairs, becomes understood as a purely verbal construction, lacking any necessary relation to anything outside itself. 'Truth' then becomes an impossibly elusive goal: the best we can hope for is to impose some meaning on data which, as it is 'given', lacks any meaning at all. 'Reality', far from being simply described in language, is itself shaped by language; and in that situation, any historical description is to be perceived as autonomous, independent of anything external to itself, and so to be validated only in its own linguistic terms. Internal coherence becomes the criterion of meaning, and such 'meaning' replaces 'truth' as the historical objective.

Once that position has been accepted, it may seem that historians, released from their previous obligation to seek conformity with an external reality, can range freely – not to say, irresponsibly – anywhere they will. One internally consistent story appears as good as any other, and the very forms of 'fact' and 'fiction' become blurred, where the only possible criterion for making respective evaluations is itself linguistic. So Gabrielle Spiegel has described the sort of impasse that can be reached, where 'the reader [of a text] is confronted, ultimately, by its final indeterminacy of meaning, its aporia, in the face of which the reader fatally hesitates, unable to decide'.[29] It is small wonder, then, that (as we shall see in Chapter 6) some historians are now contemplating the presentation of alternative accounts of the same episode, thereby avoiding any need to decide between them, and passing the buck to another reader. For such people, the historian's traditional quest for truth has been supplanted by the rather more limited objective of constructing a persuasive and meaningful hypothesis.

3.4 Language, ideology, and objectives

But to say that a work of history is to be judged in terms of its own internally consistent use of language presents further problems. For it is not only the form, but the function of language that requires consideration, not only its aesthetic but also its ideological connotations. No less than literature, it has been claimed, history itself 'participates . . . in the political management of reality'.[30] Thus, by the very act of writing, historians inevitably express some ideological commitment; for they have to stand somewhere in relation to their material, and that place (as well as that material) has been chosen by themselves. So again, as with the Rorschach ink-blot test, the choice of standpoint, and the resultant description, may tell us more about the author, or interpreter, than about the material itself. The data on which historians work is actually given its meaning by those same historians. It is they who choose it in the first place, who select it from a potentially infinite quarry, and who make some sense of it in relation to a lesson or message that they want to transmit. The written account of that data, therefore, will inevitably encapsulate the ideological commitment of its author; and, to the careful reader of the historian's language, that commitment (however unconsciously expressed) may be revealed.

A recently worked example is provided by Antony Easthope's close analysis of the language used by Lawrence Stone. An essay on the seemingly innocuous subject of 'The inflation of honours, 1558–1641' is revealed by Easthope as being far from neutral, far from the 'detached and transparent perspective on an aspect of English history' that seems initially to have been presented. Rather, a specific ideological standpoint has been consciously or unconsciously adopted; and 'since Stone and his discourse is saturated with the culture of the English gentry, his narrative is one told from the side of the winners'.[31] The very model of society assumed by Stone is shown to be significant: it is essentially mechanical, with laws of socio-economic causation simply taken as 'evident' and 'obvious'; and recalcitrant concepts (such as non-materially motivated ambitions) conversely excluded. Even the very style of the essay – 'a style which invites its style to be overlooked' – is shown to be highly rhetorical, rather than neutral as its 'academic' presentation implies. So, by contrast with what now seems to be the rather 'colourful' style of the cited primary sources, the language of Stone's actual narrative seems plain and 'factual' – almost able to 'pass itself off as unwritten'; and the conventional procedure of footnoting again contrives to give added authority for what is presented as 'just there'.[32]

Such careful reading and analysis of written texts may then itself constitute an important form of history, for embedded in those texts are the presuppositions, the attitudes and values of the age in which they were written – as manifested at least by one representative of that age. The language – not only the words, but the genre and the style and the omissions – must reveal the constitution of reality and meaning that was accepted by its author; it must indicate what were accounted possible inter-connections between the discrete objects proposed as constituents for that reality; and it must show the path towards the future that, explicitly or implicitly, was being advocated. One important historical objective might then be to un-earth or excavate just that; and it is indeed the importance of doing just that that has been shown above all by Michel Foucault.

Believing in the all-importance of language as, not only expressing, but actually constraining (even determining) the thought of any historical period, Foucault concluded that the historian's main task was to reveal the usages of language, and the reasons for and the implications of those usages; for if thoughts and attitudes were confined within the prison-house of language, then serious attention needed to be paid to the linguistic gaolers. The patrollers and controllers of the whole domain of language – its words, grammar, style, modes of analysis, and so on – are revealed as all-powerful, and as exercising power for specific (political/ideological) purposes, which themselves warrant examination. One can never reach 'the truth' about such matters, not least since historians themselves are bound within the linguistic constraints of their own time (which determine their assumptions, approaches, explanatory models, etc.); but there can be some virtue in unearthing, as best we can, the language-based constraints (and hence dispositions of power) of the past.

Thus, for example, Foucault himself researched such areas as prisons, mental institutions, and sexual practices; and he succeeded above all in clarifying the relativity of many of the concepts we continue to use in relation to these. Criminality, sanity, sexual 'normality', are all revealed as contingent, or as variables through time. Even during the last (twentieth) century, we have seen huge changes in attitudes to, for instance, the assumed 'criminality' of 'deserters' from the army – hundreds of whom, shot for cowardice in the first world war, would have been treated for mental illness in the second. And there has been a similar transition in attitudes towards (and linguistic descriptions of) homosexuality, with definitions ranging from criminality, through sickness, to normality. Foucault's point in relation to such transitions is that each description derives from an ideological position: there is no essential referent in any case, but only a culturally determined usage within an ideologically positioned discourse.

For Foucault, then:

> history serves to show how that-which-is has not always been; i.e., that the things which seem most evident to us are always formed in the confluence of encounters and chances, during the course of a precarious and fragile history . . . ; and that since these things have been made, they can be unmade, as long as we know how it was that they were made.[33]

History is thus not only a powerful discourse in its own right, as controlling 'knowledge' of the past, but, in its emancipatory role, is also centrally concerned with linguistic structures of the past. History may, for some, be more than a purely textual study, but after Foucault it is clear at all events that considerations of language must be crucial.

4 PHILOSOPHY: THE PROBLEM OF SCEPTICISM

Philosophy is sometimes seen as being quite distinct from other subjects, and empirically minded historians have tended to be on their guard against any speculative theorising from their disciplinary rivals. As with linguistics, however, some philosophies break through all attempted guards, and one which insistently intrudes is that of scepticism.

The overall thrust of philosophical scepticism tends to confirm, and to exacerbate, the parallel challenges from psychology and linguistics. The problem of scepticism is not new, nor is it by any means confined specifically to one discipline. Indeed, it dates back at least to classical antiquity, and it is of universal application. It relates to the whole question of what claims for knowledge, or for 'truth', can appropriately be made, and as such it appears to have particular importance for history and for understanding the background of the postmodern predicament in which that subject finds itself.

Can we rely upon our senses, or on our reason? Do these faculties give access to an external world? How certain can we ever be about anything? What degree of probability, what level of assent is justified in any situation? How do we balance the relative weight of two apparently conflicting statements or pieces of evidence? To what extent must dogmatic claims to certainty and truth be tempered by sceptical doubt? To what extent is confidence properly replaced by hesitancy? These are the sorts of question that apply equally to students of data relating to natural phenomena (scientists), or to students of data relating to the past (historians).

4.1 Ancient scepticism

Although often conveniently forgotten, these sceptical issues and questions surfaced at the very birth of coherent thought, of what we understand as 'philosophy', or the attempt to understand ourselves. For as soon as humans start wanting knowledge, or striving for it, or claiming to have it, they are confronted by the question of how to acquire it, and of how well substantiated, how valid, any of their claims to have reached it might be. So the earliest recorded thinkers, the pre-Socratic philosophers of sixth-century BC Greece, raised the fundamental epistemological questions with which we (not least as historians) are still concerned. Can we trust our senses? How accurately do they in fact transcribe the external world for us? Are they (and so we) never deceived, or mistaken? Do we not suffer from illusions and delusions? And is not our very 'reason' deficient – not only inherently defective, but inevitably based on first principles, or presuppositions that themselves are of questionable validity, but have by definition to remain unquestioned?

Such early questioning of any knowledge-claims culminates in the full-blown sceptical philosophy of Pyrrho (*c.* 365–*c.* 275 BC), the essentials of whose thought were conveniently recorded by Sextus Empiricus (*c.* AD 200) in his *Outlines of Pyrrhonism.* The sceptical philosophy was advocated there as a very positive way of life that should lead to 'ataraxia' or peace of mind. Having once realised our human deficiencies and having accepted the impossibility of ever deciding between equally weighted but conflicting claims for truth, we are bound to suspend our judgement, and thence supposedly, in a state of uncommitted detachment, reach 'composure and tranquillity'.

4.2 Early-modern scepticism

The recovery of Sextus Empiricus's account of Pyrrhonism in the Renaissance contributed importantly to the revival of sceptical philosophy in the early-modern period. Sextus's text in fact provided intellectual underpinning for a sceptical, relativistic attitude that was already fast becoming fashionable; and by the mid-seventeenth century there is considerable evidence for such scepticism having profoundly affected the status of natural philosophy, or science. Instead of providing a revelation of 'truth' about the essence of the natural world, science is thenceforth seen rather as offering a hypothetical explanation for observed phenomena. Since alternative explanations can always be envisaged, without there ever being clear criteria for evaluation of competing claims, science becomes relegated to the position of a provider of tentative hypotheses rather than of certain truths, of relative rather than absolute explanations for natural phenomena.

This reduced status for their theories was conceded by such practising scientists as Robert Boyle and Isaac Newton. So the former writes:

> I would have such kind of superstructures looked upon only as temporary ones; which though they may be preferred before any

> others, as being the least imperfect, or, if you please, the best in their kind that we have, yet are they not entirely to be acquiesced in, as absolutely perfect, or uncapable of improving alterations.[34]

And Newton, in one of his humbler moments, similarly emphasises the provisional nature of his own theories. It is not possible to attain real knowledge of the essences of material bodies: their 'inward substances are not to be known either by our senses, or by any reflex act of our minds'. So scientific propositions can only be considered as 'very *nearly true*, notwithstanding any contrary hypotheses that may be imagined, *till such time as other phenomena occur*, by which they may either be made *more accurate*, or *liable to exceptions*'.[35]

Acceptance of this humbler role for science becomes widespread, and is conveniently recorded in the official apologia for the English Royal Society. As their amanuensis, Thomas Sprat describes how Fellows of the Society endeavour to steer a course between the Scylla of scepticism and the Charybdis of dogmatism: they are 'cautious, to shun the overweening *dogmatizing* on causes on the one hand: and not to fall into a *speculative Scepticism* on the other'. Both banks, or extremes, have their dangers; but what is most significant about the compromise-route is that it results in scientific reports or theories, offered not 'as *unalterable Demonstrations*, but as *present appearances*'.[36] There is of course a world of difference between those respective claims. The chasm between presenting one's scientific work as 'unalterable Demonstration' and as 'present appearance', separates perhaps the mediaeval from the modern world – or else, perhaps more likely, two fundamentally distinct, perennial psychological types. But our concern must be with how historical studies more specifically are affected.

4.3 Biblical criticism

One early application of the sceptical approach to historiography lay in the field of Biblical criticism, and this soon came to be seen as having far wider historical ramifications.[37] Questioning of the scriptural record, including its actual historical authenticity and reliability, is already evident in the sixteenth century, and becomes formalised in the writings of Isaac La Peyrère (1596–1676). La Peyrère challenges in particular the well-established tradition of Moses' personal authorship of the Pentateuch (the first five books of the Bible); and what is *historically* significant here is that he argues his thesis on the basis of both internal and external evidence. That is, he points out inconsistencies in the text itself, noting for instance the difficulty that Moses would have had in recording his own death; he refers to incompatibilities between Biblical and pagan histories – with the former supposedly dating the creation to 4004 BC, whereas other accounts, as in Chinese history for example, go back at least 10,000 years; and he cites the evidence of newly discovered peoples and cultures which appear not to derive, as required, from Adam, or to have any relation to the Biblical world. The uncompromisingly sceptical conclusion of La Peyrère towards the authenticity of the biblical record is as follows:

> I need not trouble the Reader much further to prove a thing in itself sufficiently evident, that the first Five Books of the Bible were not written by Moses, as is thought. Nor need any wonder after this, when he reads many things confus'd and out of order, obscure, deficient, many things omitted and misplaced, when they consider with themselves that they are a heap of Copie confusedly taken.[38]

This heretically sceptical attitude towards Biblical authority had very obvious implications for religion itself, but ultimately its impact on historical writing more generally proved hardly less serious. The great Bible scholar, Richard Simon, knew La Peyrère and his work very well, and it was his *Critical History of the Old Testament*, first published in 1678, that sounded the death-knell of the Bible as an authoritative and reliable work of history. He carefully emphasises the original infallibility of the Scriptures as the word of God: 'No-one', he writes at the opening of his work, 'can doubt but that the truths contained in the Holy Scripture are infallible and of Divine Authority; since they proceed immediately from God, who in this has onely made use of the ministry of Men to be his Interpreters'. But he goes on to insist that human beings have been implicated in the packaging, processing, and maintenance of God's word, so that problems have inevitably intruded:

> as Men have been the Depositories of these sacred Books, as well as of all others, and their first Originals have been lost, it was in some sort impossible, but that there must needs happen some changes, as well by reason of the length of time, as the carelessness of Transcribers.[39]

It is these problems of transmission, transcription, and adaptation with which Simon is concerned, and he definitively shows that the Scriptures are historically an unreliable source. What had traditionally been claimed as a work dictated by God, now stood revealed, in Tom Paine's later words, as 'nothing . . . but an anonymous book of stories, fables and traditionary or invented absurdities, or downright lies'.[40] The resultant threat to Christian authority was obvious, but the critical historical method which provoked this theological revolution, could also be more widely applied.

The extension of Simon's approach, from more narrowly Biblical to wider historical issues, can be seen in the writings of Lord Bolingbroke to whom we have already referred. Writing in 1735, Bolingbroke explicitly refers to Simon's work, by which he had quite obviously been influenced. So, openly citing Simon, he questions the origins and nature of the scriptures, and then cynically describes them as having 'come down broken and confused, full of additions, interpolations, and transpositions, made we neither know when, nor by whom'. Reports of word-for-word correspondence between seventy-two different translations, traditionally claimed as miraculous confirmation of scriptural truth, simply have to be rejected as ludicrous: even St Jerome 'laughed at the story', and in fact 'these holy romances slid into tradition, and tradition became history'. Far, then, from providing a reliable historical record, they have been 'delivered to us on the faith of a superstitious people, among whom the custom and art of pious lying prevailed remarkably'.[41] So in Bolingbroke we see the sceptical philosophy applied uncompromisingly to the historical record of the Bible. Importantly, though, he then goes on, as we shall see, to apply it far more widely.

4.4 Historical Pyrrhonism

By Bolingbroke's time in the early eighteenth century, Historical Pyrrhonism, or the application of sceptical philosophy to historical study generally, had indeed become virtually an intellectual fashion; but that fashion was itself the culmination of earlier historical development. Some two hundred years earlier, there are already clear signs of a new, sceptically induced self-consciousness among historians. So, for example, Henricus Cornelius Agrippa, writing with a knowledge of ancient sceptical sources, includes a chapter on History in his significantly entitled treatise *Of the Vanitie and Uncertaintie of Artes and Sciences*; and after noting the numerous discrepancies between various historical accounts, together with their writers' individual partialities and suspect motivations, he concludes pessimistically that 'in no parte any credite may be throughly given to Histories'.[42] This negative assessment is shared by at least some of his European contemporaries. The Italian Francesco Patrizzi, assuming the impossibility of any historian being at the same time impartial and well informed, similarly laments how 'it is utterly and totally imposible for human actions to be known as they were actually done'.[43] And in England at the turn of the century, Sir Philip Sidney, in a defence of poetry, expresses an equally sceptical view of his disciplinary rival: the historian, he sneers, is

> loden with old Mouse-eaten records, authorising himselfe (for the most part) upon other histories, whose greatest authorities are built upon the notable foundation of Heare-say, having much a-doe to accord [i.e to show the compatibility between] differing Writers, and to pick trueth out of partiality.[44]

Whether Sidney's questioning of the validity and impartiality of historical sources derives from habitual cynicism about his disciplinary competitors, or from the sceptical philosophy by which some of his contemporaries were being influenced,[45] is not clear; but a strong tradition of specifically *historical* Pyrrhonism develops in France through the seventeenth century. François La Mothe Le Vayer, for example, applies a sceptical approach to historiography in particular. In a treatise devoted to the subject, he concludes that in the face of numerous difficulties there could be 'generally speaking, little certainty in Histories'.[46] And his fellow-countryman, the Jesuit Father Pierre Le Moyne, although repudiating the ultimate implications of such 'Sceptical Notions', himself shows a keen awareness of the problems of attaining historical truth. Having enumerated such conventional hazards as partiality and prejudice, he proceeds to note the impossibility of ever reaching a historical understanding of the inner working of past events:

> Sees he [the historian] any thing else but the Bark and Coverings of things done before his Eyes: And what serveth him the sight of the Watch, without that of the Springs and Movements; or who can convey them so Pure and Sincere, as the Publick Faith and the Truth of History demands from him?[47]

No more than scientists like Newton, then, can historians ever penetrate to the inner essence of their subject-matter. Historical 'truth' demands an explanation of the inner workings of events, but historians are necessarily confined to a study of their outer-surfaces; denied access to the *essences*, they must make do with their *appearances*.

But faced with that sceptically induced conclusion, the historian should not, any more than the scientist, simply despair. There is after all a balance to be struck, and just as Sprat described the compromise-route followed by the Fellows of the Royal Society, so Le Moyne advocates for historians 'a middle way, to be held between the Easiness of those that believe all, and the Obstinacy of those that believe nothing'. There is then no need sceptically 'to condemn all History'; but there is a need for historians to present their theories undogmatically, as corrigible hypotheses, and 'in doubtful terms, after the Sceptical way'.[48]

It is this model of history articulated by Le Moyne, that is adopted by Pierre Bayle, from whom it passes to England in the person of Lord Bolingbroke. At the turn of the century, Bayle published his influential *Historical and Critical Dictionary*, in which he uses the actual term 'Historical Pyrrhonism'; and he was one of the continental thinkers with whom Bolingbroke made contact during an enforced political exile in France from 1715 to 1723. The Englishman's awareness of Simon's earlier critical approach to Biblical history has already been noted; and he goes on, in the manner of Le Moyne and Bayle, to extend the application of scepticism to historical writing more generally. A measure of scepticism, he concedes, is quite proper in historical study, just as it is in philosophy or science. Our pieces of evidence, whether oral or written, need to be approached with 'impartiality and freedom of judgment', and even 'with suspicion . . . for they deserve to be suspected'. But one can go too far, and extremists will succeed in undermining *all* historical study. For they 'will be ready to insist that *all history is fabulous*, and that the very best is nothing better than a *probable* tale, artfully contrived, and plausibly told, wherein *truth and falsehood are indistinguishably blended* together'.

It is here that Bolingbroke sounds at his most 'postmodern', for he realises that such ultimate scepticism in relation to history is actually universalisable: it can be applied not only to ancient history (of the sort that Simon had been concerned with), but also to modern, and even 'contemporary' history. And in some respects this extremist sceptical approach is irrefutable: it does indeed have to be conceded that even 'the best [historians] are defective'. That is, one's explanations may sound plausible, and may in fact correspond with what actually happened; but equally, an alternative chain of causation may have been responsible – and who is then to choose between them? In Bolingbroke's own words: the historian 'may account for events after they have happened, by a system of causes and conduct that did not really produce them, tho it might possibly or even probably have produced them'.[49]

There is of course from a sceptical standpoint no way of discovering the ultimate 'truth' about such matters, so it could be argued that we have reached an impasse, from which it is not profitable or even possible to proceed. But that, Bolingbroke believes, is to be unduly negative: this 'endeavouring to establish universal Pyrrhonism in matters of history' is, he concludes, nothing short of 'folly'; and he reverts to an approach not dissimilar to that of Sprat and Le Moyne. So he aims again for some sort of middle path between extremes, suggesting that we are hardly justified in maintaining a position of extreme scepticism, in order to avoid the charge of extreme dogmatism: 'there is no reason to establish Pyrrhonism, that we may avoid the ridicule of credulity'. 'A reasonable man' can surely effect a compromise, and his sceptically induced impasse then becomes a starting-point for the resumption of proper historical procedures. That is, it 'becomes a reason for *examining* and *comparing* authorities, and for *preferring* some, *not for rejecting all*'. The historian does not simply give up, but rather (again like the scientist) assigns degrees of probability that are proportionate to the evidence available. So in the absence of any confirming evidence, he will naturally 'doubt absolutely'; but where there is some evidence available, he will be able to assess it and to 'proportion his assent or dissent accordingly'.[50]

Bolingbroke's recognition of the theoretically dire effects on historical study of an extremist sceptical position, together with his advised practical compromise, foreshadows much later discussion of historiography. Scepticism, it is clear, is not a problem newly discovered by postmodern theorists: it is a perennial problem, the discussion of which periodically returns to fashion. Applied to historical study, it resurfaces in the late nineteenth century in Froude's contention that history is 'a child's box of letters with which we can spell any word we please', and again in Carl Becker's assertion in 1910, that 'the facts of history do not exist for any historian till he creates them'.[51] The implication of both is that history is whatever the historian chooses to make it – that even so-called 'facts' are not 'sacred', but are no less 'free' than is 'opinion'.[52]

This sort of view continued to be maintained by a few mavericks through the twentieth century, but their sceptically based challenge has been largely resisted or ignored. In his introduction to *The New Cambridge Modern History* (1957), Sir George Clark refers to 'some impatient scholars [who] *take refuge in scepticism*, or at least in the doctrine that, since all historical judgements involve persons and points of view, *one is as good as another*, and there is *no "objective" historical truth*'.[53] Such a 'doctrine' to the traditional historian is quite unacceptable. But sceptical philosophy has refused to go away, and in the twenty-first century remains as an important ingredient of those postmodern theories that question the possibility of any historical account of the past 'as it was'.

5 CONCLUSION

Taken together the related challenges from psychology, linguistics, and philosophy, present a formidable problem for historical study, for they have served to undermine the foundations of the subject as traditionally conceived. In the face of such an assault, the instinct of historians has often been to close ranks and defend their old territory. Exponents of other disciplines, it has been claimed, have no understanding of what has become a highly specialised study, and are incompetent – and highly presumptuous – to intrude on the territory of others. One can theorise to one's heart's content, but the practical facts of history remain.

Nevertheless, the very vehemence with which historians have sometimes mounted their defence indicates a disquiet, some recognition of a real threat to the status of their subject, and to their own ability to present a record of the past 'as it was'. And that external threat has only been exacerbated by internal developments within the discipline, to be considered now in Chapter 5.

Chapter 5

Internal challenges to the old model: some major forces

> These which the inexperienced call *true*, I maintain to be only *better*, and not truer than others. (Plato)[1]

1 INTRODUCTION

The challenges to the old model of history considered in Chapter 4 could trace their roots back, in some cases as far as classical antiquity. The challenges to be identified now are more specifically modern, with Marxism growing in strength from the nineteenth century and through the twentieth, and both feminism and post-colonialism belonging essentially to our own time. These are not of course the only intellectual movements that might have been considered here, but this chapter is intended to introduce three major contemporary influences on historical study.

These three influences are clearly identifiable, and so will be treated in different sections, but they will be seen to be closely interrelated. In particular, having independently questioned the absolutist truth-claims of traditional historical accounts, they may be seen to be concerned with the relativisation of truth to which reference is made by Plato in the quotation above. Their various challenges, further, can all be interpreted as complementary to those already considered from psychology, linguistics, and philosophy. First, all three promote a different perspective on the past, a different standpoint from which to view the past and to assess it; so each deliberately indicates an alternative mode of *perception*. Second, in each case a somewhat different *language* may be implicated: since different aspects of the past are being selected for particular attention and emphasis, and a different consciousness encouraged, there is recognition of the power of language and that different modes of expression may well be needed. And third, since all three 'isms' have contrived to challenge the validity of traditional, supposedly 'objective' historical accounts, they have individually and collectively contributed to that *relativisation* which we have seen to be long associated with sceptical philosophy.

One more general issue needs to be confronted at the outset. In view of their challenges to prevailing orthodoxies, the forces here reviewed have provoked considerable opposition. That is not surprising, for each in turn has questioned the validity of previous perceptions, offering alternative visions not only of the past but of the future. That can be disturbing. Our personal and professional security is often based on, or derived from, commitment to one particular position. Just as some conventional astronomers in the early seventeenth century refused to look through Galileo's telescope for fear that they might see something that undermined their own long-held position, so some historians might now be expected to reject any need to expose themselves to the possibility of re-thinking their subject. Whether in history or science or any other subject, where a long-serving framework still survives, within which to fit data and provide interpretations, potential rivals are bound to be resisted. To have the bedrock of one's discipline questioned, is to be unsettled; and when stability is threatened, aggression usually follows. Why should we be required to view the processes of history as dependent upon factors that we have previously overlooked, or whose importance we have minimised? Why should we turn our attention to groups of people who have long been ignored as historically unimportant, whether they be the 'lower orders', or women, or slaves, or foreigners, or ethnic minorities? Why should we be encouraged to look at the past in terms other than those with which we have been brought up, when it is they that have provided the foundation for what we think we have become? By questioning the validity of our previously accepted historical emphases, interpretations, and accounts, our three intellectual movements force us to question ourselves; and that can be an emotionally as well as intellectually unsettling experience.

But it can also be exciting, for opportunities are offered for new perceptions, imaginative alternatives, and creative possibilities. Admittedly, there is some danger of enthusiastic proponents of each new 'ism' believing that they uniquely have found the final route to truth, and their sometimes strident advocacy can be presented in the unhelpful convolutions of a virtually private language.

But a calm appraisal of the issues considered here, does indicate that, even if the whole of history does not need to be re-written, some new chapters at the very least are needed. For each 'ism' can be seen as potentially shedding fresh light on the infinitely complex shadow of history; each has its part to play in our interpretative dreams; each supplies another lever by means of which we may move the weight of the past, in order to examine it in other ways, from other aspects; and each therefore extends the range of living possibilities, not only in relation to that past, but also to our future.

2 MARXISM

> He [Marx] made a tremendous contribution by altering the whole fashion of historical thought. (L. Kolakowski)[2]

Few would deny that claim. Marxism may now, by the twenty-first century, seem to many to be little more than an irrelevant corpse, but no historically conscious thinker can avoid confronting the revolutionary and lasting challenge which Karl Marx (1818–1883) made to traditional views of history. It remains highly problematic to define precisely what that challenge has been, since the label 'Marxism' has proved contentious and highly ambiguous. Marx's writings have been plundered by widely differing theorists (including historians), who have used his (not necessarily consistent) ideas for their own purposes; and varied interpretations of his words and works have served to provide justifications for many different positions. But the very breadth and variety of his influence indicate the vital importance of a man who has given his name to what remains perhaps the most respected and hated 'ism' of the last century. No attempt will be made here to examine Marxism in any detail: our purpose rather is to indicate the force of its challenge to the conventional model of 'history' identified in Chapter 2.

That challenge was quite consciously made. Marx deliberately set out to replace conventional or 'bourgeois' history with his own, and that replacement was to be effected for an explicitly 'ideological' purpose: his revised account of the past was presented as underpinning for a political programme for the future. The function of philosophy, Marx believed, was not simply to interpret the world, but actually to change it; and in his practical ambitions for the future, a key role was to be played by his theories of past history. He knew well that, for future change to be encouraged, some understanding had to be given that people's own situation was not static, but a part of an on-going historical process; and, like other historians, he interpreted that process in such a way that his own desired outcome would seem to be natural and necessary.

So Marx criticised earlier historians for the inadequacies of their own theoretical approaches. They had tended to over-emphasise the importance of individual figures; they had over-estimated the power and significance of abstract ideas, including those of religion; and they had correspondingly under-estimated the factors that seemed to him to be most fundamental: 'Writers of history have so far paid very little attention to the development of material production, which is the basis of all social life and therefore of all real history.'[3] The 'development of material production', then, seemed to Marx to provide the key to an understanding of historical developments, and it was this insight that provoked the rather extravagant claim by his friend Friedrich Engels, that 'Just as Darwin discovered the law of evolution in organic matter, so Marx discovered the law of evolution in human history'.[4]

In fact, the discovery of 'the simple fact . . . that mankind must first of all eat and drink, have shelter and clothing, before it can pursue politics, religion, art, science, etc.', was made rather earlier, and might be attributed to Aristotle. But Marx's own emphasis on 'the development of material production' as the crucial element of historical change, was particularly important, since it implied that that change did not come about purely by chance: rather, it resulted from the operation of certain observable laws. And those laws were economic. For the social and political structure of society at any given time was determined by its economic structure; and that had to do with production, with 'labour', and with the way humans first subsisted and later earned their livings.

The actual development of economic structures was recorded in history. First, there were primitive communes where land and property were shared, and there was little need for any division of labour. Then in ancient societies where there was some increase in productivity, private property developed, so that divisions arose between different classes – between rich and poor, owners and slaves. Those class-distinctions were further elaborated under the next social structure of mediaeval feudalism, in which people were ordered in hierarchies that were supposedly divinely sanctioned. Then feudalism in turn was replaced, through significant technological improvements in the means of production, by capitalism; and that was importantly characterised by new social relations between capitalists themselves, who owned the means of production, and the wage-labourers whom they employed and whom they were in a position to exploit.

The most significant factors in historical development, then, derived from those interactions with nature which were necessitated by people's need physically to survive. As those interactions changed, through the application of new modes of production, so correspondingly did the structure of society change. That was not to say that people were totally *determined* by their physical situation, or by their social and economic relations: ultimately they remained as free agents. But they were free only within certain constraints, and in particular they were bound within those constraints that their own time had inherited from previous generations: 'Men make their own history, but they do not make it just as they please; they do not make it under circumstances chosen by themselves, but under circumstances directly encountered, given and transmitted from the past.'[5] Those inherited circumstances included most importantly the relationship that humans had developed with nature and with one another, in order physically to survive. Thus, 'every succeeding generation finds itself in possession of the productive forces acquired by the previous generation'; and these productive forces become the very 'basis of all their history', and give history its 'coherence'. For, again, it was from the mode of production that social and individual intellectual life was derived: 'The mode of production of material life conditions the social, political and intellectual life process in general. It is not the consciousness of men that determines their being, but, on the contrary, their social being that determines their consciousness.'[6]

This prioritisation of 'the mode of production of material life' justified Marx in the description of his own approach as 'the materialist conception of history'; and his emphasis on *material* factors (or even determinants) has continued to provoke controversy. It seems likely that Marx himself sometimes over-stated his position in response to his opponents; or it may be that, like many of us, he was himself torn about the extent to which human behaviour *is* determined. At all events, history was not to be de-personalised: of itself, it does nothing; it is made by human beings. And, as we have seen, within certain constraints humans do 'make their own history'. They make it, not so much as individuals, but as members of social classes; and it is central to his revolutionary programme that different social classes are locked in a continuing struggle. So as he emphasises in his *Communist Manifesto* (1848), 'the history of all hitherto existing societies is the history of class struggles'.[7]

Class struggles again derived obviously from different economic situations and interests. As technologically based means of production had improved, so there had developed a surplus to immediate requirements; and that surplus was appropriated by the class which owned the means of production, at the expense of any other. In the contemporary historical phase, then, there was an obvious and essential distinction between those 'capitalists' who owned land or the means of production, and the 'proletariat' who had only their labour to sell; and the gap between these classes, Marx thought to be inevitably widening. For the dominant class was in a position to consolidate its dominance: economic power gave political power; and productive power entailed intellectual power – power over the minds of the oppressed:

> The ideas of the ruling class are in every epoch the ruling ideas: i.e., the class which is the ruling *material* force of society, is at the same time its ruling *intellectual* force. The class which has the means of material production at its disposal, has control at the same time over the means of mental production, so that thereby, generally speaking, the ideas of those who lack the means of mental production are subject to it.[8]

That insight is crucial to Marxism's relationship with history, and it returns us to the theme of self-consciousness. For it was the self-consciousness of their membership of one class in opposition to the other, that Marx believed would provide the motor for future revolution and historical change. And that self-consciousness was to be informed by an understanding of history – its underlying laws, and its clarification that capitalism was only one phase in a continuing development. Just as feudalism had given place to capitalism, so too capitalism itself would in turn be superseded by socialism.

That illumination and that programme provoked or consolidated a change in historical interest and emphasis, at least among some historians. Well before Marx, in the early eighteenth century, Macaulay had appealed to historians to extend their interests from 'palaces and solemn days', to 'ordinary men as they appear in their ordinary business and in their ordinary pleasures';[9] and this more popular approach was re-affirmed in the 1870s, when the English historian J. R. Green rebelled against what he called 'drum and trumpet' history with its traditional political and military preoccupations. As its title implied, Green's *Short History of the English People* (1877) was designed to be a history 'not of English Kings or English conquests, but of the English *People*'. And this tendency was re-emphasised when Jean Jaurès in France openly acknowledged the influence of Marx, and published a provocatively entitled '*socialist*' history of the French Revolution. This was directed specifically at 'workers and peasants', with the aim of enlightening them about factors relating, not only to the past, but to a *forthcoming* proletarian revolution.[10]

During the twentieth century the more 'populist' approach associated with Marxism continued gradually to gain converts, and history as a narrative of past events is now seen to include a recognition that those events have affected and will affect not only the 'great', but also 'ordinary' men and women. As the Marxist playwright Bertolt Brecht expressed the point in a poem:

> Even in legendary Atlantis
> Didn't the drowning shout for their slaves
> As the ocean engulfed it?
> The young Alexander conquered India.
> He alone?
> Caesar beat the Gauls.
> Without even a cook?[11]

One publication that addressed those questions raised by Brecht was E. P. Thompson's enormously influential work, *The Making of the English Working Class* in 1963, still widely regarded as a Marxist landmark. In this historical account of the emergence (through the late eighteenth and early nineteenth centuries) of an identifiable and self-conscious 'class', Thompson significantly professed a concern 'to rescue' some of history's 'losers', and to describe a 'process of self-discovery and of self-definition'. This deliberate change of focus on his part was intended most obviously to establish the importance of many who had been previously ignored – a class of English people whose own identity, he believed, could be forged by reference to such historical antecedents as the early-modern Levellers and Diggers. But there was an additional, less obvious yet more important point: that, with their newly found identity and historical self-consciousness, these people could see that history can actually be affected; so they themselves could become, not merely a sociological category but more a moral agency, working for a better future.

Thompson's work, then, was inspired by political conviction and fired with personal moral commitment. His belief in a supposedly homogenous and unified 'class', has now been challenged not least by theories of ethnicity and gender arising from the other 'isms' to be considered below. But *The Making of the English Working Class* remains a seminal study; and, with its clear moral standpoint, it is, like so much serious history, as much about the future as the past.

That a Marxist historical approach could be fruitfully directed towards much earlier periods was demonstrated by the ancient historian G. E. M. de Ste Croix. *The Class Struggle in the Ancient Greek World* (1981) showed that, with proper attention to the shifting concept of 'class', the analytic tools and techniques derived from Marxism could profitably be applied here too. And de Ste Croix showed further that parallels could be drawn between the respective aims of the ancient Greek historian Thucydides and of Marx who was himself a student of the classics. In particular, both men were concerned to enable students of history to perceive the underlying laws of human societies, for it was only by understanding the constraints imposed by those laws, that they might to some extent be liberated from them.

Marx's related insistence on the need for some awareness of one's own historical situation, and his highlighting of the contingency of that situation and the consequent possibility of future change, have been centrally important in his challenge to conventional historiography. Marx proposed what his later followers E. P. Thompson and Geoffrey de Ste Croix actually set out to provide: a new perspective on the past. By doing that, and by adopting an alternative focus for their studies, Marxist historians have changed the criteria for what is to be selected as historically significant.

That change of emphasis and new perspective are derived, as we have seen, from a vision for the future; and despite the crumbling of Communism and the relegation of Marxism to (as we say) 'history', those ideals and aspirations do remain for those who refuse to accept Francis Fukuyama's identification of liberal-capitalism as the culmination of historical development. The perceptual switch of Marxist historians is deliberately made for 'ideological' reasons, and like many others, they interpret the past in such a way that it appears as a path towards the future they desire. As we shall see, such a belief that history needs to be re-written from the starting-point of a more desirable future, has been shared by proponents of our other 'isms'.

3 FEMINISM

> Then all the stories would have to be told differently, the future would be incalculable, the historical forces would, will, change hands, bodies; another thinking as yet not thinkable will transform the functioning of all society. (Hélène Cixous)[12]

That quotation from Hélène Cixous indicates the revolutionary potentialities of feminism, and not least on historical studies. As with Marxism, the term 'feminism' has attracted many meanings, but in general it is clear that the feminist movement over the last decades of the twentieth century resulted in another fundamental challenge to the traditional picture of history as outlined in Chapter 2.

One essential point is very simple: as Virginia Woolf observed, women have been 'all but absent from history'. So it has been argued that past histories have generally been written by men about men, and that women have been rendered almost invisible, their roles, contributions, and achievements correspondingly minimised or totally ignored.

While in general terms that is undoubtedly true, it is worth noticing that there have been some notable exceptions to the standard male-orientated pattern. Long before the modern feminist movement, a few women did succeed in breaking through the conventions of their day to become historians, and a few male historians did contrive to pay specific attention to the roles and achievements of women. Women historians to have received attention over the last few years include Christine de Pisan. Early in the fifteenth century she was commissioned to write a history of the French king Charles V, and she later went on to write the work for which she is best known, *The City of Ladies*, printed in an English translation in 1521. Another woman historian to re-emerge after long neglect is the eighteenth-century Catherine Sawbridge Macaulay. Her contemporary reputation earned her the honorary title 'Dame Thucydides',[13] and resulted in the erection of a statue in her likeness, actually entitled 'History'. But in an eight-volume *History of England* she made no attempt to conceal her strong republican sympathies. Scorning conventional submission to authority, she wrote openly 'in the cause of liberty and virtue' – an ideal she derived from her own reading of Greek and Roman history, and one that found more favour in revolutionary France, where her work was translated in 1791–1792, than in her own country.[14] In addition to her political provocation, Catherine Macaulay feared that she

Figure 5 Catherine Macaulay (1731–1791) as 'Dame Thucydides': statue of an eighteenth-century historian, now in Warrington Town Hall.

might be censured for encroaching on male territory; and both issues are indicated in Dr Johnson's reported comment that 'she is better employed at her toilet than using her pen. It is better she should be reddening her own cheeks, than blackening other people's characters'.[15] But despite such discouragement, a number of other women historians continued through the nineteenth century to make their own contributions to the subject, confident that they could, in the words of Alice Stopford Green in 1897, 'open new horizons where man's vision has stopped short'.[16]

There have, too, been some male historians concerned to include women in their own accounts of the past. As early as the seventeenth century, Gilles Ménage, believing that women had been unfairly neglected in the history of philosophy, discovered in his researches no fewer than sixty-five examples for inclusion in his *History of Women Philosophers*. In 1752, George Ballard included essays on such eminent women as Margaret Cavendish, Damaris Masham, and Mary Astell, in his *Memoirs of Several Ladies of Great Britain who have been celebrated for their Writings or Skill in the Learned Languages, Arts, and Sciences*; and a generation later, William Alexander produced a far more ambitious work on the history of women from antiquity to his own time, purporting to give 'some account of almost every interesting particular concerning that sex among all nations'! During the nineteenth century, notable treatments importantly include that of W. E. H. Lecky, who concluded his *History of European Morals* with a weighty chapter devoted to 'The Position of Women', in which he showed a personal concern, not only with their past, but also with the possibility of future change.[17]

Nevertheless, despite such exceptions, the male-orientated focus of most past historical writing is indisputable, and attempts to redress that imbalance have included the introduction of specifically women's history, or narratives of the past in which the scales are deliberately tipped the other way, towards 'positive discrimination'. Such counterbalancing histories are obviously no less biased than those of the past, but the bias is openly admitted and the ideological standpoint clarified. Thus, for example, two American historians expressed an aim 'to counter the subtly denigrating myth that women either "have no history" or have achieved little worthy of inclusion in the historical record', and they presented, specifically on behalf of women, *A History of Their Own*.[18] Another writer explicitly defined her objective as being 'to demonstrate that women have not been "all but absent" from history . . . [but]

have played a crucial role, producing, processing, and reproducing the cultural and economic resources of each generation'.[19] The motivation, in such cases then, is clear, and the choice of focus has been made with a particular agenda in mind.

The related claim that 'the result will be a retelling of the human past enriched and *made complete*, a retelling that will give us for the first time *a true history of humanity*',[20] is clearly problematic. It goes against the argument of this book that any account of the past could ever be 'complete', and that the concept of one 'true history of humanity' is even meaningful. But the feminist strategy must certainly serve to *enrich* history, and it has already served to recover some previously lost aspects of the past. Feminist historians, no less than their Marxist colleagues, have (following new answers to the question 'Why?') refused to accept conventional judgements about who and what should be studied. Just as Marxist historians have declined to focus exclusively on one 'higher' social group, and so have recovered many long-forgotten individuals and movements, so feminists have encouraged a reversal of traditional values by insisting on the relevance of *women's* roles in past societies. Once again it has been shown how historians fail to see what does not suit them, and conversely find what they are looking for. Far more evidence has been found to exist, both from women and about women, than was previously thought possible, and recent writers have not only retrieved from obscurity many long-forgotten figures, but have also been enabled, with their changed emphasis and concerns, to put a new complexion on important past events.

A few examples may be taken from the seventeenth century. In 1980, Carolyn Merchant questioned the 'triumphalist' account of the Scientific Revolution, in which the earlier 'organic' model of nature was superseded by the 'mechanical'; and she initiated a reconsideration and re-assessment of that development from a specifically feminist and ecological standpoint that has subsequently become far more fashionable. One result is the perceived need for some historiographical re-evaluations: of the whole concept of 'progress', for example, and of the definition of an 'age of reason' for a period when numerous women were still being burned as witches. In parallel with such re-visions, long-ignored women have been retrieved for scholarly attention: the playwright Aphra Behn (1640–1689) has undergone a major revival, with her works newly published and performed; Margaret Cavendish (1624–1673) has been studied as scientist, playwright and poet; and as a philosopher and scientist, Anne Conway (1630?–1679), following re-publication of her major work after a lapse of some three hundred years, has been re-introduced into the history of science and has been assessed in philosophical terms as 'perhaps the keenest metaphysician in England' of her time.[21] So in such obvious ways – by the recovery and re-introduction of long-forgotten figures and by the revival of long-ignored concerns – feminism is changing the orientation of much historical study.

It is, though, in their insistence on the impossibility of *any* value-free account of history, that feminists have most profoundly challenged historiography, and it is here that they can be seen to confirm and contribute to the overall challenge of postmodernity. The essential point here refers back to our discussion of language. In Chapter 4, section 3.2, the theory was outlined that our words have no divinely authorised applications, no essential referents or external objects to which they correspond. So that our language, rather than reflecting 'reality', actually comes to define that reality, in what must be an arbitrary or at least contingent way (a way that could be different). Language, then, inevitably expresses one specific viewpoint on the world (our own), and it thereby necessarily excludes alternative possibilities. If we spoke and wrote another language, we might experience the world quite differently. And the same applies to history, or our experience of the past.

That point is central to feminist critiques of historiography, for it is argued that our whole history – our whole past and our account of that past – is written in a language that derives from and in turn underpins an essentially 'patriarchal' structure. That is, men and male attitudes have long been dominant in western societies, so that those attitudes perceived as being 'male' have been deliberately fostered, with corresponding values transmitted through our very language. History, then, has come to be written, not only *with* a certain emphasis, but *in* a language or 'discourse' that confirms that emphasis. So, it is claimed, historians are all trapped, often unconsciously, within a linguistically confirmed conceptual and chronological framework that minimises the value of the 'female'.

Conventional periodisation in historical study, for example, identifies the so-called 'Renaissance' (the recovery or 're-birth' of classical learning) as the great turning-point that marks the end of the dark Middle Ages and heralds the illumination of modernity. The Renaissance has always been associated with a very positive and progressive political, social, and cultural development: it marks the consolidation of nation-states, the end of feudal social structures, the emergence of the self-conscious and self-formed individual. That positive perception remained essentially unquestioned until, from her feminist perspective, Joan Kelly asked whether *women* had actually participated in that programme – whether indeed *they* had enjoyed a 'Renaissance' at all. By asking that question, Joan Kelly was not, of course, asking whether women had lived through the historical period referred to as the Renaissance: of course they had. The point was to ask whether women's experience of that time was to be seen in the glowing terms that conventional history described. And her own researches indicated that, in a number of respects, the position of women, far from improving, had actually declined at that time. Whereas in the preceding mediaeval period she found women enjoying a measure of respect, independence, and political and cultural influence, by the fourteenth century their position appeared actually to have deteriorated. In political, cultural, and personal matters, Italian Renaissance women had become reduced to a subordinate position: 'the modern relation of the sexes [had] made its appearance'; so that, she concluded, 'there was no renaissance for women – at least, not during the Renaissance'.[22]

The point, then, is again that feminism has challenged the chronological and conceptual frameworks within which history has conventionally been done. For the feminist, those frameworks, which define (if not determine) the history we write, have been essentially patriarchal; and they have been confirmed not least by the patriarchally based language by which they are described and understood. Even grammatical structures, it has been suggested, can be revealing in this respect. Michel Haar, for example, has claimed that 'at bottom, faith in grammar simply conveys the will to be the "cause" of one's thoughts'. That is, the active voice, 'I think', expresses (or implies, or even presupposes) personal agency: there is a self-conscious self, or 'I', who does the thinking; whereas an equally valid way of expressing the same experience might be in the passive form of 'It occurs to me . . .'.[23]

Deriving as it does from seventeenth-century scientific developments and their aftermath, that language of supposedly enlightened 'rationality' (which embraces also the ecological domination that characterises modernity) has, then, been construed as essentially male orientated. The much-vaunted clarity of style, advocated and adopted by such early Fellows of the Royal Society as Joseph Glanvill, no doubt had many advantages, but it may be seen to have had its 'downside' too. 'Univocality' – the understandable attempt to avoid any possibility of ambiguity by ensuring that each word carries one single meaning – can be attained only at the price of effecting those 'closures' against which some feminists and postmodernists now rebel. It is argued that a more 'poetically' inclined language might avoid such preordained and sometimes premature closures, and thereby open up the possibility of multiple meanings that better express or reveal complex realities.

Another function of that sort of poetic language might be to prioritise, not such traditionally 'masculine' virtues as rationality and order, but rather the previously repressed or marginalised 'feminine' qualities that have sometimes surfaced as mysticism, magic, and madness. But this is another potentially explosive issue, for it invites the exploration of alternative potentialities in matters both personal and political. Chris Weedon has clarified how 'once language is understood in terms of . . . competing ways of giving meaning to the world, which imply differences in the organisation of social power, then language becomes an important site of political struggle'.[24] So any linguistic reform or revolution would indeed constitute a major challenge to the existing social structure as well as to the historiography that supports it. As Hélène Cixous indicates in the passage from which our heading quotation is taken, it would 'threaten the stability of the masculine edifice which passed itself off as eternal-natural. . . . What would become . . . of the great philosophical systems, of world order in general, if the rock upon which they founded their church were to crumble?'[25]

There is an important sense, then, in which feminism is contributing to the de-stabilisation of historical study. It has already served for many to change the emphasis of historical concern, and to bring into focus aspects of the past that had previously been largely ignored. But of greater significance in the longer term, is its confirmation of a more general relativism, its recognition of the inevitable partiality and contingency of any historical account, and its 'de-centring' of any historical narration. It provides thereby for the possibility of some fundamental re-definitions – of 'femininity', of the 'self', and even of 'reality'. All those terms, after all, can be seen, through historical study itself, to be contingent: linguistic labels are imposed, perpetuated, adapted, used, abused, within specific cultural contexts – those contexts from which they derive and which in turn they help to maintain. The character and experience of 'womanhood' itself, or 'femininity', is far from being necessarily fixed and immutable through time and space, but is constantly re-defined – even possibly in the course of a single life. 'One is not born a woman', wrote Simone de Beauvoir, 'but rather becomes one'; and the becoming (its direction and culmination, and the construction of individual identity) is, at least to some extent, a matter of choice. The deliberate adoption of an identity can then become an important socio-political gesture, potentially made in defiance of historically and culturally imposed categorisations. There might, for instance, be no need to be constrained by overly tidy categories implied by such binary opposites as 'male' and 'female', when the construction of those categories itself becomes a subject for historical investigation.

Feminism develops here into the wider study of gender, for men, no less than women, have lately come to see the historical contingency of their own identification as *men*. By that I mean that what constitutes their 'masculinity' – the attributes that make them 'men' – does not exist like an ideal Platonic form, timeless, and eternal, and unchanging; nor yet as a more earthbound but predefined 'essence' in nature. Masculinity, rather, is something that itself has a history – something that has been very different, and could be something else.[26]

Thus, even in the western tradition and in the last half century (easily within one man's living memory), the concept of masculinity has been transformed, with stiff upper lips traded in for more flexible tear ducts, and increasing acceptance of the propriety of publicly expressed (and privately felt) emotion. As (in the developed world) international competition is transferred from military battlegrounds to corporate boardrooms, imperialistic and entrepreneurial qualities are not confined to men, and the old stereotypes of 'male' and 'female' are giving way to something far more fluid, with potentialities for development unconstrained by earlier expectations. Both femininity and masculinity thus enter the mainstream of a reformed historical study, as they become revealed as contingent constructions, with pasts that need to be understood, in order for their futures to be consciously negotiated.

4 POST-COLONIALISM

> The trouble with the Engenglish is that their hiss hiss history happened overseas, so they dodo don't know what it means.
>
> (Salman Rushdie)[27]

> The question is this: from what base do we look at the world?
>
> (Ngugi wa Thiong'o)[28]

In the sixteenth century, François Baudouin noted how 'Diodorus Siculus attacked the ancient historians who wrote the history only *of a single nation*, because they were writing not history but only a certain disconnected piece of history';[29] and in 1699 Thomas Baker, noting that the Spanish conquistadors had reported on the Amazons as being giants and cannibals, suggested that their underlying motivation might have been economic (their love of gold), and that they represented the people 'as Monsters' in order to have a better excuse 'to destroy them'.[30] It is essentially these criticisms, of a cynically parochial (often economically motivated) presentation of a partial view, that still concern 'post-colonial' writers, and that is illustrated in the stammering words of Salman Rushdie's drunken character quoted above. That is to say again, it is claimed that history has been written by 'winners' for their own self-justificatory purposes, and that in particular it has been written by spokespeople of imperial powers, and of then dominant nations. As a result, the 'history' which has been recorded, has been derived from a specific ideological perspective, while the greater part of what has happened in the past, has been left well alone and out of sight, ignored or not comprehended, or simply not noticed. Existing histories, then, have been 'partial' in both senses of that word: first, they have presented only one small *part* of an infinitely complex whole; and second, that part itself has been narrowly interpreted, with its focus consciously or unconsciously determined by the writer's own position and prejudices. So the basic question becomes again, in Ngugi's words above, 'From what base do we look at the world?' And what is now sought is re-assessment from other, previously less privileged bases, a re-focusing that does not necessarily replace the original, but that can at least be seen as complementary, opening other eyes and mouths, other dimensions and possibilities.

The need to re-write history from a post-colonial perspective arises, then, from the rather unoriginal recognition that the thrust of past narratives has been determined by a specific ideology – in this case the ideology of a dominating power, usually European, but in the twentieth century increasingly American too. Thus, modern history has explicitly or implicitly reflected and expressed and consolidated the ideas and ideals of nineteenth- and twentieth-century imperialism. These include in particular the assumed superiority of western white culture and its civilising mission, a belief in 'progress' grounded in specific social, economic and technological theories, a commitment to the supposed religious truths of Christianity, and a more secular but no less certain faith in 'liberal capitalism'. It was their confidence in the absolute validity of such ideas that served for many to justify imperialism and imperialistic behaviour, and history was generally written from the standpoint of those who had accordingly and, it was assumed, altruistically shouldered 'the white man's burden'.

The unitary coherence of such a view has now been challenged, fragmented by the break-up of empires and by increasingly insistent demands that appropriate recognition be given to those numerous minorities, whose perceptions do not necessarily conform to other people's expectations and interests. By what criteria, it is asked, was European culture judged to be 'superior' to those 'native' cultures which it endeavoured to dominate and to erase from history? Who is to say that western ideas of technologically based 'progress' are to be preferred over all others and universally imposed? Is Christianity the *only* valid religion, with a unique route to truth that justifies attempts at universal conversion and the destruction of more 'primitive' belief-systems? Is there not something deeply ironic about professedly 'democratic' powers trying to bomb other peoples into submission? Some of these issues are well illustrated by the reported response of an Indian leader, Smohalla, to the late nineteenth-century American Government policy to force all Indians to become farmers:

> You ask me to plough the ground; shall I take a knife and tear my mother's bosom? Then when I die she will not take me to her bosom to rest. You ask me to dig for stones; shall I dig under her skin for her bones? Then when I die I cannot enter her body to be born again. You ask me to cut grass and make hay and sell it and be rich like white men; but how dare I cut off my mother's hair?[31]

A fundamental clash of cultures is exposed in those words. Smohalla is expressing a value-system diametrically opposed to that which he is being directed to adopt. His (non-Christian) *religion* forbids the exploitation of the land which is dictated by *economic* interest, and he is resisting assimilation into the alien (and 'masculine') perspective of '*white men*'.

This stand against the imperialistic imposition of alien values goes to the heart of post-colonialism, in relation to which alternative perceptions such as those of the American Indians, are to be accepted as valid in their own terms, even when – perhaps especially when – they seem 'anomalous' and cannot be immediately fitted into the previously accepted scheme of things. The autonomy of minority and non-conforming views is to be respected, not only now but in their past; so that a whole new history has to be written to accommodate and justify them. And once that is done, once their voices have been retrieved, it will be seen to be not only their own history that has been affected. In addition, that other self-justifying history, from which they had been excluded, will need to be rewritten; for it can now be seen that its coherence and persuasiveness were bought only at the price of exclusions that can no longer be tolerated.

Such enlargement of the historical consciousness poses both threats and possibilities, and post-colonial revisionism is bound therefore to meet with a very mixed reception. The most obvious threat is to that stable 'self', which has been individually and collectively constructed over the years with so much self-concern. In other words, as we have seen in our discussion of perception in Chapter 4, section 2, one of our primary needs is to build up an interpretation of the world, and to evolve a framework in terms of which we can make sense of experience and of ourselves. Our history – both personal and national – forms an important part of that construction: a meaningful path is needed to justify what we currently are, so our assessment of the past deliberately bolsters our self-constructed 'self'.

Now as we all recognise, our own identity is forged importantly by reference to other people. Those in solitary confinement, deprived of the possibility of such reference, commonly go mad. So our historically constructed self inevitably includes as an integral part the intertwining history of those with whom we have had relationships; but of course *our* history of those others will inevitably differ from *their* history of themselves. There must, after all, inevitably be a difference in relative perspectives. So the imperialist's history of another country will be perceived and written as a part of the history of his or her own country; the colony will then be seen not so much as an end in itself but rather as a satellite of some 'metropolitan' centre. So, as Frantz Fanon writes:

> The settler makes history and is conscious of making it. . . . Thus the history which he writes is not the history of the country which he plunders, but the history of his own nation in regard to all that she skims off, all that she violates and starves.[32]

There is, then, an obvious sense in which 'colonial' history has generally been written from a coloniser's (necessarily limited) perspective, but there is also a sometimes subtler way in which colonial peoples themselves have been defined in terms that suit the coloniser. For again, we define ourselves in relation to other people, and it is convenient to classify and identify some 'others' in a way that boosts our own self-image. John Tosh has described how the idealised 'masculinity' of imperial Britain was forged through contrasts drawn with variously 'effeminate' subordinate races.[33] Such characteristics as idleness, docility, and affection were attributed to the 'other' of colonials – partly perhaps as a (possibly unconscious) projection of sublimated facets of their own selfhoods, but partly too in order to justify their imperial role of domination.

Imperialists, then, have often been guilty of imposing inferiority (of one sort or another, and however defined) and even 'subhumanity' on subject classes and races, whose 'otherness' has served effectively to consolidate 'imperialist' identity and to keep the subject in their 'proper' place. As Jean-Paul Sartre put it, 'The European has only been able to become a man through creating slaves and monsters'[34]; or in the more recent words of Homi Bhabha, it was in the colonisers' interests 'to construe the colonized as a population of degenerate types on the basis of racial origin, in order to justify conquest and to establish systems of administration and instruction'.[35] Natives can be seen as lazy and incompetent and primitive, and eager to receive salvation from those whose organisational and technological expertise will guarantee progress. So the past was distorted, with the devaluation of precolonial times specifically designed to show the continuing need for the coloniser, in order to prevent any relapse or any reversion to that uncivilised past in the future. In the words of Fanon again, speaking at the time of the Algerian uprising against the French (1959):

> The effect consciously sought by colonialism was to drive into

> the natives' heads the idea that if the settlers were to leave, they would at once fall back into barbarism, degradation and bestiality. . . . Colonialism [sought] . . . to be considered . . . as a mother who unceasingly restrains her fundamentally perverse offspring from managing to commit suicide and from giving free rein to its evil instincts.[36]

The characterisation of colonial peoples in this way has obviously been achieved only at great cost. For the characteristics of 'otherness' attributed to them have been *imposed* – not indeed arbitrarily, but with specific social and political motivation; so that the 'colonial' character has not been freely self-chosen but has been defined and imposed from without. And, further, it has been argued that in order to satisfy the needs and convenience of the imperialist, that character has often been assumed to have a *static* quality and to require a *homogeneity* which in actuality it lacked. The imposed fixity denied any possibility of subsequent development, and any actual diversity of 'native' societies was seen as one of those weaknesses from which deliverance could be provided. So it was reported from the great Imperial Assemblage in Delhi in 1876, that 'those Princes, chiefs and nobles [were invited] in whose persons the *ambiguity of the past* is associated with the prosperity of the present'. As Bernard Cohn notes, it was made clear that 'the Viceroy, standing for the empress, represented the only authority which could hold together the great diversity inherent in the "colonial sociology" ', and which could consequently guarantee present and future prosperity.[37]

With any system of categorisation, classes can be defined and pigeon-holes neatly filled only by deliberate exclusions. To aid our definitions, we choose to prioritise or to take into account certain qualities of an object or person, but that choice implies that many other qualities (which we might equally have chosen) will be deliberately ignored. We might, then, categorise people in terms of their income or skin colour or nose length, in which cases their sex will be irrelevant. Post-colonial critics are now affirming the importance of precisely those qualities which were previously ignored or discounted, and emphasising the 'hybridity', the variety and heterogeneity, of what has previously been subsumed within an assumed but spurious 'unity'.

Through such revision of the nature of the 'other', post-colonial theorists may already seem to pose a threat to the stable identity of western personality and history, but additional anxieties may derive from their assault on the whole concept of 'culture'. Historically, non-European cultures have not infrequently influenced individual European artists: for example, nineteenth-century Impressionists acknowledged the influence of Japanese prints, and in the earlier twentieth century, such renowned painters and sculptors as Picasso and Matisse were fascinated and influenced by newly imported works of art from Africa. Musically, too, as is well known, the effects of such non-European forms as jazz have been enormous. But on the whole, it has been presupposed that culture is still to be defined in western terms, and any influences have been safely accommodated within that still dominant tradition. The viceroy of India in 1877 indicated that imperial administrators would 'continue to form the most important practical channel through which the arts, sciences and *the culture of the West . . . may freely flow to the East*', and a much more recent African report has described how that country 'was taught to look on Europe as her teacher and the centre of man's civilization, and herself as the pupil'.[38] Aspects of European culture have been exported, not always without some incongruity, on the assumption of their superiority; and it was by traditional European standards that other assuming cultures were assessed, and generally found wanting. Inevitably, therefore, indigenous native cultures have been under-valued, or discounted and ignored, their past often seen 'as one wasteland of non-achievement'.[39]

Again, then, post-colonialism presents a challenge to previously accepted values and criteria. If the old Eurocentric standards are to be renounced, what shall we be left with? Accepted boundaries that gave security through their consolingly sharp definitions, are exposed for what they always really were: not absolute at all, but arbitrary, contingent, relative, and with a newly perceived fluidity that invites erosion and even necessitates replacement. As recently as 2001, South Africans are reportedly preparing 'to take [the] burden of history off the white man', by incorporating alternative perspectives into narratives about their past. For generations of South Africans, history began with their equivalent of Columbus – a European who had supposedly 'discovered' the country in 1652 (in this case, a Dutchman, Jan van Riebeek). A new 'more balanced' version of the past is now to be prepared, giving greater emphasis to the indigenous Bushmen (who had lived in the region for millennia), to Bantu tribesmen, and to the liberation struggle against apartheid. And those modifications to history textbooks are being supplemented by proposals to change some names that no less encapsulate (and symbolise) an outgrown past: South African post-colonialists might well question whether it is any longer appropriate for the name of their largest city, Johannesburg, to commemorate an unknown, long dead Afrikaner.[40]

In all this revision and reassessment, not even the very linchpin of western civilisation is immune. 'Rationality' itself, in terms of which 'science' has evolved and 'progress' been assumed, comes under question. Not, it has to be said, for the first time by any means: the validity of reason was questioned in Greek antiquity, and its relativism has been sporadically noted from the early-modern period on (not least more recently, as we have seen, in the context of feminism). But the post-colonial attack is somewhat different, inasmuch as 'reason' is identified as a western artefact which has underpinned imperialist pretensions. Its assumed monolithic nature has, it is alleged, been used again as a standard, in relation to which other societies may be judged and alternative cultures found ineffective, so that any refusal to accept the terms of western rationality 'has been seen as . . . the final proof of the cognitive inferiority of the non-white races'.[41] With those non-white races now questioning the very basis of western scientific and technological civilisation, it is hardly surprising that one post-colonial spokesman can write of how 'the struggle against colonial oppression . . . changes the direction of Western history'.[42]

5 CONCLUSION

Changing the direction of western history can seem a frightening possibility or programme, but at the same time it can have a very positive and practical outcome. It is in the end what all our 'isms' are concerned with. Marxism, feminism, and post-colonialism are, or were, themselves the product of a time and place, so subject to their own historical development, and destined for replacement by yet another 'post-'; for 'isms' themselves fragment or lose their cutting edge. 'Marxism' now already has a curiously dated air, and feminism's phases follow each other fast and sometimes furiously. But, however rapidly aspects of these movements may be replaced and disdainfully discarded, a central message remains. For what all share is a recognition that conventional historical accounts of the past can be challenged, inasmuch as a change in perspective results in a new perception, which in turn opens the way to new interpretations and narratives. The realisation of that possibility entails a recognition that history – our accounts of the past, present, *and future* – could be different. History, in short, is not fixed: change is possible.

This view of history opens up new possibilities for the underprivileged, for it invites re-assessment from the standpoint of those previously overlooked or viewed through a distorting lens. It offers the possibility of re-definition: an opportunity is provided for retrieving from their traditional obscurity those 'others', whether slaves or workers or women or 'colonials' or any other minority, who have previously been relegated to the status of 'people without history'.[43]

In relation to post-colonialism, but with equal relevance to Marxism, feminism, and other 'isms', Edward Said has called for a new 'contrapuntal perspective'. By that he means that, instead of adopting one standpoint and interpreting from that one necessarily exclusive perspective, we should remain aware of the innumerable alternatives that we might equally have adopted:

> That is, we must be able to think through and interpret together experiences that are discrepant, each with its particular agenda and pace of development, its own internal formations, its internal coherence and systems of external relationships, all of them co-existing and interacting with others.[44]

This sort of approach would theoretically refuse to privilege any one position, any one narrative; and such a refusal is of course entailed by a postmodern perspective. For the narratives of our 'isms' are no less immune than any others to charges of inevitable partiality, of incompleteness and one-sidedness. And the foci in any case, the temporarily privileged – whether social classes, women, ethnic groups, or whatever – are themselves, when subject to analysis, found to be less than the coherent entities ideally required for their function. So while our 'isms' have all made their contributions to our current postmodern position, they themselves suffer some fragmentation in its light. But they have helped to raise the level of historiographical awareness, and to deliver the *coup de grâce* to any lingering belief in the possibility of a historical account of the past 'as it was'.

Chapter 6

What and why? The future of history

> History is 'reporting on what they [historians] believe happened in the past interpreted in the light of their own prejudices and opinions.'
>
> (Claire Rayner)[1]

> No one is quite sure of the ground on which they stand, which direction they are facing, or where they are going.
>
> (Michael Keith and Steve Pile)[2]

1 THE POSTMODERN PREDICAMENT

Claire Rayner has a point. In the light of the various challenges considered in Chapters 4 and 5 – challenges presented by psychological theories of perception, by new accounts of language, by philosophical problems of scepticism, and by such movements as Marxism, feminism, and post-colonialism – the traditional model of history as an 'objective' record of the past 'as it was' has been clearly superseded. Historians in fact may seem to be in a situation like that described in the second quotation above – in a postmodern predicament where the foundations and direction and future of their subject have all come under question.

No-one has been more responsible for the overturning of old historiographical certainties than the genial postmodern guru, Hayden White. Since the publication of his *Metahistory* in 1973, White has achieved fame and notoriety as a main spokesman for postmodernism's implications for historical study – applauded and reviled above all for his own alleged erosion of that most fundamental distinction between 'fact' and 'fiction'. This is not the place for another assessment of White's work,[3] but a brief look at some of his ideas may help to clarify the nature of our 'postmodern predicament'.

First, then, it's for his critique of *narrative* that Hayden White is probably best known, and his essential point in relation to this is that historical narratives are not (as often presupposed) simply 'found' already fashioned, *in* the past; but they are, rather, invented and imposed *upon* the past by historians, ever anxious to endow that past – or the still surviving traces of that past – with some sort of sense and coherence, meaning, purpose, and direction. The narrative chosen may take any form, whether romantic, tragic, comic, or satiric; and (since all these forms are epistemologically equivalent, one being as good as another in its representational ability) that choice can be made only on the grounds of aesthetic or moral preference. That choice (whatever it is) will then, and obviously, determine the *form* of the 'history' (selecting and shaping the elements in a way to suit its purpose); and it will also (though less obviously) determine the *content*, in that (as we have considered before) the historian's viewpoint and focus will provide the criteria for what evidence is to be accounted relevant, for what is to be included. The crux of the matter is, then, that historians have to take an imaginative step, in order to choose their own way of 'emplotting' the past in narrative form; so they need to remain aware that alternative descriptions are always available, and that their work is thus akin to any other work of fiction.

A second and important point about narrative (of whatever nature), according to White, is that it implies 'closure'. In other words, historical narrative has the effect of tidying up the chaos of the past, so that we can all feel comfortable with it – aesthetically satisfied, and reassured. The remains of the past are constrained within a structure, sporting a beginning, a middle, and an end; so we are left with the feeling that that is how it was because that's how it was bound to be. That's how it's made to appear. And that has implications for the present and the future, since it's only an apprehension of the past's contingency that seems to open up the possibility of future choice. White argues, then, that history should somehow avoid narrative closure and 'educate us to *discontinuity*' – showing us, that is, that things not only could have been, but could be, different.

Implicit then, in the third place, is a criticism of the historical discipline as it has evolved over the last two centuries. It has become, according to White, a rather bland vehicle for maintaining the *status quo*. Far from being ideologically neutral, as its practitioners persistently claim, it is essentially conservative, its very language constricting the range of what is to be accounted acceptable and possible. History is made to accommodate past complexities and apparent anomalies, and so smoothes the way for a perpetuation in the future of things as they have been and are. It 'has become increasingly the refuge of all those "sane" men who excel at finding the simple in the complex and the familiar in the strange.'[4] But, White argues, while it has been accounted one of history's positive virtues to overcome (or conceal) the inherent meaninglessness of the past, such concealment is actually vicious, since it deprives people of any liberating vision of alternative possibilities and choices for their own futures. A better function for history is, again, to highlight the discontinuities and contingencies, and so empower people, in the cause of a visionary politics.

So are we left, as Claire Rayner implies, with history as nothing more than a mere vehicle for historians' self-indulgence? And if that is what history *is*, what now can be the *point* of it all? In other words, we are brought back to our original questions of *what* history is and *why* we should study it.

Some aspects of the situation are, as we have seen, very far from new, and in particular some scepticism about historical 'truth' is as old as the subject itself. Over a hundred years ago, William Stubbs, for all his affected repudiation of philosophy (noted in Chapter 1), questioned the possibility of ever reaching a definitive and conclusive account of the past: 'History knows that it can wait for more evidence and review its older verdicts; it offers an endless series of courts of appeal, and is ever ready to re-open closed cases.'[5] More recently Pieter Geyl has similarly concluded that historical hypotheses must always remain tentative and corrigible, and that 'History is an argument without end.'[6] Both these historians, then, are careful to refrain from making the dogmatic claims for their subject that are identified with the older model. But both would reject Claire Rayner's description of what it is that they do, for both continue to work to some extent within a previously accepted framework. Stubbs's resort to the image of the law court implies that there is an agreed structure or forum within which debate can proceed according to mutually agreed rules, and Geyl's position similarly at least admits of the possibility of an 'argument', presumably again within agreed parameters. The problem now is that even those vestiges of possible methodological compatibility have come under question, and the postmodern predicament seems to imply that effectively '*anything* goes'. A radical 'de-centring' necessitates the acknowledgement that no one focus can either embrace the whole or claim an inherent superiority over any other; and in such a situation historical explanation, in Tony Bennett's words, 'turns out to be a way of telling stories without any particularly convincing means, where such stories differ, of deciding between them'.[7]

This is related to the questioning at last of some long-lived Aristotelian diktats. In fact, historical studies may be seen very belatedly to be undergoing their own 'Copernican revolution'. Admittedly, previous upheavals in the subject have been identified, notably by F. S. Fussner, who described the revolution in historical writing and thought that took place in the early-modern period.[8] But there is a sense in which the Aristotelian dictatorship, many facets of which were gradually overthrown during the intellectual revolution of the seventeenth century, still awaits its *coup de grâce* in relation to history. At least three aspects of Aristotelian influence persist: these relate to chronology, canon-formation, and cultural categorisation; and each is questioned by postmodernism.

1.1 Questioning chronology: past, present, and future

> Time present and time past
> Are both perhaps present in time future,
> And time future contained in time past.
>
> (T. S. Eliot)[9]

Those lines of T. S. Eliot express a truth that has often been forgotten by historians, who have long continued to accept Aristotle's seemingly obvious distinction between past, present, and future. As we saw in Chapter 2, section 2.1, the past was defined by Aristotle as the proper subject-matter of history; and more than satisfied with such a generous (and constantly extending) birthright, subsequent historians have been careful to retain it. But in order to defend their territory, they have carefully fenced it off from its chronological neighbours, and have often affected to repudiate any interest in the present and future.

So one American historian in the middle of this century boasted of his own immersion in historical texts, coupled with total isolation from contemporary concerns. He had carefully read the Elizabethan Poor Law and Calvin's theological works, but had only 'rather haphazard notions' about such present concerns as the Social Security Act and existentialist writings. With these priorities, he claimed, he could avoid 'the passions, prejudices, assumptions and prepossessions, the events, crises and tensions of the present dominating [his] view of the past'. The past, that is, was to be carefully fenced off to prevent any intrusions from the present (let alone the future), for the historian's perception of its essential nature could only be distorted by any such chronological trespassing. And with a similar attempt to retain an 'innocent eye', Herbert Butterfield too makes a virtue of a chronological *cordon sanitaire*, re-emphasising the need to keep one's account of the past untainted by considerations of the present: for 'the study of the past with one eye, so to speak, upon the present is the source of all sins and sophistries in history. . . . It is the essence of what we mean by the word "unhistorical"'.[10]

Butterfield's own main concern was with what he referred to as 'Whiggishness', a characteristic he ascribed to the then fashionable approach to English constitutional history, whereby past political developments were assessed and evaluated in contemporary terms. In particular, such developments were interpreted as being steadily 'progressive', inasmuch as liberals had succeeded in extending human rights in the face of conservative opposition. Butterfield's complaint was that liberal or 'Whig' historians were thus describing the 'present as the inevitable outcome of a triumphant historical process' – producing thereby not a simple or neutral historical account of the past ('as it was'), but rather its 'ratification, if not . . . glorification'. These historians were, in other words, guilty of interpreting the past in terms of themselves – their own political standpoint and values; and Butterfield himself went on more broadly to condemn the general historical approach whereby the past was in this way studied 'with reference to the present'.[11]

Butterfield later, in his own study of early-modern science,[12] applied this historiographical point to the history of science more specifically. 'Science' does admittedly seem to be one area of human experience where the concept of 'progress' has some meaning, but that, he argued, does not justify us in evaluating past scientific theories in terms of our own superior knowledge. That again would amount to 'Whiggism', inasmuch as we would be assessing past achievements with the benefit of hindsight, and with a view to their contribution to our own position. As in the case of politics, that would involve us in a judgement on the past – illegitimate because derived from a present position. The past must be assessed not in our terms, but rather in its own. So generations of subsequent historians have taken meticulous care to avoid any such sin, and one result has been a form of supposedly 'strictly descriptive' writing, in which, it has been claimed, 'not a hint of contemporary relevance intrudes'. The professed historical aim is then to describe 'the entire milieu', and 'to present "the total picture"', in a 'value-free' way.[13]

It is only comparatively recently that criticisms have been levied in turn against this attempted anti-Whiggish style of writing. Ernst Mayr, for example, has questioned the validity of transferring the Whig-critique from politics to science. In his own history of biology, he remains unapologetic about emphasising 'the background and the development of the *ideas dominating modern biology*', though he notes that 'such a treatment justifies, indeed *necessitates, the neglect of certain temporary developments in biology that left no impact on the subsequent history of ideas*'. In this context, he cites with approval the historians of logic, W. and M. Neale, who confess their primary purpose to have been similarly 'to record the first appearances of those ideas which seem to us most important in the logic of our own day'.[14] In accordance with such an approach, then, the historian of science, or of logic or whatever, blatantly selects data on the basis of what is thought to be important today. Such historians have little sympathy with 'exploring every forgotten blind alley', since alleys that have proved blind and been forgotten have been, as it were, bred out in the evolution of ideas, and are therefore, by definition, not worthy of further consideration. It is conceded that one has to avoid bias against specific scientists or theories (as, for example, a creationist might be biased against Darwinism), that one must beware of distortions which might derive from chauvinism (emphasising British authors, for example, at the expense of their continental contemporaries), and that one should refrain from making illegitimate value-judgements with the benefit of hindsight. But, it is maintained, by starting from a knowledge of what is currently acceptable, one can maintain a sharp historical focus. In Mayr's words:

> What a scientist is most interested in when doing historical studies is to illuminate or reconstruct the pathway of the currently prevailing ideas. . . . It is only common sense for a historian to devote most attention to that particular conjecture that turned out to have had the greatest "fitness", that is, which had the greatest subsequent impact.

The historian can then with a clear conscience refrain from being 'deflected by non-essentials', for there can patently be 'nothing wrong with omitting something that is irrelevant'.[15]

That, however, is precisely the problem. For how in fact do we know what *is* 'non-essential' and 'irrelevant'? When can we possibly know *what* alleys have ultimately proved 'blind', or *which* ideas have had most 'subsequent impact'? What is to be our time-scale here? And is there anyway not some positive value in retaining *alternatives* to 'currently prevailing' perceptions? Might not this even be the whole *point* of our historical study?

We are, then, faced here with a very real problem. On the one hand, it seems intolerably limiting to view the past from our own parochial perspectives, and we can hardly be justified, as Mayr seems to advocate, in deliberately closing our eyes to those aspects of the past which seem to be (but may not be) unrelated to our own good selves. But on the other hand, the insistence that the past should be treated 'in its own terms', without any reference to contemporary interests and values, is in practice meaningless. For no more than anyone else can the historian operate like some sort of assumed mechanical sensor, in an emotional and chronological vacuum. Any perception of the past will, as we have seen in Chapter 3, necessarily involve interpretation, and that interpretation will in turn necessarily derive in part from a perceiver – a perceiver who is human and who is living in a present, with at least some thought of a future. Impaled upon the horns of this dilemma, our only relief can come from awareness of our own discomfort. For while it seems clear that our present concerns should not be allowed to dominate our histories, it nonetheless seems inevitable that our view of the past will be affected by them. It is in historical practice impossible to maintain any rigid distinction between past and present and future.

As T. S. Eliot recognised, there is anyway a far greater chronological fluidity than seems to be allowed by the rigid boundaries proposed by Butterfield and his many followers, and imposed or presupposed by our grammatical tenses. The seventeenth-century philosopher Leibniz noted what we all accept, that 'The present is big with the future and laden with the past.'[16] What we *are* is determined by what we *have been*, and determines in turn what we *will be*; and it is impossible ever to grasp 'the present' in isolation, as it slips irrevocably into the past, even as we turn to it. Tidy chronological distinctions cannot in practice be maintained, and in historiographical terms, 'such is the unity of all history that anyone who endeavours to tell a piece of it must feel that his first sentence tears a seamless web'.[17]

That quotation from the Victorian historian Frederic Maitland refers in part to the geographical extension of the subject-matter. England, for instance, is a part of Great Britain, which is a part of Europe, and so on; so that we cannot study local history without becoming involved in the history of the world. But there is also a chronological dimension to Maitland's point: that we cannot isolate the past from the present and future; for as soon as we look at any one historical event, we are carried ever backwards and forwards along potentially infinite chains of causality, with any final stopping-place only arbitrarily selected.

One of the historian's first problems, then, is to decide how and where to insert an analytic knife into that seamlessness of time, and to recognise the motivations for whatever incision is made. The presumed birth of Jesus Christ has long provided one convenient marker (between BC and AD), but only for those within the Christian tradition; and the reign of monarchs has seemed appropriately to delineate some epochs (such as Elizabethan or Victorian), but in an even more parochial context. Decades and centuries suggest another skeleton framework for our time-scales, but it is sometimes hard to squeeze what seems relevant into such externally imposed constraints: for English political historians the seventeenth century may start a touch belatedly in 1603 (with the accession of James I), but for others, with other interests and concerns, the starting-point may need to be pushed back to, say, 1543 (the publication date of Copernicus's epoch-making astronomical treatise). As a poet, Philip Larkin may have ironically pinpointed 1963 as the year when 'sexual intercourse began', but historians would be rash to claim any such chronological precision.

Our choices of starting-point, though, do seriously affect our subsequent interpretations. For just as we choose our standpoint from which to perceive our world or our historical data, so too we choose the chronological parameters or boundaries of our narrative, in order to construct a meaningful account of what has happened. And in that construction, the present and the future will play an important part. Our perception and our story of the past will depend both upon our present position and upon our vision of the future.

Samuel Gott recognised in 1648 that, 'In writing history, there is quite as much need of *foresight* into coming events as of *recapitulation* of the past.' More recently Homi Bhabha has defined a 'breakdown of temporality', in terms of which the serial and progressive narrative of histories is brought into question, as depending of course on a particular perception of the present and future. Without some such sense of the present and future, our grasp on the past too becomes tenuous. For in John Forrester's words, 'the reorganisation of the past *and* the future go hand in hand . . . the past dissolves in the present, so that the future becomes (once again) an *open question*, instead of being specified by the fixity of the past'.[18]

A desire to avoid 'fixity' and embrace an 'open' future underlies the proposal by Elizabeth Deeds Ermarth that historians might utilise a model taken from the visual arts.[19] A collage, she suggests, brings together a wide variety of different materials that haven't been juxtaposed before – that haven't seemed to fit together. An artist can select seemingly incompatible and even incongruous ingredients, and blend them into a whole that not only proves aesthetically pleasing but also encourages the viewer to see things (often familiar things) in an entirely new way. Historians might similarly exercise their own creative imagination, by shaking together their kaleidoscopic facets of past, present, and future, and fashioning them once more into an agreeable pattern (a potentially rich, if unexpected, historical narrative). That model of collage has the virtue of liberating historians from the constraints of linearity, or from the representation of events in such a way as to suggest an inevitability of outcome.

Challenges to traditional chronological distinctions and to the conventional representation of time, thus open up future possibilities, and constitute one exciting ingredient of postmodern historical study.

1.2 Questioning the canon: 'winners' and 'losers'

> Hippo no one would think fit to include among these thinkers, because of the paltriness of his thought. (Aristotle)[20]

Any re-vision or blurring of chronological categories may have implications too for whom we choose to study. A changed standpoint in time affects our relative evaluations of past actors on the stage of history, and re-assessments of our so-called 'canon' form another part of the postmodern predicament. That is, re-definitions are required of our 'heroic' figures – of who is great or important or significant; of who are properly identified as 'winners', who as 'losers'. For in these matters fashions do change. As we have seen in Chapter 5, among other influences, Marxism, feminism, and post-colonialism have provided three stimulants for change in this area, so that historical attention has now largely shifted from kings and queens to more 'ordinary' people, to women, and to other groups of the 'historically displaced'.

That new emphasis in *social* history has parallels elsewhere, and in particular the concerns of *intellectual* history are at last receiving some attention. For here too the influence of Aristotle continues to show. Aristotle himself was not only a philosopher. He was also the earliest known historian of philosophy, and as such he often still serves as a historiographical role model. In the opening chapter of his own work on metaphysics, he surveys his predecessors, enumerating those who seem to him to have made a significant contribution. Those whom Aristotle listed are still known to historians of philosophy, but who has ever heard of Hippo? As the quotation above indicates, the unfortunate Hippo is effectively dismissed by Aristotle, and excluded from the canon of significant thinkers; and as a result of that unilateral judgement, his name has virtually been lost to history.

The quality of Hippo's thought is not the issue here. The point is that the history of philosophy has derived a canon of significant thinkers from the past, and the formation of that canon has sometimes been quite arbitrary – depending in this case on the judgement of a single philosophical 'dictator'. And Aristotle was making his judgement from his own personal standpoint, viewing his predecessors as stepping-stones leading to himself, and excluding as irrelevant anyone who diverted from that path. A meaningful direction had been imposed on history, but at the expense of those who failed to conform to Aristotle's own perceptions. However 'paltry' Hippo's thought appeared to Aristotle, it might conceivably have been of some interest to students of intellectual history in the twenty-first century.

But the formulation of any canon, of any list of people thought worthy of historical attention, will necessarily exclude more than are included. So it becomes of first importance to assess the criteria by which admission is gained. 'Historians of philosophy naturally limit their attention to the ablest thinkers', wrote Leslie Stephen in 1876; and over a hundred years later A. L. Rowse agrees: 'As for thought, one doesn't really want research into the thinking of those who can't think; only the reflections of the few elect spirits who *can* have any value.'[21] Like Aristotle, then, Stephen and Rowse would blackball anyone who might be charged with 'paltriness of thought'. But the question remains as to who is to define 'the ablest', and who 'the few elect spirits'; and that raises in turn, and once again, the whole question of what the purpose of such study is. If the aim is to confirm our own self-importance, by showing how past developments necessarily culminate in our own good selves, then the Whiggish approach of Aristotle and his many successors is fully justified: history reveals, in Milan Kundera's words, 'a relay race, in which everyone surpasses his predecessor, only to be surpassed by his successor'.[22] And as we breast the tape at last, we are gratifyingly identified with the 'winners'.

But another function for history could be envisaged, which has to do with 'losers': namely, as Nietzsche proposed, to keep alive 'the memory of the great fighters *against history*' – those who have failed to conform to the 'unconscious canon of *permitted* sagacity' and who have repudiated the rules of the 'relay race'.[23] Some of life's apparent 'losers' in the short term can then be revealed as highly significant within a longer perspective. Socrates was in one sense defeated by his enemies, and paid the price by drinking hemlock. But who now celebrates his prosecutors, Meletus, Anytus, and Lycon? And, as has been noted in another context, there might have been people present at Jesus Christ's crucifixion on Calvary two thousand years ago for whom 'the only people of any consequence . . . would have been Pontius Pilate and the Roman legionaries'.[24] Both Socrates and Jesus were in one sense short-term 'losers', but their doomed protests against the values of their time have in the longer term had incalculable effects.

It is precisely such non-conforming eccentrics who might offer alternative perceptions, and who might thereby point a way forward for those who are not altogether satisfied with history's seemingly inevitable direction. Like Hippo, they may in many cases have been all but lost to history, but the questioning of canonical categories remains another important part of the postmodernist's programme.

1.3 Questioning cultural categories: reason and imagination

> The so-called 'historical method' [implies the avoidance of] imaginative excess (i.e. 'enthusiasm') at any price. (Hayden White)[25]

The third area in which Aristotle's views are now being questioned relates to his disciplinary distinction between history and poetry. We have seen that he described historical study as a rather mechanical procedure, concerned with particular instances rather than with the more general truths to which poetry aspired. From this derived the long-lived perception of history as an empirical study of 'factual' data, to the interpretation of which *reason* should be properly applied, with the potentially distorting faculty of *imagination* rigorously excluded. As we saw in Chapter 2, section 2.2, this rigid antithesis between scientific reason and speculative imagination was reinforced within the influential Baconian tradition, and then became one of the hallmarks of the eighteenth-century Enlightenment. As an Enlightenment spokesman, Voltaire therefore specifically forbids in history the use of a 'figurative style', as being derived from such truth-obscuring characteristics as 'ardent imagination, passion, [and] desire' – characteristics more appropriately reserved for poetry; and in the quotation heading this section Hayden White has noted in our own time how respectably academic historians must continue at all costs to repudiate 'enthusiasm' or 'imaginative excess'.

The potentially debilitating effect of such an attitude is shown by Hayden White to be illustrated in George Eliot's *Middlemarch* (1871–1872), where the heroine renounces the antiquarian scholar Casaubon for the sake of a young artist. In this novel, 'artistic insight and historical learning are opposed, and the qualities of the response to life which they respectively evoke are mutually exclusive'.[26] And this view of a fundamental *contrast* between history and the imaginative arts, has continued through the twentieth and into the twenty-first century. In two illuminating articles, Martin Davies has argued for the primacy of poetry, in view of history's inadequacy in the context of our own malaise. In his eyes, the one subject is to be set against the other and compared. Whereas, he claims, history is by definition 'closed' inasmuch as it purports to present one coherent story, poetry remains 'open' and receptive to a whole range of various interpretations; and whereas history is used to vindicate particular political interests, poetry reserves its own 'space' and autonomy and independence. Poetry alone therefore can continue genuinely to represent human authenticity and interests:

> History tries to construct meaning from the flawed autonomy of man; but poetry . . . offers the sole prospect of liberation from the labyrinth of inconclusiveness that history is. . . . Where Clio [history] offers inconclusive knowledge of the past for the self-

> interest of the living, Orpheus [poetry] in the end proposes for the living solidarity with the dead for what they once were.[27]

The life-denying view of history described by Martin Davies and represented by George Eliot's Casaubon, derives from historians' own aspirations to be seen as respectably 'scientific'; for (as we have seen) they have frequently tried to validate their own activities in terms of a model attributed to the natural sciences. That theoretical model derives in turn from a mistaken apprehension of the nature of science itself, but it has historical roots in Francis Bacon's professed belief that the human understanding needs to have its imaginative wings clipped and to be 'hung with weights, to keep it from leaping and flying', in order to attain 'a true knowledge of the world, such as it is in fact'.[28]

In practice, of course, scientists have been no less imaginative creators than those working in any other field, and a good corrective to the Baconian misapprehension is provided by an actual scientist of some eminence in the nineteenth century (though now largely forgotten). William Carpenter (1813–1885) was a marine zoologist and comparative physiologist; he was a Fellow of the Royal Society from 1844, and became Professor of Forensic Medicine and then Registrar at the University of London. As President of the British Association, he gave the annual address in 1872, at the very time when scientism was at its most fashionable; but the picture that he draws of science totally belies its traditionally assumed relationship with imaginative arts. So he records:

> the general belief – in many . . . the confident assurance – that the Scientific interpretation of Nature represents her not merely as she *seems*, but as she *really is*. But when we carefully examine the foundation of that assurance, we find reason to distrust its security; for it can be shown to be no less true of the Scientific conception of Nature, than it is of the Artistic or the Poetic, that it is *a representation framed by the Mind itself* out of the materials supplied by the impressions which external objects make upon the Senses; so that to each Man of Science, *Nature is what he individually believes her to be.*[29]

Carpenter's view of science thus corresponds at a number of points with the view of history being presented in this book. In particular, both scientists and historians are seen to be imposing their own beliefs upon any perceptions of their respective materials, so that, far from neutrally describing what is there, they actively contribute to what can only be personal interpretations of data or phenomena. The essential point is, then, that the scientist in this respect closely resembles the artist or poet. In neither case does it make any sense at all to affect a methodology that repudiates the 'imaginative . . . at any price'.[30]

A rejection of the scientistic tradition in historiography, and an alternative approach, does periodically surface. It notably becomes evident in the thought of Giambattista Vico, whose *New Science* was first published in 1725. The conventional Aristotelian disciplinary hierarchy is there overturned, for Vico believes that truth can be reached by history rather than by science. The natural world, having been made by God, lies beyond any possible reach of human understanding, whereas the past conversely must be comprehensible as having by definition been made by human beings themselves. The truth about the history of that past is revealed, however, not to reason but rather to imagination: it is, Vico believes, by *imaginatively* entering into the mental life of other people, that we can gain our knowledge of them.

Resistance to the Baconian downgrading of 'imagination' was similarly offered by such Romantics as the poet William Blake, for whom indeed 'Bacon's philosophy has ruined England'. And the new, more imaginative emphases of the Romantic movement come to have an important effect on historiography. The significance of Sir Walter Scott's hugely popular novels, for example, was noticed by Carlyle:

> These historical novels have taught all men this truth, which looks like a truism, yet was unknown to writers of history and others, till so taught: that the bygone ages of the world were actually filled by living men, not by protocols, state papers, controversies and abstractions of men.[31]

As being essentially concerned with *people*, historical understanding requires something more than the application of mere 'reason'. In fact reason by itself could positively mislead. So it was argued by Macaulay that Enlightenment historians such as Hume and Gibbon had been 'seduced from truth, not by their imagination, but by their reason'; and he concluded, in terms that an Aristotelian or Baconian would have found hard to understand, that 'A history in which every particular incident may be true, may on the whole be false.'[32]

For Romantics, in other words, the historical whole remains more than the sum of its parts. Somehow to enter into the 'reality' of the past requires, not so much orderly steps of rational analysis, but rather an imaginative leap. This, again, has partly to do with the attempted imposition of our own frameworks upon an essentially amorphous mass of data: we schematise the whole, identifying 'causes' and 'effects', and thereby reading some sense into what has happened. But, in Carlyle's words, whereas 'narrative is *linear*, Action is *solid.* Alas for our "chains" or chainlets, of "causes and effects", which we so assiduously track through certain hands-breadths of years and square miles, when the whole is a broad, deep Immensity, and each atom is "chained" and complected with all!'[33]

This problem of causation to which Carlyle refers had been discussed in philosophical terms by David Hume, and even earlier by Joseph Glanvill, who came to the sceptical conclusion that the essential unity of nature implied that an understanding of any particular within it necessitated an understanding of its total context: 'all things being linkt together by an uninterrupted chain of Causes . . . we can have no true knowledge of any, except we comprehend all'.[34] But in Carlyle, the scepticism previously applied to our potential for knowledge of the natural world, is specifically turned to problems of historiography, where too a knowledge of discrete atomic 'facts' can never yield a unitary historical truth.

The continuing search for such a truth has brought some thinkers back to poetry. Even in the nineteenth century, the eminent historian J. A. Froude (1818–1894) went so far as to assert that poetry might actually prove to be the best history. In particular, he claimed that Shakespeare's plays constitute 'the most perfect English history which exists'; and he went on to suggest that historians might learn from poets with regard to 'being true to nature', and even 'in difficult matters, leaving much to reflection which cannot be explained'.[35] Nearer to our own time, the popular social historian G. M. Trevelyan (1876–1962) writes similarly of 'the poetry of history'. The 'poetry' derives from the fact that history ultimately consists of what other *people* have done, and people in short are human – 'men and women, as actual as we are today, thinking their own thoughts, swayed by their own passion', and just as mortal as we are. The task of history then becomes to understand such people, and the best equipped historian will therefore have not only intellect, but also 'the warmest human sympathy, the highest *imaginative* powers'. Trevelyan unsurprisingly praised Scott and Macaulay, and Carlyle, who had revealed aspects of history about which 'generations of dispassionate historians . . . had unerringly missed the point'. 'Dispassionate', supposedly 'scientific' historians were bound to miss the point about a past that was itself 'full of passion', and Trevelyan therefore concluded that the muse of history, 'Clio should *not* always be cold, aloof, impartial'.[36]

This 'romantic' view of history has long been out of fashion, but is now returning, partly as a result of postmodern critiques of any 'scientific' aspirations towards objectivity and absolute reality. So, it has been claimed, 'the real is as imagined as the imaginary'.[37] Even what we assert to be 'real', that is, has no 'objective' reality, but gains its supposed authority only through our own imaginative interpretations. And if we grant the impossibility of *any* value-free descriptions, we may legitimately concede, if not encourage, imagination's role in any historical construction. So the Aristotelian distinction between the disciplines of history and poetry is at last becoming blurred. If 'judgement' or reason can no longer meaningfully aspire to historical truth, imagination or 'fancy' may be given freer rein.

Thus, experiments with a more literary, if not 'poetic', approach to history have been made by Simon Schama, who claims in *Dead Certainties* (a book about two supposed historical 'certainties') to have written 'a work of the *imagination* that chronicles *historical* events';[38] and despite professional accusations of having in this way deliberately obliterated 'the difference between archival fact and pure fiction',[39] his attempts have met elsewhere with critical acclaim. Along similar lines, Peter Burke has proposed for the historian a novelist's technique of adopting more than one viewpoint, or of leaving open or alternative endings to one's narrative, thus allowing individual readers to draw their own conclusions;[40] and Antony Easthope has gone one stage further by recommending that, in their use of novelists as models, historians should 'move away from George Eliot and become a bit more like James Joyce'.[41] Some years ago, in fact, Theodore Zeldin openly repudiated any attempt to attribute simplistic historical causation, preferring, as he put it, '*juxtaposition*, so that the reader can make what links he thinks fit for himself'.[42] Hayden White, whom we considered earlier, has not only assimilated history and fiction, but has envisaged 'the possibility of using impressionistic, expressionistic, surrealistic, and (perhaps) even actionist modes of representation for dramatizing the significance of data'.[43] And more recently Thomas Söderqvist has foreseen the possibility of at least one branch of history – that of science biographies – becoming 'as adventurous and experimental as modernist novels . . . and particularly contemporary movies'. The time is ripe, he suggests, 'to experiment with stylistic inventions, such as collage, narrative discontinuity, multigenre narratives, unsuspected time-shifts, with stream of consciousness, symbolism, poetical reconstructions, and polyvocal texts, and so forth'.[44]

Paradoxically, then, historical study seems now to be becoming less autonomous, or less than ever constrained within the imposed (and, again, contingent) boundaries of a single disciplinary structure; and the old Aristotelian distinctions between history and poetry, reason and imagination, are becoming increasingly eroded.

2 HISTORY AS HYPOTHESIS

2.1 Dogmatism, doubt, and style

> They have not reported, as *unalterable Demonstrations*, but as *present appearances*.
> (Thomas Sprat)[45]

Thomas Sprat in 1667 was writing about scientists. In the face of the early-modern sceptical crisis, Fellows of the Royal Society are described as accepting an amended status for their theories. No longer can such theories be presented dogmatically as certainly true and unalterable. Rather, they should be considered as provisional descriptions, as tentative hypotheses, proposed with due humility. And that is one model of science which historians might appropriately emulate.

This is not to deny the need for some agreed framework within which historians can work. Without that, the future of the discipline might well seem to be in jeopardy. In fact there would be some danger of losing the very notion of a 'discipline', a notion that inevitably implies (as Hayden White has described[46]) some 'systematic repression'. For in any discipline, certain constraints are accepted, so that while some things are admitted, others are excluded. Some boundaries have to be agreed, some territory mapped out as potential subject-matter; and methodological parameters need to be established, in terms of which there are criteria for what are to count as admissible procedures and as 'valid' historical evidence. As in science, so in history, without some publicly agreed framework, it is impossible for work to proceed; and it is the threatened removal from historical study of any such framework or rules, 'repression' or 'discipline', that has provoked contemporary criticism and professional concern.

First, though, it may be argued that history need not assume an all-encompassing homogeneity: there may, after all, within a broad church, be room for more than one sect; historians may be permitted some individuality. This, as Glenn Burgess has argued, may imply their having a different 'end' in view as they survey the chaos of potentially available evidence. *Some* 'end' has to be selected, to provide a viewpoint and a pathway through the data, but it can be a positive advantage when a *variety* of such ends is provided. For the result will be a variety of narratives, each valid in its own terms, though each inevitably incomplete; and while the individual explanation must inevitably remain defective, it can at least contribute with – rather than against – its 'competitors' towards a fuller understanding of the whole. Again in relation specifically to the problematic English Revolution (to be considered further in section 2.2 below), Burgess notes how a different *chronology* will inspire a different historical account:

> The type of story you are telling, and the things relevant to it, will alter dramatically if you switch from thinking of the English revolution as a process culminating in the emergence of radicalism in the late 1640s, to thinking of it as a process culminating in the restoration of the Stuarts in 1660. The two views will produce different causal chains running through the same years, and both may well be correct. There are many different true stories that can be told about what appear to be the same events.

One may question Glenn Burgess's use of 'true' here, as well as the criticism which he seems to go on to make of alternative accounts which show (inevitably) 'signs of . . . incompleteness'. But he is surely right to abandon decisively any 'monocausal' model, to stress the impossibility of writing history without the adoption of some standpoint, and to conclude with an integrative approach in terms of which historians produce 'not competing but different stories', each of which 'explains things that the other cannot'.[47]

This may seem to imply, again, that *anything* goes, and that historians need only carry out Claire Rayner's prescription of reporting their own beliefs about the past, as viewed in the light of their own prejudices. In that case we may well be left with manipulative historians who feel justified in denying a past that by others is all too well remembered, and, as we shall go on to consider in the Postscript, there is already some evidence of these. There is indeed a real problem here, for while it may be undesirable in history or in physics or in any other discipline to outlaw the maverick, the unconventional non-conformist by whom breakthroughs are usually made, the whole notion of a breakthrough loses its meaning without the postulation of something to be broken through. So some sort of compromise is needed – a compromise between those who continue to maintain a naively empirical view of history as a record of the past 'as it was', and those who carry sceptical postmodern arguments to their ultimate and conclude that the history of the past can be, or even must be, constructed simply as we want it.

The essential point reduces to the question of whether or not historians are to accept the existence of a past 'reality' that is at least hypothetically accessible to their own investigations. Does such a past exist independently of us and of the evidence by which it is represented, or do those representations actually constitute that past, to which we then have no alternative access? If there is assumed to be no reality external to the language by which it is described, then the whole of history becomes nothing more than a linguistic study, and there is no external (extra-linguistic) referent by which the validity of alternative versions of our histories may be assessed; and history then becomes an imaginative language-game, a form of poetry, 'a little theatre in which the representations of the past are assigned their part'.[48] But if some belief is maintained in an external reality – a social, political, economic, cultural reality, which may owe much to its linguistic portrayals but is ultimately independent of them – then some goal remains for historical investigation; and it remains possible in principle to aspire to some understanding of that actual independently existing past.

The problem with the latter position is that, although common sense indicates that an actual past existed, it was never a simple entity that could be easily comprehended, perceived or understood. It was always possible to view it from innumerable standpoints, to select from it different items as important and significant, to trace different causal chains; an infinity of interpretations was always potentially available. Any evidence deriving from that past is therefore inevitably partial – partial in the sense of being only a part (an infinitesimal part) of what it might be, and partial in the sense of being not impartial, not 'objective'. All we can do with that evidence, therefore, is to evaluate it, make some provisional sense of it, and then use it to give an account that seems to us to have meaning. Our history will then be recognisably personal and provisional, our own description of 'present appearances', rather than a supposedly factual, final, and 'unalterable demonstration'. So as with Sprat's scientists it will be presented not as dogma but as hypothesis.

Such humility, deriving from a recognition of the ultimate limitations of the subject, by no means needs to be seen as negative. Admittedly there follows a need to avoid any pretentious claims to be able to reconstruct the past 'as it was', but that does not imply a need for silence. And the best contemporary historians, while unlikely to concede the validity of an extreme postmodern position, do write with a full awareness of the problematic issues by which they are constrained. As in the case of Sprat's scientists, that has implications both for their manner of writing and for any claims they make respecting 'truth'.

That point may be clarified by considering one specific example.

2.2 An example: causes of the English Revolution

The search for the causes of the mid-seventeenth-century upheavals in England, has long been a problematic area for historians. Indeed, investigations and speculations on that subject have continued at least from the time that Clarendon began writing his *History* in 1646, right up until today. There seems little prospect of any diminution of interest in that historical study, but what can be noticed is a changing attitude towards its status and the aspirations of historians themselves.

It is hardly surprising that Clarendon's work itself exemplifies some of the characteristics of what we have defined as the 'old model' of history. Believing that an account of the 'mischiefs' of the time should be useful as a warning for future generations, Clarendon enumerates his own qualifications for giving a truthful narrative, and providing a clear vision of 'the hand and judgment of God'. He was himself a member of parliament at the material period, and has subsequently been close to royalty; so he is in a position to give 'an equal observation of the faults and infirmities of both sides'. He will refrain from any personal assessments motivated by 'private provocation, or a more public indignation', and will duly observe 'the rules that a man should, who deserves to be believed'. For, he concludes, 'I know myself to be very free from any of those passions which naturally transport men with prejudice.' Clarendon, then, sees himself as an impartial observer and recorder of events, and as such he feels competent to disclose those 'natural causes and means' which are the instruments of Providence. That providential government is presupposed. As with the natural philosophy of his time, so too in history, a belief in the possibility of reaching truth is underpinned by a religious conviction of God's presence and power, and that remains unquestioned. So in the case of the civil war, 'the immediate finger and wrath of God must be acknowledged in these perplexities and distractions'.[49] It is that 'reality' which Clarendon sees and describes in his account of the past 'as it was'.

Such providential causation, however, was firmly rejected by Clarendon's own near-contemporary Thomas Hobbes. Writing just after the restoration of the monarchy, Hobbes drew his own more secular lessons from the civil war, and his historical analysis unsurprisingly served to confirm the validity of political theories he had previously formulated. So far as he was concerned, God was not needed to account for an evil caused by purely human interventions and deficiencies. Rather, the government needed to be so structured as to avoid such evils in the future, and that meant essentially having it strong enough to withstand threats from competing individuals and institutions. In their challenge to the king, people had been variously corrupted, their minds seduced by seven identifiable factors. Presbyterian ministers of the church had personally claimed divinely legitimated authority; Catholics had characteristically had their loyalties divided between king and pope; sectarians had asserted the validity of their own anti-monarchical interpretations of the scriptures; educated men had been corrupted through reading books by republican authors of the classical period; traders had been beguiled by the current model of republicanism in the Netherlands; opportunists had simply sought to make their own profits from a war; and people in general had just been ignorant of their proper duties to the king.[50] People had behaved, in short, as people do; and the evidence of their behaviour, as perceived by Hobbes, justified the very political remedies that he himself prescribed. His perception of the war thus served to validate his theories.

The contemporary accounts of Clarendon and Hobbes, then, were both in a sense self-justificatory, with each historian seeing past events as confirmation of his own theological, psychological, and political position. Since then, political, social, economic, and intellectual historians have all made their contributions to the continuing debate, all from their various standpoints. The Victorian S. R. Gardiner concentrated on religious and institutional concerns: the upheaval, he believed, resulted essentially from a Puritan challenge to the established church, with its royal and aristocratic support. And he, again, was well qualified to judge the matter. Living long after the events in question, he could remain detached in his analysis, undistracted by either the 'buoyant hopes' or 'melancholy despair' displayed by those living at the time.[51] Such claims for detachment have not been made by all, and some subsequent social historians have deliberately taken the revolutionary people and events of the mid-seventeenth century as models for the future. Christopher Hill, for example, has enthusiastically embraced what he calls 'the worm's eye view', which has enabled him to disinter some of the long-buried, and re-emphasise the historical importance of such groups as the Levellers and Diggers, Fifth Monarchists and Muggletonians. Deliberately focusing attention on these alternative heroes, he has openly expressed 'gratitude to all those nameless radicals who foresaw and worked for . . . the upside-down world' to which he himself aspires in the future.[52] His histories of the period, then, have been unashamedly partisan, but legitimately so inasmuch as their counterbalancing function has been quite explicitly expressed.

More recently, the English Revolution has been treated by historians who have shown themselves increasingly aware of the historiographical issues discussed in this book. Lawrence Stone, in his 1972 investigation of the revolution's causes, may have expressed surprise that it was still 'very hard to find a succinct account of just why it happened'; but he nevertheless avoids any claims for his own work providing any such 'definitive solution'. He notes in particular the need to extend one's geographical and chronological ranges, in order respectively to avoid English insularity and any narrowly circumscribed causal explanations. In both contexts he emphasises the need to adopt a 'multi-causal' approach, together with a 'multiple variability of categorization'. In other words, he accepts that no single cause could ever be found for any complex effect or historical event, and that, in the face of innumerable possibilities, any classifications of people or events necessarily derive from a specific and arbitrary point of view. The rigid distinction maintained by Stone between his own avowedly 'analytic' approach, and the 'narrative' way ascribed to those who are less conscious of what they are doing, now seems questionable. But he clarifies the essential problem: that to make history intelligible, some 'oversimplification' and some 'over-assertive dogmatism' are inevitable; yet that any account appearing as 'too orderly' must for that very reason be suspect. So to make sense of the data and to provide some coherent explanation, he neatly provides for analysis three types of factor: the long-term preconditions, the medium-term precipitants, and the short-term triggers; and he deals with each in term. But while this gives an impression of control, Stone himself concedes that any 'rank-ordering', or any attempt to evaluate the respective importance of these factors, must depend on the individual historian's bias; so that he finally presents his work as 'one scholar's *inevitably imperfect* version'.[53]

This tentative approach has been more recently demonstrated in relation to the same vexed subject, by Professor Conrad Russell. Without going into the detail of his arguments, we can note some main features of the historiographical stance adopted in his *The Causes of the English Civil War* (1990). First, he warns of dangers inherent in the title itself, noting that the categorisations used there may already serve to predetermine certain historical judgements. To talk of a specifically *English* civil war, may in itself be misleading, inasmuch as it narrows the geographical parameters within which the subject is expected to be studied. In particular, it may discourage any attempts to explore possibly related factors outside England itself – whether in Britain, including Scotland and Ireland, or in Europe more widely. Second, to talk of *the civil war* suggests that what is to be studied is a discrete entity, and easily definable; whereas the reality might have been far more messy, with even the definitions of beginning and end remaining as matters of debate.[54] And, further, if there are problems with that seemingly uncontroversial part of the title, how many more there are with the admittedly difficult concept of *causation*.

Before any speculation on causes, Conrad Russell argues, it is obviously necessary first to identify *effects*; and to simplify subsequent investigation of the causal chain, those effects must be as simple and unitary as possible. The identification of such simple effects, though, is already highly problematic. It involves numerous categorisations which are themselves contingent, or which might have been made in quite other ways. To further complicate the issue, effects may include not only actual events but also their absence, or those *non-events* where we might have expected more positive or alternative outcomes – as, for example, in the case of the failure to achieve a political settlement in 1641. That was a 'highly unusual' failure which 'cries out for explanation'. But the problem of such 'non-events' is compounded by other elusive objects of study, including what Professor Russell describes as 'mythologies' and 'unrecordable personalities'. The former include beliefs, unfounded perhaps, but played upon, appealed to, and utilised to practical effect. The latter are those highly personal characteristics, ill defined and even undescribable, which yet determine how we present ourselves, and what reactions therefore are provoked. So 'mythologies', he claims, 'recruited as many troops as facts'; and the unfathomable personality of Charles I, including 'his ability to rub people up the wrong way', provided at the least one 'necessary condition of the Civil War'.[55]

'Non-events', 'mythologies', and 'personalities' are, of course, themselves effects requiring causal explanations; and this highlights the problem of causal chains that lead forever back, and out in all directions. Our problem may be that we have, not too few, but too many plausible explanations, and that 'all of them may easily be made to look perfectly convincing' (p. 12). Just, then, as Joseph Glanvill had noted in the seventeenth century itself, our aspiration to have knowledge of one small part of anything, is seen to involve us in a potentially infinite task of comprehending the *whole* of which it forms a part.

From his self-consciously sceptical standpoint, Glanvill was writing about what he perceived as inevitable limitations in natural philosophy, but the point has obvious parallels in historical study, and Conrad Russell's position exemplifies recognition of the problem in our own time. Just as Glanvill then despaired of ever reaching complete knowledge of nature, so Russell now renounces any claim to have arrived at final truth in history. Having worked on the period for nearly thirty years, he is more than ever in a position to recognise the complexities; and so he repudiates any belief in the validity of 'a simple picture', modestly restricting his hopes to the provision of an account which '*may have some approximation* to the truth'. Having shown, not least importantly, the enormity of the historical task on which he has been working, he presents his conclusions as provisional, or as an 'interim finding' (p. 25).

That tentative approach is reiterated throughout Professor Russell's study. Like Stone, he warns against a picture that appears 'too tidy to be credible', and against 'imposing an artificial pattern on . . . contingent decisions' (p. 21); he concedes that his various lists (e.g. of members of the Commons for and against further reformation in 1642) cannot 'pretend to any objective precision', not least because different historians would classify differently. Then, 'since people are individuals, criteria will often conflict' (p. 220), so that 'classifications should be regarded as provisional, and subject to future revision, refinement, and refutation' (p. 221). Emphases, too, can change, and what appears unimportant at one time can come to assume great significance at another: 'We can now see that James's programme was made up of a series of items, sometimes pursued by changes so small that *at the time they barely appeared worth comment*' (p. 46); and sometimes it is precisely the apparently unimportant which may need particular emphasis. Scottish aspirations to force the English to accept their own church structures are 'perhaps the hardest thing in the story for an English historian to understand', and for that very reason 'demands the lion's share of the space' (p. 31); and religious considerations, as being so alien to late twentieth-century (or now twenty-first century) readers, may require particular elucidation.

Aware, then, of the numerous and intractable historiographical problems by which he is confronted, Conrad Russell refrains from dogmatically asserting his conclusions, but writes in the deliberately diffident manner of a Robert Boyle. Just as the sceptical chemist had laboured his use of such qualifying terms as 'perhaps' or 'probably' or 'it seems to me', so too the (post-) modern historian remains self-consciously diffident: avoiding dogmatism, 'it *seems* that the political explanation *may* be paramount' (p. 12); and, in another context, 'religion was an explanatory tool for *imposing an order* on an otherwise *unintelligible mass* of material' (p. 21).

If Conrad Russell concludes with a recognition of the impossibly huge task that awaits historians in his own limited domain of the causes of the English civil war, that conclusion does not necessarily lead to a sceptically induced abandonment of hope or motivation. For, even without any further belief in the possibility of an account of the past 'as it was', some insights may still be afforded; and his own book exemplifies that very point. One lesson deriving from the search for causes, is that the causal chain leads decisively out of the parochial confines of England. The civil war in question may have taken place on English soil, but it is by no means an atomistically isolated event. Seen rather as a part of a very much wider whole, illumination is provided by relating it to events in other parts of

Britain. So Russell draws attention particularly to the Irish Rebellion, and to the crisis in Scotland that began in 1637; and he notes the important parallels and interconnections between events in all three countries.

This leads in turn to a recognition of the need for collaboration: the historian may, and often does, plough a solitary furrow, but comfort can be taken from providing some contribution to the turning of the whole field. The process will never be complete: there is no final solution; even solid concrete cracks in time and provides a route for weeds. But at least new fertilisation can result in a more luxuriant crop, and enjoyment can be attained from the harvesting.

The illumination provided by Conrad Russell's work indicates that the study of history is far from dead. By casting additional light on the past, the historian can clarify our present and even give tentative sign-posts to the future. Thus, although Professor Russell's primary objective may not have been didactic in the sense of those earlier historians who deliberately incorporated some moral 'message' in their work, yet certain attitudes and values are inevitably revealed. We are not being preached at, but by the end of Russell's book we probably feel more wary of oversimplifications and excessive intellectual tidiness, of exclusive categorisations, of chronological parochialism and geographical insularity.[56]

These are important lessons, and particularly so at our moment of 'historical crisis', when it is to just those vices that we might feel most tempted to succumb. At a time of increasing insecurity, historical study resembles a balancing act between avoiding those refuges of the narrow minded on the one hand, and the need to make some sense of the past on the other. Confronted by this dilemma, what is anyway the point of history? *Why*, again, should we engage in its study? This is the subject of the following section.

3 THE POINT AS 'EMPOWERMENT': AFFECTING AND EFFECTING THE FUTURE

> Among the aphorisms of the ancients . . . the most remarkable was that of Clio, one of the seven sages . . . : Know thyself. Now this knowledge depends upon history. (Pierre Droit de Gaillard)[57]

> History . . . enables man to make a world for himself, corresponding to the presumptive needs of his own existence. (Martin Davies)[58]

'History is not a practical subject', writes Peter Lee, in a paper published in 1991, and 'political concerns [are] extrinsic to teaching history'. But he goes on immediately to claim that 'History changes our whole view of the world, of what the present is and of what human beings are and might be, and in so doing has the potential to change ends.' The apparent confusion here probably derives in part from Lee's deference to the British empirical tradition, which has generally sought to minimise the role of ideas in historical development; and it is of course, further, politically incorrect, or inexpedient, to assign to history any possible political role in education. But it is hard to see how a change in our whole viewpoint on the world, and on human beings themselves, can remain a purely intellectual construction, and irrelevant to how we act. History inevitably becomes a matter of social and political commitment. Lee's curious plea that 'political and social goals must be clearly distinguished from and remain firmly subordinate to *genuine historical criteria*' is hard to understand, but if it implies the clear distinction between 'political and social goals' and historical study, it is clearly incapable of fulfilment. His own retention of the traditional ideal of teaching '*real historical knowledge*' is also linked with another questionable attempt – this time, to separate individuals from society: 'the reason for teaching history is not that it changes *society*, but that it changes *pupils*'. He does not clarify how the one can fail to result in the other, but does concede that, 'as political leaders are quick to recognise, [history] is dangerous'.[59]

It appears, then, that Peter Lee is caught between two stools: he is trying at once to assert the educational importance of historical study, and to protect that study from political interference by denying it any political role. But to be educationally important, history must of course play a practical role in human life – changing individual perceptions and thence enabling change within society. And it is preferable that that whole process be effected openly and consciously. For, as Pierre Droit de Gaillard implies in the quotation heading this section, we need to know who we are, and what we are doing and why, in order to determine further where we wish to go.

To be of any practical benefit, historical study must result in some effect upon the future; it must facilitate, enable, and direct the course of future change. This is not in any way to suggest that our future is predetermined by our past, but (as Martin Davies suggests in our other quotation) that our perception of the past can be used to validate and re-inforce the future that we want. For the events of past history are themselves neutral, like Epicurean atoms or the letters of the alphabet: initially lacking any qualities of their own, they can be combined in innumerable ways, to constitute such diverse creations as tragedy and comedy. So, as recent ideological re-interpretations of the past have shown, history can underlie or justify anything: 'It teaches precisely nothing, for it contains everything and furnishes examples of everything';[60] and it is for us to choose its lessons.

Those lessons may be both social, concerned with the direction we think society ought to take, and highly personal, relating to the sort of persons we think we ought to be. For the former, Eric Hobsbawm's thought-provoking study of the twentieth century[61] seems to have been motivated by the author's perception of a need for some change in the direction our society is taking. At this 'point of historical crisis', as Hobsbawm describes our current position, some knowledge of how we got here may facilitate adaptation in the face of an uncertain and unpredictable future. We may not be enabled to prophesy the future, but in the face of uncertainty we would at least have the benefit of some self-consciousness to aid assessment of strategies for future survival.

On a more personal level, Thomas Söderqvist has indicated how historical study, and in particular biographies of scientists, might provide lessons for the individual. As we have seen in Chapter 3, section 3.2, the records of people's lives have often been used by historians as moral examples, indicating good things to be imitated and bad to be avoided. But writing within the context of postmodernity, Söderqvist is concerned with how biographical models might assist with fundamental existential choice. He argues that by detailed study of a person's life, one might gain some insight into how such important choices had been made – choices of career, of lifestyle, of whether or not to conform to intellectual and social pressures. And through gaining that insight or empathy, one might be helped when confronted by such issues in one's own life: 'life stories not only provide us with opportunities to understand ourselves, intellectually as well as emotionally, but may also change and create ourselves'.[62]

The changing and creating of ourselves may seem an unlikely objective for historical study, but what else is education ultimately for? The choice of what we may wish to change into, of whom we may wish to create, remains highly problematic, but it is a choice that does have to be made, and again it is better made self-consciously.

One requirement for the postmodern future appears to be an ability to resist dogmatic pressures to accept any one single truth, or answer, or 'reality' (of past or present). Aspiration might rather point towards a tolerance of many truths and answers and descriptions, without a corresponding need to deny the validity of those that fail to fit our own requirements. When writing of the requisites for poets, John Keats advocated the characteristic of what he called 'negative capability', by which he meant 'when a man is capable of being in uncertainties, mysteries, doubts, without any irritable reaching after fact and reason';[63] and it is just this that seems to be the quality required by those (and not only poets) living in a postmodern era.

In the vital educational objective of encouraging such an ability, just as in the aim to be aware and to make choices with the benefit of some self-consciousness, historical study has a crucial role to play.

3.1 The limits of contemporaneity

History's unique contribution in the context of such aims lies in its potential to unshackle minds from the constraints of the present. For it offers alternative perceptions of what has been in the past and so of what might be in the future. An important role for history therefore is simply to liberate its students from chronological constraints, and it is precisely that potentially liberating function of history that is denied by an emphasis on so-called 'contemporary' history. Almost by definition, of course, the contemporary seems more immediately accessible to the ordinary reader or student, and its supposed popular appeal has long been recognised. 'I know', writes Sir Walter Raleigh in the Preface to his *History* (1614), 'that it will be said by many, That I might have been more pleasing to the Reader, if I had written the story of *mine owne times*.' The instant appeal of contemporary history is, then, no new thing, but as Raleigh himself goes on to note, there are associated problems: 'that whosoever in writing a moderne History, shall follow truth too neare the heeles, it may haply strike out his teeth!' – the potential kick in the teeth coming from the very proximity of the source-material and the obvious involvement, and consequent partiality, of the witnesses. As Lord Bolingbroke later wrote, 'contemporary authors are the most liable to be warped from the straight rule of truth, in writing on subjects which have affected them strongly'.[64]

But quite apart from such practical difficulties, the 'contemporary' hardly needs reinforcement by historians. It can well look after itself, for it is of course impossible to avoid. As Nietzsche warns: 'Everything contemporary is importunate; it affects and directs the eye even when the philosopher does not want it to; and in the total accounting it will involuntarily be appraised too high. That is why . . . the philosopher must *deliberately under-assess it.*'[65] If we succumb to the easy allure of 'contemporary' history, we are liable to be confirmed in our own tunnel-vision, avoiding confrontation of just those issues which most need our attention. Historians may please their readers, but at the cost of failing to perform one of their most important functions. As a historian of philosophy has noted, concentration on the contemporary might actually help 'to reinforce the prejudices of the present by insulating us from that in the past which would most disquiet us'.[66]

3.2 Future-focus

This is the very opposite of what should be the case. Rather than insulating us in that way, an important function of history is to expose us to other possibilities, to enable us to distance ourselves from our immediate present, and to view ourselves in a wider perspective; for we may then be made aware of alternative options for the future. The past and present and future are then once again seen as indissolubly interconnected, and our preferred options for the future can determine our apprehension of the past. In Hobbes's words, 'No man can have in his mind a conception of the future, for the future is not yet: but of our conceptions of the past, we make a future'.[67] Or as Antony Easthope suggests, 'our choice of ancestors [might be] . . . also a decision about what future we desire'; and citing the Homeric example of Odysseus' revitalisation of dead spirits in order to empower his future, he argues that the postmodern historian's function may well be to construct, in Nietzsche's words, 'a past from which one would wish to have descended'.[68] As indicated, again, in Martin Davies' quotation heading section 3 above, history might then enable us to make the sort of world we think we want.

If that takes us back to Claire Rayner, we should at least now be in a position to approach her criticism positively. It is difficult to see what else historians can be expected to do than report on the past in the light of who they are, but that is no bad thing so long as they are aware of what they are doing and why. For at some point a decision has to be taken about what is important: even if all such decisions are 'relative', they do have to be made. Extremists may speculate about the desirability of living with a past that is recognised as meaningless, but on both personal and public levels any attempt actually to do that seems doomed to result in failure, or insanity. It seems to be simply impossible to accept meaninglessness with equanimity. As with a Rorschach ink-blot test, we are bound, if only for our own creative satisfaction, to make some sense of what we see, to interpret data in such a way as to elicit meaning from it, so that we know how, within its context, to proceed. The interpretation may tell us more about ourselves than about any 'objective' reality, but at least we will have avoided simply accepting a convention from the past, and will have made our own conscious and deliberate decision.

It is this sort of positive step that some feminist and post-colonial historians can be seen to be taking. Detecting alleged omissions and distortions in previous accounts, they are looking again at the past from a quite different perspective. So that not only does new data come to light, but the old is seen to be in need of drastic re-interpretation or at least supplementation. The past has to be re-constituted, or even literally re-membered. And this is undertaken, not as a theoretical game, but in furtherance of a practical programme. The rehabilitation of those who have previously been long lost to history is not to be seen simply as an academic musical-chairs, in which turns are taken to play at being placeless; but rather there is a serious underlying purpose. In each case, a serious imbalance is to be redressed and a whole new system of values accepted. For some feminists, the ultimate objective is a revolution in the power-structure of society; and for post-colonialists similarly, due recognition is to be given to those groups whose members have been underprivileged and ill defined (in the sense both of being out-of-focus and of being mis-represented). Both feminism and post-colonialism, then, from a consciously adopted programme for the future are concerned with changing values and perceptions of the past (just as Marxism too has been).

These 'isms', further, are concerned with a re-definition of the self. Through an examination of the past, we can be helped to see how we became what we currently are. For past ideas of social class, femininity, masculinity, dominance, and subjection, and innumerable other factors, have all contributed to our make-up, to the way that we are perceived by others and by ourselves. If we wish to change those present perceptions and actually to reconstitute ourselves for the future, then we shall need to re-interpret, re-perceive the past, as leading rather to our new ideal.

That is not as impossible or as irresponsible as it may sound, for it is, on a personal level, what we all do all the time. That is to say, we constantly modify our perceptions and interpretations of our own past experiences – from a virtually infinite totality, recalling some 'lost' memories, reconstituting or obliterating others, and periodically seeing events and other people and ourselves in 'a new light'. So we mould our own narrative thread in such a way that our past leads in a meaningful way to ourselves in the present. And at least to some extent, that re-moulding can be consciously achieved, and with an eye to the future.

That brings us back to our Platonic starting-point, and the need for self-examination and awareness. In both our personal and public lives, that remains the prime objective. For our public problems derive in the end from our personal selves, so that what is needed is a study of how we came to be the sorts of people that we are, of why we have the perceptions, the outlooks, and the attitudes that we have. Such a study must clearly in large part be historical, but it needs to include practical as well as theoretical dimensions, sciences and social sciences as well as arts. It would constitute the ultimate humanistic discipline, in which nothing human was to be considered 'alien' or irrelevant, and the various contributions would be seen, not as competing or mutually inconsistent, but rather as complementary visions that provide illumination from their various perspectives.

To conceive of historical study in these terms may sound grandiose and pompous. Historians and others have become accustomed to equating academic respectability with specialisation: to lay claim to more than a very narrow field has come to savour of territorial aggressiveness and intellectual arrogance. It may also sound excessively idealistic, or 'unrealistic', in the sense of being impossible to achieve; and it must of course be conceded that no one historian could ever make more than a minute contribution to any imagined whole that was to be constructed on this basis.

But that is no reason not to have a goal. If our ultimate educational goal is to escape from Plato's 'unexamined life', then historical study can provide one route in the required direction, one focus from which to try to make sense of ourselves. And, most importantly, history can thereby help to determine the future that we want.

Postscript

Since the first publication of this book, postmodernism has become more prominent as an historical (and more widely a cultural) concern, and reactions against it have grown. This postscript is added in an attempt (a) briefly to assess 'pomophobia', or what sometimes seems to be a real *fear* of postmodernism; (b) to counter any suggestion that postmodernism, in relation to historical study, might result in the denial of the reality of past events, including especially the Holocaust; and (c) to add a few concluding words on history's place in a postmodern future.

1 POMOPHOBIA: THE FEAR OF POSTMODERNISM

'Pomophobia' is a fear of postmodernism; it is quite literally a dis-ease – an unease, or lack of ease with postmodernism, an anxiety about it, or (as the Greek origin of the word suggests) an actual *fear* of it. Unsurprisingly, it is often suffered by modernist (traditional) historians in a particularly virulent form; for as we have seen in chapter 1, empirically orientated historians have often been wary about 'philosophy' or 'theory' in general, and postmodernism might well seem to be an extreme form of that, undermining, as it does, many (if not most, or even all) of the foundations of modernist history.

Negative and fearful reactions to postmodernism can now be seen worldwide. In Britain, Geoffrey Elton, whom we earlier took as exemplar of the old (modernist) model of history, described it as 'the intellectual equivalent of crack': proffered to innocent young people 'by devilish tempters', it resulted in a 'frivolous nihilism which allows any historian to say whatever he likes', and threatens the historian's very 'claims to existence'.[1] More recently, Felipe Fernández-Armesto has urged his readers ('perplexed', as they may be about the truth) not to abandon their children to be 'victims of delusions or doubt'. It's time, he insists, 'to prise ourselves free' from a pernicious intellectual movement which threatens to drag us all back to the Dark Ages. Civilisation itself is endangered: the barbarians, in the form of contemporary postmodern 'truth vandals', are already at the gates.[2] And Richard Evans has published his 'defence of history' against the 'disintegrative attack' of postmodernism, believing, in the words of his blurb, that 'under the onslaught of postmodernist theory, the profession of history is in crisis'.[3]

On the other side of the Atlantic, Allan Bloom has similarly referred to 'an intellectual crisis of the greatest magnitude, which constitutes [nothing less than] the crisis of our civilisation';[4] and Gertrude Himmelfarb has stressed what she sees as 'the basic incompatibility of postmodernism and historical study', with postmodernism appearing to her as 'not so much a revision of modernist history as a repudiation of it'. She is one of a large group of eminent American historians who have joined together with the aim of 'reconstructing history', in the belief that their subject is 'under siege' by postmodernists, with historians themselves condemned 'to a growing irrelevance'.[5]

Better irrelevant than dead, which is the prospect envisaged by the Australian historian Keith Windschuttle, whose book, *The Killing of History* (1997), is presented as a defence of 'the traditional practice of history' against 'a potentially mortal attack'. Postmodernism, Windschuttle believes, constitutes 'a lethal process [that is] well underway'; and 'if historians allow themselves to be prodded all the way to this theoretical abyss, they will be rendering themselves and their disciples extinct'.[6]

Amongst historians at the opening of the third millennium, then, postmodernism is a divisive issue, representing for some a challenge, but for others a cause for real concern and even fear; and there is some justification for that fear. Modernist history's foundations have indeed been challenged and largely (if not entirely) undermined. Thus, such foundational concepts as 'truth' and 'fact' and 'objectivity' have been exposed as, at worst, meaningless, and at best in need of radical redefinition; some postmodernists have condoned (and even welcomed) interdisciplinary seepage that has seemed to threaten professional 'disciplinary' standards and procedures; while others have gone so far as to question the very point of persisting at all with what can be seen as an effectively outdated enterprise.

The most basic fear, though, derives from the loss of a meaningful notion of 'truth'. We have seen how early-modern natural philosophers (scientists), when confronted by the challenge of newly revived scepticism, felt at a loss about how to proceed. Deprived of any criterion for distinguishing truth from error, they could see no reason for accepting one hypothesis rather than another. The consequent state of indecision could not be tolerated, at a professional or personal level; which is to say that it at once precluded the possibility of intellectual advance and induced extreme emotional anxiety. The solution at both levels was to accept a 'common-sense' approach, whereby the goal of certainty was pragmatically replaced by 'degrees of probability': some things, that is, on the basis of one's own experience, seemed more likely to be right than others; and, where evidence had to be taken at second hand, some people seemed more likely to be reliable than others. 'Truth', then, was redefined: instead of being an absolute (as Plato had insisted), it became what could best be taken on trust.[7]

Historical study, some four centuries on, is at a parallel point: with the concept of any absolute historical 'truth' removed, historians are left floundering between competing hypotheses (still believing that one has to be preferable to any others), and increasingly worried about the distinction between 'fact' and 'fiction' – the distinction that has always been claimed to underpin their discipline and to mark it off from others (such as literature).

History's problem in this respect can be most clearly seen in popular manifestations of the subject – in so-called 'docudrama', film, and sites of 'heritage'.[8] First, then, the very word 'docudrama' announces the problem, referring as it does to some sort of hybrid – something that is in part 'documentary' (and therefore supposedly 'factual'), but in part also 'drama' (where intrusions of 'fiction' are permissible and even expected). The difficulty lies in clarifying those distinctions. Writing, for instance, of the BBC television programme 'Rebel Heart' – supposedly an account of Irish history between 1916 and 1922, and shown in January 2001 – one critic observed: 'The main problem here is that nowhere is it stated where fact ends and fiction begins'. Admittedly, then, the action is supposedly based on 'real historical events', but those events themselves have to be viewed from some perspective: their *historical* description is not just 'given'; and here they are presented from the standpoint of the Irish 'rebels'. Opposing British soldiers, therefore, are depicted as 'anonymous, heartless, robotic villains', in actions whose dates have been shifted to suit *dramatic* purposes.[9]

Dramatic purposes, though, are not all. According to David Trimble, current First Minister of Northern Ireland, the drama has its own clear (and highly questionable) social and political agenda. Over-simplification and one-sided presentation of issues, polarisation of attitudes, and glamourisation of violence, all combine as a force that can cause positive harm, by damaging the present peace negotiations. With its 'artistic licence taken with the factual history', David Trimble concludes, 'Rebel Heart' 'functioned not as "television drama" but as a political tract'.[10]

Altogether, then, the 'docudrama' highlights some of the problems associated with history more generally. It does more blatantly what historians do anyway – namely, take some story from the past, and make some sense of it for their own ideological or aesthetic or moral purposes; and as such, it will inevitably please some viewers or readers, while offending others.

The same thing happens in the case of films that purport to represent (re-present) some historical episode from the past. 'Truth is first casualty in Hollywood's war', reads an English newspaper headline over a report of 'The Patriot', a film in which the American War of Independence is shown as a conflict between heroic freedom fighters ('thoughtful and merciful') on the one side, and bloodthirsty war criminals ('snobbish . . . nasty . . . and thuggish') on the other – a Manichaean contrast that makes better drama than history.[11]

Rebellions and wars are particularly prone to revision in that way, for nationalistic or patriotic (or, again, simply dramatic) purposes. The reputation of Michael Collins, for example, the Irish republican leader during the Easter Rising and civil war in 1921, was updated in ways that proved less than uncontentious in the film of his name. And the second world war has suffered historical casualties in such films as 'U-571', which claimed for Americans the capture of the German Enigma code machine, which had been taken by the British before America entered the war; 'The Colditz Story', where a major role in escaping from the prison is assigned to Americans, none of whom actually succeeded in getting away; and 'Saving Private Ryan', in which the British were denied their part in the capture of Omaha beach in 1944. The last case has resulted in protests by surviving participants at the honorary knighthood bestowed on the film's director, Steven Spielberg.[12]

Finally, and perhaps more surprisingly, that other great site of historical interest – the ever expanding 'heritage industry' – has only added to public confusion about the categories of 'fact' and 'fiction'. In the west of England, for example, the well known prehistoric site of Stonehenge, with its orderly circles of giant stones, is not quite what tourists are led to believe. It has, according to recent reports, been 'modified' through the years, with leaning stones straightened up, lintels removed and replaced, and concrete added as necessary, all in the interests of safety and aesthetics. So that, it is now claimed, Stonehenge has actually 'been created by the heritage industry and is not the creation of prehistoric peoples'.[13] Similar cases of the tidying up (and in some cases reconstruction) of ancient sites can be seen, for instance, in Egypt (where columns of the Luxor Temple have been repositioned; to say nothing of the wholesale re-location of Abu Simbel and other structures threatened by the Aswan High Dam), and in Greece (where the English archaeologist Sir Arthur Evans notoriously re-built part of the temple of Cnossos in Crete). In these latter cases relating to archaeology, no attempt is made to conceal what has been done in modern times, and there is an analogy here, perhaps, with written histories: we may be initially disappointed to learn that the past wasn't quite as it is now presented, but in the end we'd rather know when liberties have been taken; we don't want actually to be deliberately deceived.

Deception, though, might relate, not only to us as we visit ancient sites in the present, but also to the people who have lived in those sites in the past. That is to say, it might be argued that we are guilty of deceit if we knowingly *misrepresent* the past of others. (We may concede our inability ever fully or 'truthfully' to represent that past, without repudiating responsibility for deliberate *mis*representation.) This relates most obviously to written history, but might apply also to 'heritage' sites that have been so sanitised as to give little idea of what actually took place in them. A recent example of this is the Lithuanian 'deportation experience', in a Stalinist theme-park organised by an entrepreneur who seems determined to capitalise on comparatively recent horrors; but earlier models might be cited at Auschwitz and the Bridge on the River Kwai in Thailand – both sites of appalling experiences within living memory, and already transformed into major tourist attractions. A question to ask, then, is to what extent we have betrayed the memories of those who suffered, by reducing their experiences to something with which we, as voyeuristic tourists, can easily cope.

The most extreme example of potential betrayal, and the one most often cited by pomophobes concerned with the erosion of historical 'truth' and of the distinction between 'fact' and 'fiction', is Holocaust denial – a subject that came to particular public prominence early in the new millennium, with the David Irving/Deborah Lipstadt libel trial.

2 HOLOCAUST DENIAL

There's nothing new about denying history – denying that traditionally accepted accounts of the past are valid or true; nothing new either in maintaining that such accepted accounts have been deliberately designed and perpetrated in order to mislead. We have already cited Dion Chrysostom's rejection of Homer's account of the Trojan War, and another such revisionist-denier is Jean Hardouin (1646–1729), described by one detractor as 'the Darling of the Jesuitical Order'. Allegedly in order to advance his Order's fortunes in the 'illiterate Barbarism, and . . . Ruin of Letters' that would follow, Hardouin promulgated the theory that many of the supposed authors of classical antiquity had actually been invented in the Middle Ages. He referred, for example, to the Roman writers Ovid, Statius, Martial, and Tacitus as 'pretended Antients' who are in fact 'modern and suppositious' [sic]; and Virgil's great Latin epic, the *Aeneid*, he insisted, 'appears to have been compos'd about the Year 1230, after Christ'. Virgil himself is granted existence during what had always been assumed to be his lifetime in the first century AD, and his authorship of the *Eclogues* and *Georgics* is not disputed; but there were, Hardouin claimed, good reasons to deny his authorship of a poem that revealed inconsistencies, anachronisms, neologisms, inappropriate speeches, imperfect verses, and chronological faults. And Horace similarly had to be denied authorship of many of the works ascribed to him, which exemplified verse forms that were not even invented until the fourteenth century (some thirteen hundred years after he supposedly wrote). In short, Hardouin was inclined to believe his friend who had reported having discovered that 'a certain Club of learned and ingenious Men, a few Centuries ago, had combin'd for compiling fictitious Histories . . . , and imposing them on future Generations'.[14]

Apart from the chronological time-scale, Hardouin and his friend sound not unlike contemporary conspiracy-theorists and deniers of the Holocaust, who repudiate the generally accepted historical record – in this case of comparatively recent events – claiming again that in important respects they are 'fictitious' and are being imposed 'on future generations' in order to mislead them. These matters have been debated now for some decades, and in fact ever since the end of the war in 1945. But they have recently been coming to a head in academia, not least in the context of post-modernist critiques of history, which have sometimes seemed to lead to the 'anything goes' position described by Claire Rayner;[15] and they have now impinged much more widely on the general public as a result of the David Irving trial and related commentary.

First, then, it has to be clarified that postmodernism does imply Clio's essential promiscuity, or that, in Keith Jenkins' words, history will 'go with anyone'. In other words, as we've already seen in chapter 3, section 5, it's possible to take 'the past' and use (or abuse) it for virtually any purpose at all – which is precisely what makes history so powerful and so important. But it does not follow from that, that 'anything goes'. We may interpret and 'emplot' the traces of the past in various ways: in fact, we have no option but to do so, if we write them into history. So elements of the history of the Nazi Third Reich have been consolidated into a narrative entitled 'Holocaust' (defined by Michael Shermer and Alex Grobman as 'the systematic bureaucratically administered destruction by the Nazis and their collaborators during the Second World War of an estimated six million Jews based primarily on racial ideology'[16]). That name was not used at the time; nor were the events embraced by that term viewed as an historical 'entity' until well after the end of the war. 'There was', as Hans Kellner has written, 'no Holocaust for anyone to experience or witness; it was *an imaginative creation*, like all historical events'.[17] But that doesn't imply any scepticism about the singular events which came to constitute that 'imaginative creation' having actually happened. It is possible to view them, and describe them, and force them into narrative form, in many different ways (though our inadequacies in making any sense of them at all have often been noted); but it is not possible, without denying the standards of evidence by which we live as both historians and human beings, to deny that something (that we can refer to as the Holocaust) *did* happen. It is, again, possible to question such matters as the numbers of individuals who died, and when, and how; and these remain matters of empirical investigation. But no post-modernist, by virtue of postmodernism, would be bound to deny that *something* (now referred to as the Holocaust) did actually take place.

That sort of denial was what the David Irving libel case was largely concerned with; and it has been said that the trial itself performed a disservice to historical study by publicising such views – giving prominence to 'bad' history in general and to Holocaust denial in particular. (Already in 1994, it was reported that '22 percent of all Americans believe it's possible the Holocaust never happened. Another twelve percent say they don't know'.[18]) But there should, on the contrary, be some far more positive outcomes for the discipline, since the case, while highlighting some of the weaknesses of the traditional 'modernist' position, has focused attention on a number of important historiographical issues that warrant further discussion.[19] In particular, anyone who followed the trial proceedings must have been forced to consider such fundamental matters as the nature and reliability of historical evidence, the relative reliability of oral and written testimony, the importance of ideological factors in the writing of history, the relevance of personal morality, and the whole matter of history's importance – of why we need to bother with it anyway.

Thus, the revelation that a respected historian such as David Irving[20] can challenge the record of such a recent and cataclysmic event as the Holocaust, inevitably raises questions about the status of historical knowledge more generally. He may, in this case, have gone beyond the bounds of conventional revisionism, but his might be seen as only an extreme example of reinterpretation; and continuing re-visions of this kind about the past might well then provoke doubts about the possibility of ever reaching a final and definitive account of what has happened. As Montaigne observed in relation to sixteenth-century cosmology, if one system (the Ptolemaic) is replaced by another (the Copernican), we may surely expect that the latter will in turn be replaced by something newer and supposedly better. So is it appropriate here to talk of 'truth', or, in historical terms, to aspire (as Ranke again) to tell it 'as it was'?

Such challenges to previously accepted accounts, whether of planetary motions or of historical events, immediately raise questions about the reliability of evidence: what makes the new story more persuasive than the old? David Irving's appeal to the 'archaeological' evidence of the physical remains at Auschwitz typifies the 'empirical' approach that has been taken, in both science and history, at least since the seventeenth century. Astronomical observations finally confirmed the validity of the Copernican hypothesis, and the alleged absence of holes in the roof of the relevant buildings at Auschwitz was claimed by Irving to disprove the possibility of using gas for mass extermination. Irving's empiricism further (though paradoxically) led him to prefer documents to people as sources of evidence. He is not alone in that preference: Eric Hobsbawm, for example, has described oral history as 'a remarkably slippery medium for preserving facts'.[21] But many have argued conversely that oral testimony is somehow closer to an event than any literary documentation can be. That was, for example, the basis of early-modern Catholic claims for the superiority of their own oral tradition to Protestant reliance on the written scriptures. Whether in the case of early Christianity or of the second world war, witnesses can report what they have experienced directly through their senses, and reliably pass that information on through the generations; whereas documents are suspect as being subject to mistranslation, misinterpretation, and deliberate or inadvertent fabrication.

At all events, David Irving – although himself apparently relying on oral testimony when that suited his purpose (as when he interviewed and took evidence from Nazi officers, concerning Hitler's role in 'the final solution', after the end of the war[22]) – emphatically reiterated his preference for written evidence, and even went so far as explicitly to express his distrust of any oral testimony from those who claimed to be Holocaust survivors.[23] That (selective) repudiation of what would seem to many to be empirically derived evidence, will no doubt serve to re-fuel the on-going debate on the relative reliability of oral and literary evidence.

Another main area of historiographical dispute will have been re-activated by Irving's obvious ideologically based motivation. Recognition that his right-wing political views and his admiration for Adolf Hitler (not to say his racism and anti-semitism, as described by the Judge[24]) influenced his historical interpretation, will have revealed to a wider public how any written history is liable to be (if not bound to be) affected by its author's ideological commitments. It is, of course, impossible for human beings not to have such commitments, but historians have traditionally been thought to be able, *qua* historians, to discard that aspect of their personality (or humanity) and to retain a professional 'detachment' that enabled them to work in an ideological vacuum. At the conclusion of the trial, then, the military historian John Keegan wrote of David Irving's apparent duality: on the one hand, the respected historical researcher 'who sticks to the facts', and on the other hand, 'the thinker' who is altogether more human. But of course no historian can avoid those human attributes that, in Keegan's assessment, 'cloud his [or her] mind'[25]; and it should now be apparent that historians are no less human than anyone else. So that inevitably history will be written from a certain perspective, and be somehow ideologically 'positioned'.

Related to that is another vital matter that arose in the David Irving case: the relevance of morality to the historian's work, in at least two important ways. First (as noted above) is the possible need to respect the 'alterity' of the past – the otherness of the past (with its inhabitants). Postmodernists may wish to deny any *intrinsic* value there, but that does not preclude the deliberate ascription or donation *to* it of some value. The past, after all, consists of the stories of other individuals, and our chosen morality may demand that those stories be recognised.[26]

This seems particularly obvious in the case of the Holocaust, and it's related to a second point specifically concerning personal moral values: the whole question of trust. It's significant that Irving was actually branded by his opponents as someone who could not be trusted. Deborah Lipstadt had originally described him as someone whose partisanship for Hitler had resulted in him 'skew[ing] documents and misrepresent[ing] data in order to reach historically untenable conclusions'[27]; and he was branded by the defending lawyer Richard Rampton as someone who couldn't be trusted – as 'a falsifier . . . [or] to put it bluntly . . . a *liar*'. That meant that he was guilty of 'invention, misquotation, suppression, distortion, manipulation and – not least – mistranslation'. And that charge was supported by Professor Richard Evans, who reported having been taken aback by the 'sheer depth of duplicity' in Irving's treatment of sources (adding words to some quotations, excising words from others, as suited his own case).[28]

Such charges clearly go further than any professional accusation of being an incompetent historian: they refer to standards of personal morality. And this serves to highlight an important point about history: that its whole practice and validity depends on a shared structure of moral values – a morality shared, that is, not only by practitioners who need to be able to rely on each other's findings, but also by those eyewitnesses and record-makers who are responsible for history's actual source-material. Such dependance is always bound to be problematic, since experience teaches that not everyone *can* be trusted – that people *do* falsify memories and records, sometimes deliberately and sometimes quite unwittingly; and whether or not they falsify, they can anyway give only a partial description of any event in which they've been involved. But on the whole, we live on a basis of trusting each other, and what is significant in this respect, again, is David Irving's total repudiation of any evidence presented by direct participants (or, in this case, survivors). Thus, for example, in the key matter of mass-killings in Auschwitz, Irving rejected the whole body of eye-witness evidence, describing it as 'totally demolished' by his own research.[29]

As we have seen, the methodological issues raised by the Irving case are by no means new; but they have now been brought to a wider public, and debate about them opened up – and that can only be to the benefit of historical study as a whole. It should have been beneficial, too, to be reminded by the case that history actually *is* important. It does matter that the Holocaust took place, and it's important to refute those who deny it. We may no longer be confident in our ability to transmit 'the truth' of that event, or even know what it might mean to try to do that. But we can and need to be concerned with the transmission of an historical record, which has been based as reliably as possible on the evidence of those with direct experience. That is the least that is due to those who suffered in the past, and it's also what is owed to the future as our generation's lesson in self-knowledge.

3 THE FUTURE OF THE PAST[30]

The postmodern challenge to historical study can't just be ignored. Ostriches may choose to think that postmodernity is another passing phase that will have left the historical desert and moved on by the time they get their heads out of the sand; but postmodernity is a *condition*, and it's the one we're privileged (or condemned) to live in. Rather, then, than surveying at length the colossal wrecks of abandoned heroic projects from the past, it's surely time to set about our own construction. That implies first a need to formulate some answer to the questions of what it's all *for* – the 'why' of history. The time for an unreflective study of the past – with no thought, that is, for why we're doing it, or what it is we're doing – has passed; it's 'history'. It's time (as I've argued elsewhere) to replace the ideal of a study that is 'purposeless' with one that can be employed, in Nietzsche's words 'for the purpose of life!'[31]

That, of course, does not mean that there is, or ever could be, only one purpose. Indeed, history can take on rather sinister connotations when we think of it in such terms: a single-track of history leading to some foregone or preordained conclusion in the future is the way to an Orwellian (or Nazi or Stalinist) nightmare. But within the labyrinth, we do, as individuals, need a thread; or, to change the metaphor, we do need to know in which direction, over the boundless ocean of the past, to throw our lifeline. And that means having some idea of whom or what we want to save, and why.

That doesn't preclude the possibility of antiquarian research for those who find such work attractive. There may still be plenty of students who wish to burrow away in the archives, with no other purpose than to find out what the records 'say', or reveal to them about a past that supposedly has its own intrinsic interest and value. Living in and for the past is not without its attraction. For some, as for Geoffrey Elton, 'The future is dark, the present burdensome; only the past, dead and finished, bears contemplation'.[32] There might, though, be some danger of spending too much time 'with the dead', as the novelist George Eliot's 'dried up pedant' Mr Casaubon came to realise;[33] and there might, too, even be some moral virtue in utilising historical study, as Nietzsche proposed, for the purpose, rather, of *life*.

If that is so, responsibility is left with historians for the choice of a path that leads from the past to a future; and the direction of that path will be determined by the future that they themselves select from another infinite range of possibilities. Some may see the end of history already reached, so will view the past as leading to a culmination in our own good selves; others may still envisage further struggle to attain a future characterised by such (variously problematic) virtues as 'order', 'equality', or 'justice'[34]; in which case their historical trajectories will be imposed in such a way as to make the attainment of such goals seem possible, or probable, or even necessary. The point in any case, though, is to have some personal vision that gives some sense of purpose to our lives – and hence a sense of purpose also to our histories. That's surely how to give the past – and history – a future?

Notes

1 INTRODUCTION: HISTORY, PHILOSOPHY, AND HISTORIOGRAPHY

1 Edward Gibbon, *An Essay on the Study of Literature*, London, T. Becket & P. A. De Hondt, 1764, p. 107.
2 Plato, *Apology* 38a, in *The Dialogues*, transl. B. Jowett, 5 vols, Oxford, Clarendon Press, 1875, vol. 1, p. 371.
3 William Stubbs (Regius Professor of Modern History at Oxford, 1866–84), quoted by J. R. Hale (ed.), *The Evolution of British Historiography*, London, Macmillan, 1967, p. 56.
4 Leslie Stephen, *The English Utilitarians*, 3 vols, London, Duckworth & Co., 1900, vol. 3, p. 341.
5 Herbert Butterfield, *Man on His Past. The Study of the History of Historical Scholarship*, Cambridge, Cambridge University Press, 1955, p. 139.
6 Mark Cousins, 'The practice of historical investigation', in D. Attridge *et al.* (eds), *Post-structuralism and the Question of History*, Cambridge, Cambridge University Press, 1987, p. 130.
7 G. R. Elton, *The Practice of History*, London, Fontana, 1969; Raphael Samuel (ed.), *People's History and Socialist Theory*, London, Routledge & Kegan Paul, 1981, p. xl; Arthur Marwick, inaugural lecture at the Open University, 5 October 1993; *The Nature of History*, London, Macmillan, 1970, p. 215.
8 For useful multi-disciplinary anthologies, see Charles Jencks (ed.), *The Post-Modern Reader*, London, Academy Editions, 1992; Lawrence Cahoone (ed.), *From Modernism to Postmodernism*, Oxford, Blackwell, 1996.
9 Terry Eagleton, *Literary Theory: An Introduction*, Oxford, Blackwell, 1983, p. 143.
10 I am particularly indebted for what follows to James Duncan and David Ley (eds), *Place/Culture/Representation*, London, Routledge, 1993.
11 So Ann Wordsworth: 'there is no real object "history", only a philosophy of history; the historian's work reduces to its ideological positions'. 'Derrida and Foucault: writing the history of historicity', in Attridge *et al.* (eds), *Post-structuralism*, p. 116.

12 Keith Jenkins, *Re-thinking History*, London, Routledge, 1991, p. 69. Jenkins provides a good, short introduction to postmodernist historiography.

2 WHAT WAS HISTORY? THE PAST AS IT WAS

1 Lucian of Samosata, as quoted by Thomas Hobbes in the Preface to his translation of Thucydides, *The History of the Grecian War* (1629), 3rd edn, London, D. Brown, 1723.
2 The word 'history' is also often applied to the past itself, as when we talk about ourselves or our country having a 'history'. It should be clear from the context how the word is being used here.
3 Lucian, quoted by D. R. Kelley (ed.), *Versions of History*, London, Yale University Press, 1991, pp. 66–67.
4 J. H. Plumb, *The Death of the Past*, London, Macmillan, 1969, p. 145.
5 R. Aldrich (ed.), *History in the National Curriculum*, London, Kogan Page, 1991, p. 21.
6 Thucydides, *The Peloponnesian War*, I.3, 9–10; III.104; II.41, transl. R. Crawley, London, J. M. Dent & Sons, 1910, pp. 2, 4–6, 95, 181–182.
7 Aristotle, *Poetics* II.vi in Aristotle, *Poetics and Rhetoric*, (ed.) T. A. Moxon, London, J. M. Dent & Sons, 1953, p. 20 (my emphases).
8 Aristotle, *Metaphysics* I.i–ii, in *Metaphysics*, transl. H. Tredennick, London, Harvard University Press, 1933, pp. 5–13.
9 Quoted by J. M. Levine, *Humanism and History: Origins of Modern English Historiography*, Ithaca and London, Cornell University Press, 1987, p. 50 (my emphases).
10 Sir Philip Sidney, *An Apologie for Poetrie* (1595), ed. E. S. Shuckburgh, Cambridge, Cambridge University Press, 1948, p. 17.
11 Francis Bacon, *The Advancement of Learning* (1605), II.iv, 2, London, Oxford University Press, 1951, pp. 96–97. Cf. Gibbon: 'the characters of great men should doubtless be held sacred; but Poets, in writing their history, may be indulged in giving it us, rather as it ought to have been, than as it actually was'. *An Essay on the Study of Literature*, London, T. Becket & P. A. De Hondt, 1764, p. 70.
12 See R. F. Jones, *Ancients and Moderns*, Berkeley and Los Angeles, University of California Press, 1961, Ch. IX.
13 Walter Charleton, *Two Discourses, the First, Concerning the Different Wits of Men*, 3rd edn, London, William Whitwood, 1692, p. 14.
14 Quoted by John Hope Mason, 'Thinking about genius in the eighteenth century', in Paul Mattick (ed.), *Eighteenth-Century Aesthetics and the Reconstruction of Art*, Cambridge, Cambridge University Press, 1993, p. 218.
15 So e.g.: 'Hypotheses are not to be regarded in experimental Philosophy.' *Opticks*, ed. I. B. Cohen, New York, Dover Publications, 1952, p. 404; cf. p. 369.
16 Quoted by I. Kramnick (ed.), *Lord Bolingbroke: Historical Writings*, Chicago, University of Chicago Press, 1972, p. xxvi. Fontenelle goes on

to decry such an approach: 'I had as soon a man acquired exactly the history of all the clocks of Paris.'

17 J. B. Bury, 'The science of history' (1902), quoted by F. Stern (ed.), *The Varieties of History*, New York, Meridian Books, 1956, p. 216.

18 Thucydides, *Peloponnesian War* I.21–22, p. 11.

19 Quoted by H. Baker, *The Race of Time*, Toronto, University of Toronto Press, 1967, p. 18.

20 Thomas Blundevill, *The True Order and Methode of Wryting and Reading Hystories*, London, William Seres, 1574, unpaginated.

21 Quoted by Baker, *Race of Time*, pp. 20, 21.

22 Ephraim Chambers, *Cyclopaedia* (1728); Voltaire in Diderot's *Encyclopédie* (1751–1765); Edward Gibbon, *An Address*, quoted in Kelley, *Versions*, pp. 440, 442, 461 (my emphases).

23 Condorcet, *Sketch for a Historical Picture of the Progress of the Human Mind* (1794), quoted in Kelley, *Versions*, p. 495 (my emphasis).

24 Hugh Trevor-Roper, *The Rise of Christian Europe*, London, Thames & Hudson, 1965, p. 9.

25 Quoted by Stern, *Varieties*, pp. 57, 59.

26 Quoted by P. Geyl, *Use and Abuse of History*, New Haven, Yale University Press, 1955, p. 45.

27 Hippolyte Taine (1828–93), quoted by Geyl, *Use and Abuse*, p. 47.

28 Quoted by Peter Novick, *That Noble Dream: The 'Objectivity Question' and the American Historical Profession*, Cambridge, Cambridge University Press, 1988, p. 38.

29 Quoted by Novick, *Noble Dream*, p. 27.

30 Novick, *Noble Dream*, pp. 37, 40.

31 Quoted by Stern, *Varieties*, p. 215 (my emphasis).

32 G. R. Elton, *Return to Essentials*, Cambridge, Cambridge University Press, 1991, pp. 52–53, 9; *The Practice of History*, London, Fontana, 1969, p.74; cf. p. 86.

33 *Practice*, pp. 68, 19 (my emphasis).

34 J. R. Hale (ed.), *The Evolution of British Historiography*, London, Macmillan, 1967, pp. 60–61 (my emphasis).

35 E. H. Carr, *What Is History?*, Harmondsworth, Penguin, 1964, p. 123. For a critique, see Keith Jenkins, *On 'What is History?': From Carr and Elton to Rorty and White*, London, Routledge, 1995.

36 John Tosh, *The Pursuit of History*, London, Longman, 1984, pp. 111, 124. (A third edition was published in 2000.)

3 WHY HISTORY? PAST ANSWERS

1 David Hume, 'Of the study of history' (1741), in E. F. Miller (ed.), *David Hume: Essays Moral, Political, and Literary*, Indianapolis, Liberty Classics, 1985, p. 566.

2 Livy, *Roman History*, transl. W. Gordon, Edinburgh, Bell & Bradfute, 1809, p. 14.

3 See Pierre Le Moyne, *Of the Art Both of Writing and Judging of History*, English transl., London, R. Sare & J. Hindmarsh, 1695, pp. 35–36.

4 Ranulphus Higden, *Polychronicon* (fourteenth century), quoted by E. Rhys (ed.), *The Growth of Political Liberty*, London, J. M. Dent & Sons, 1921, p. 1.
5 Henry St John, Lord Bolingbroke, *Letters on the Study and Use of History* (1752), London, Alexander Murray, 1870, p. 130. Bolingbroke contrasts Herodotus in this respect with Thucydides and Xenophon, by whom 'you are *taught* indeed as well as *entertained*' (my emphasis).
6 Herodotus, *The History*, transl. G. Rawlinson, 2 vols, London, J. M. Dent & Sons, 1910, vol. 1, p. 1.
7 Herodotus, *History*, vol. 2, p. 134.
8 Thucydides, *The Peloponnesian War*, II.22, transl. R. Crawley, London, J. M. Dent & Sons, 1910, p. 11 (my emphasis).
9 Alexander Ross, *The History of the World*, London, John Clark, 1652, Preface.
10 Le Moyne, *History*, p. 59.
11 All quotations in this and the following paragraph are taken from the Preface, in William Whiston's translation of Josephus, *The Wars of the Jews*, London, J. M. Dent & Sons, 1906.
12 Jan Karski, *Story of a Secret State*, London, Hodder & Stoughton, 1945, p. 319; Primo Levi, *If This Is a Man*, London, Abacus, 1987, p. 398.
13 The original authorship of this much-cited maxim is attributed to Dionysius of Halicarnassus in the first century BC, *De arte rhetorica*, XI.2.
14 Richard Braithwait, *A Survey of History*, London, Jasper Amery, 1638, p. 2.
15 Braithwait, *Survey*, pp. 21–22; and *passim*.
16 So e.g. Thomas Heywoode advises women specifically in his *Nine Bookes of Various History Concerninge Women*, London, Adam Islip, 1624. However, he does claim to deal with the whole gamut of women, ranging from goddesses, muses and prophetesses, to Amazons, adulteresses, and wantons, and he aims to provide a range of exemplary models for his readers: 'Wives may reade here of chast Virgins, to patterne their Daughters by, and how to demeane themselves in all Coniugall love towards their Husbands: Widowes may finde what may best become their solitude, and Matrons those accomplishments that most dignifie their gravitie' ('To the reader').
17 Braithwait, *Survey*, pp. 382, 414.
18 Braithwait, *Survey*, pp. 130–132, 71.
19 Degory Wheare, *The Method and Order of Reading both Civil and Ecclesiastical Histories* (1635), transl. E. Bohun, London, Charles Brome, 1685, p. 320. Cf. Alexander Ross in the Preface to his *History* (1652): 'What can be more profitable than to learn Wisdom by other mens follies, to get experience by other mens cost and labours, and to be safe by other mens dangers.'
20 Wheare, *Method*, pp. 323–324.
21 Wheare, *Method*, p. 360.
22 Plutarch, *Lives*, transl. J. and W. Langhorne, 6 vols, London, Lackington, Allen & Co., 1803, vol. 1, p. xiii.
23 See Plutarch's 'Life of Alexander', in *Lives*, vol. 4, p. 133.

24 Giorgio Vasari, *Lives of the Most Eminent Painters, Sculptors, and Architects* (1550), transl. J. Foster, 5 vols, London, Henry G. Bohn, 1880–1885, vol. I, pp. 7, 33.
25 Izaak Walton, *The Lives of Dr John Donne; Sir Henry Wotton; Mr Richard Hooker; Mr George Herbert; and Dr Robert Sanderson*, London, Bell & Daldy, 1866, Epistle to the Reader. Cf. Thomas Lincoln's comment on Walton's Life of Robert Sanderson, Bishop of Lincoln: 'Sure I am, that the life and actions of that pious and learned Prelate will afford you matter enough for . . . the imitation of posterity.' Letter dated 10 May 1678, included in the edition published, significantly, by the Society for Promoting Christian Knowledge (London, undated), p. 371.
26 William Wotton, *History of Rome* (1701), Dedication, quoted by J. M. Levine, *Humanism and History: Origins of Modern English Historiography*, Ithaca and London, Cornell University Press, 1987, p. 172.
27 Thomas Carlyle, *On Heroes, Hero-Worship, and the Heroic in History*, London, Cassell & Co., 1908, p. 11.
28 Samuel Smiles, *Self-Help; with Illustrations of Conduct and Perseverance*, London, John Murray, 1890, Introduction to the 1st edition, 1859, p. x.
29 Smiles, *Self-Help*, p. 371 (my emphasis).
30 R. G. Collingwood (1946), *The Idea of History*, Oxford, Oxford University Press, 1961, p. 50. On providential history, see C. A. Patrides, *The Grand Design of God*, London, Routledge & Kegan Paul, 1972.
31 Anon., *God's Judgements upon Drunkards, Swearers and Sabbath-Breakers . . .*, London, E. Tyler, 1659, p. 25.
32 *Ecclesiastes* 1,9.
33 See e.g. early-Christian rejection of well-established Greek ideas on the sphericity of the earth.
34 St Augustine, *City of God*, transl. John Healey, 2 vols; London, J. M. Dent and Sons, 1945, XII.xiii (vol. 1, p. 356).
35 Bede, *The Ecclesiastical History of the English Nation*, London, J. M. Dent & Sons, 1958, pp. 11–14. Bede's account of the martyrdom was based on an earlier Life of St Alban, now lost. On Bede and mediaeval historiography, see Antonia Gransden, *Historical Writing in England, c. 550 to c. 1307*, London, Routledge & Kegan Paul, 1974; and *Historical Writing in England II, c. 1307 to the Early Sixteenth Century*, London, Routledge & Kegan Paul, 1982.
36 *The Life and Miracles of Saint Cuthbert* is appended, in the Everyman edition, to the *History*, pp. 286–348.
37 John Foxe, *The History of Christian Martyrdom* (1554), ed. J. M. Crombie, London, Gibbings & Co., 1903, p. 442.
38 Josephus, *Wars*, Preface, p. 3, n. 1.
39 See Cotton Mather, *Magnalia Christi Americana* (1702), quoted by C.A. Patrides, *The Grand Design of God*, London, Routledge, 1972, p. 120.
40 Statement by Institut vuur Christelijke-nasionale Onderwijs, quoted by Marc Ferro, *The Use and Abuse of History*, London, Routledge & Kegan Paul, 1984, p. 2.

41 Voltaire, quoted in D. C. Lindberg and R. S. Westman (eds), *Reappraisals of the Scientific Revolution*, Cambridge, Cambridge University Press, 1990, p. 7 (my emphases).
42 Livy, *Roman History*, transl. W. Gordon, Edinburgh, Bell & Bradfute, 1809, p. 14.
43 Quoted by John Hope Mason, 'Thinking about genius in the eighteenth century', in P. Mattick (ed.), *Eighteenth-Century Aesthetics and the Reconstruction of Art*, Cambridge, Cambridge University Press, 1993, p. 230.
44 Bolingbroke, *Letters*, pp. 69, 79, 100–101, 104 (my emphases).
45 View ascribed to Lévi-Strauss by Hayden White, *Tropics of Discourse*, London, Johns Hopkins University Press, 1978, p. 104.
46 Dion Chrysostom, *Discourses*, transl. J. W. Cohoon, 5 vols, London, Heinemann, 1932, vol. 1, pp. 517, 541, 561.
47 Juan Luis Vives, *De causis corruptarum artium* (1531), quoted by J. H. Franklin, *Jean Bodin and the Sixteenth-Century Revolution in the Methodology of Law and History*, New York, Columbia University Press, 1963, p. 94, n. 13.
48 Quotations from *Mein Kampf* are taken from Ferro, *Use and Abuse*, pp. 100–101.
49 See J. Habermas, *The New Conservatism: Cultural Criticism and the Historians' Debate*, ed. and transl. S. W. Nicholsen, Cambridge, Polity Press, 1989, pp. xi, xvii, 233–235.
50 P. Geyl, *Use and Abuse of History*, New Haven, Yale University Press, 1955, p. 57. Cf. Oakeshott: 'The removal . . . of the name of Trotsky from the official Bolshevik emblematic past, or that of the explorer Stanley from the practical past of Zaire, was part of an undertaking to construct a symbolic vocabulary of practical discourse which would not prejudice an approved practical present.' *On History*, Oxford, Blackwell, 1983, p. 43.
51 In 1988 and 1989 school history examinations had to be cancelled pending such revisions of the Stalin and Brezhnev eras. R. Aldrich (ed.), *History in the National Curriculum*, London, Kogan Page, 1991, pp. 3–4.
52 Ferro, *Use and Abuse*, pp. 114, 118, 122.
53 Report in *The Daily Telegraph*, 25 April 1995.
54 Kenneth Baker (1988), quoted in Aldrich (ed.), *National Curriculum*, p. 95.
55 J. Anthony Lukas, correspondent of *The New York Times*, quoted by Peter Novick, *That Noble Dream: The 'Objectivity Question' and the American Historical Profession*, Cambridge, Cambridge University Press, 1988, p. 416.
56 Novick, *Noble Dream*, p. 416
57 David Eakins, quoted by Novick, *Noble Dream*, p. 426
58 Ferro, *Use and Abuse*, pp. 227–228.
59 John Tosh, *The Pursuit of History*, London, Longman, 1984, p. 4. On post-colonialism and history, see Ch. 5, section 4.
60 Alexander Ross, *The History of the World*, London, John Clark, 1652, Preface.

61 *Sunday Times*, 16 February 1992, under the headline 'Europe rewrites history as bunk'. Lord Acton had earlier advised prospective contributors to the 1902 *Cambridge Modern History*, that 'our Waterloo must be one that satisfies French and English, Germans and Dutch alike'. F. Stern (ed.), *Varieties of History*, New York, Meridian Books, 1956, p. 249.

62 George Orwell, *Nineteen Eighty-Four*, Harmondsworth, Penguin, 1987, pp. 30–31, 126; cf. pp. 35, 62, 76.

63 Charles Nicolle, quoted by W. I. B. Beveridge, *The Art of Scientific Investigation*, London, Heinemann, 1957, p. 27.

64 Sir Walter Raleigh, *The History of the World*, London, W. Burre, 1614, p. 457.

65 Pascal, *Pensées*, transl. W. F. Trotter, London, J. M. Dent & Sons, 1931, p. 48.

66 Cf. David Hume: considering the same theme, again in its relation to the Roman Empire, but with a different anatomical example, he suggests that 'Some small touches, given to Caligula's brain in his infancy, might have converted him into a Trajan'; or, looking at external factors, 'One wave, a little higher than the rest, by burying Caesar and his fortune in the bottom of the ocean, might have restored liberty to a considerable part of mankind.' *Dialogues concerning Natural Religion*, ed. N. Kemp Smith, Oxford, Clarendon Press, 1935, p. 254. For further examples, see E. H. Carr, *What Is History?*, Harmondsworth, Penguin, 1964, p. 98.

67 Galileo, *Dialogue concerning the Two Chief World Systems*, ed. S. Drake, Berkeley, University of California Press, 1970, p. 400.

68 John Selden, *Historie of Tithes*, London, 1618, Preface, p. vi. This work has been described by a modern historian as 'the best expression of history written with a view to its political utility'. F. S. Fussner, *The Historical Revolution: English Historical Writing and Thought, 1580–1640*, London, Routledge & Kegan Paul, 1962, p. xvi.

69 A handwritten copy of Selden's 'submission' to the court on 28 January 1618, is in the front of the British Library copy of the *Historie* (517.b.4).

70 Bolingbroke, *Letters*, pp. 25–27. Cf. Alexander Ross, who believed that a wide historical perspective enables us to escape from that childish myopia, by which we are constrained to see only what lies immediately in front of us and take account of nothing else. *History of the World*, Preface.

71 Bolingbroke, *Letters*, p. 403.

72 See Plato, *Republic*, Book III, in *The Dialogues*, transl. B. Jowett, 5 vols, Oxford, Clarendon Press, 1875, vol. 3, pp. 292–293.

4 EXTERNAL CHALLENGES TO THE OLD MODEL: SOME INTERDISCIPLINARY PERSPECTIVES

1 Dr Johnson, quoted by D. C. Douglas, *English Scholars*, London, Jonathan Cape, 1939, p. 358.
2 R. W. Emerson, *Essays and other Writings*, London, Cassell & Co., 1907, p. 24. The essays were originally published in 1841 and 1844.
3 A good introduction is still R. L. Gregory, *Eye and Brain: The Psychology of Seeing*, 4th edn, London, Weidenfeld & Nicolson, 1990.
4 Emerson, *Essays*, p. 362.
5 W. H. Auden quoted by N. R. Hanson, *Patterns of Discovery*, Cambridge, Cambridge University Press, 1961, p. 181, n. 3.
6 Cf. Emerson: 'It is the fault of our rhetoric that we cannot strongly state one fact without seeming to belie some other.' *Essays*, pp. 39–40.
7 Primo Levi, *The Drowned and the Saved,* London, Abacus, 1989, pp. 22–23. Cf. Emerson again: 'things are, and are not, at the same time. . . . All the universe over, there is but one thing, this old Two-Face, creator–creature, mind–matter, right–wrong, of which any proposition may be affirmed or denied'. *Essays*, p. 363.
8 Glyndwr Williams, reviewing A. Grafton, *New Worlds, Ancient Texts: The Power of Tradition and the Shock of Discovery*, in *The Times Higher Education Supplement*, 29 January 1993.
9 Levi, *Drowned*, pp. 20–21.
10 Galileo, *Dialogue concerning the Two Chief World Systems*, ed. S. Drake, Berkeley and Los Angeles, University of California Press, 1970, p. 400. On the replacement of conceptual frameworks or 'paradigms', see T. S. Kuhn's influential work, *The Structure of Scientific Revolutions*, Chicago, University of Chicago Press, 1962.
11 Quoted by Richard Rorty, *Contingency, Irony, and Solidarity*, Cambridge, Cambridge University Press, 1989, p. 38.
12 Hanson, *Patterns*, pp. 7, 15.
13 F. J. Levy, *Tudor Historical Thought* (1967), quoted by J. H. Preston, 'Was there an Historical Revolution?', *Journal of the History of Ideas*, 1977, vol. 38, p. 364. Cf. Hegel's perception that periods of happiness are represented in history as blank pages.
14 M. Oakeshott, *On History*, Oxford, Blackwell, 1983, p. 5.
15 Compare, however, J. R. Hale: 'Partly because of German scholars, who were interested in the Teutonic origins of Anglo-Saxon England, early medieval history attracted greater attention among professional historians at the end of the nineteenth century than any other period.' *The Evolution of British Historiography*, London, Macmillan, 1967, p. 65.
16 E. H. Carr, *What Is History?*, Harmondsworth, Penguin, 1964, p. 24.
17 Thomas Fuller, *The Church History of Britain*, quoted by Preston, 'Historical Revolution?', p. 364.
18 Stephen Greenblatt, à propos Sir Philip Sidney's assertion that 'there is nothing so certain as our continual uncertainty', has described how he considered writing a dissertation on uncertainty – 'to make a virtue of my own inner necessity'. *Learning to Curse: Essays in Early Modern Culture*, London, Routledge, 1990, p. 1.

19 *What Is History?*, p. 36. Carr draws the reasonable implication that 'anyone wishing to understand what 1848 did to the German liberals should take Mommsen's *History of Rome* as one of his text-books' (p. 37). See further on Meinecke's psychological development in relation to his chosen historical subjects, pp. 40–41.

20 J. Burckhardt, *Judgements on History and Historians*, quoted by Carr, *What Is History?*, p. 55.

21 Lucian (second century AD), quoted by Thomas Hobbes in the Preface to his translation of Thucydides, *The History of the Grecian War*, 3rd edn, London, D. Brown, 1723.

22 This term was coined by Gustav Bergmann, according to Richard Rorty, who used it as the title for an anthology in 1967. See letter, *London Review of Books*, 4 November 1993, p. 4.

23 See J. E. Toews, 'Intellectual history after the linguistic turn: the autonomy of meaning and the irreducibility of experience', *American Historical Review*, 1987, vol. 92, p. 882 – to whom, however, this view is not to be ascribed.

24 Toews, 'Intellectual history', p. 906.

25 Plato, *Cratylus* 438, in *The Dialogues*, ed. B. Jowett, 5 vols, Oxford, Clarendon Press, 1875, vol. 2, p. 264.

26 Plato, *Dialogues*, vol. 2, p. 262.

27 So Louis Montrose, quoted by G. M. Spiegel, 'History, historicism, and the social logic of the text in the Middle Ages', *Speculum*, 1990, vol. 65, p. 70.

28 D. Attridge, 'Language as history/history as language', in D. Attridge *et al.* (eds), *Post-structuralism and the Question of History*, Cambridge, Cambridge University Press, 1987, p. 188.

29 Spiegel, 'History', p. 62.

30 Jean Howard, quoted by Spiegel, 'History', p. 71, n. 43.

31 A. Easthope, 'Romancing the stone: history-writing and rhetoric', *Social History*, 1993, vol. 18, pp. 240, 242.

32 Easthope, 'Romancing', p. 245. In fact, of course, the very description of seventeenth-century people in twentieth-century language anachronistically assimilates their attitudes and motivations to our own, with inevitable distortions.

33 Michel Foucault, quoted by Alec McHoul and Wendy Grace, *A Foucault Primer: Discourse, power and the subject*, London, UCL Press, 1995, pp. 11–12. Recognition of Foucault's relevance to historical study was slow in coming: see Allan Megill, 'The reception of Foucault by historians', *Journal of the History of Ideas*, 1987, vol. 48, pp. 117–141. But for a 'first attempt to address at length the issue of how Foucault's vision has been affecting the professional writing of history' over the last two decades, see Jan Goldstein (ed.), *Foucault and the Writing of History*, Oxford, Blackwell, 1994.

34 Robert Boyle, *Certain Physiological Essays*, in *The Works*, ed. T. Birch, 6 vols, London, J. & F. Rivington, 1772, vol. I, p. 303.

35 Isaac Newton, *Principia*, ed. F. Cajori, 2 vols, Berkeley and Los Angeles, University of California Press, 1966, vol. 2, pp. 546, 400 (my emphases).

36 Thomas Sprat, *History of the Royal Society* (1667), ed. J. I. Cope & H. W. Jones, London, Routledge & Kegan Paul, 1959, pp. 101, 108.
37 See R. H. Popkin, *The History of Scepticism from Erasmus to Spinoza*, Berkeley and Los Angeles, University of California Press, 1979, Ch. XI.
38 Isaac La Peyrère, *Men before Adam* (1656), quoted by Popkin, *History*, p. 217. See also R. H. Popkin, *Isaac La Peyrère (1596–1676): His Life, Work and Influence*, Leiden, E. J. Brill, 1987, Ch. 4; and A. Grafton, *Defenders of the Text: The Tradition of Scholarship in an Age of Science*, Cambridge, Mass. and London, Harvard University Press, 1991, Ch. 8, on 'Isaac La Peyrère and the Old Testament'.
39 Richard Simon, *A Critical History of the Old Testament*, English transl., London, Walter Davis, 1682, pp. 1–2. The theological consequences were profound, affecting in particular the 'rule of faith' debates between Protestants and Catholics; for 'Instead of believing with the Protestants that the shortest and most certain way of deciding the questions of Faith is to consult the Holy Scriptures, we shall on the contrary find in this Work that if we join not Tradition with the Scripture, we can hardly affirm any thing for certain in Religion.' (Authour's Preface.)
40 Thomas Paine, *The Age of Reason, Part the Second, being an Investigation of True and Fabulous Theology* (1795), quoted by Popkin, *History*, p. 221. For the earlier view of the Bible as the supreme historical record, cf. the advice given to Oxford undergraduates in 1623 – that 'it is the Sacred History onely which discovers the secrets of the most remote Antiquity, and never lies: It is the Sacred History alone, which gives a faithful testimony of the Succession of times from the very beginning of all things, and never makes one false step. She alone is the most shining light of the Eternal Truth'. Quoted by H. Baker, *The Race of Time*, Toronto, University of Toronto Press, 1967, p. 35.
41 Lord Bolingbroke, *Letters on the Study and Use of History* (1752), London, Alexander Murray, 1870, pp. 69–72.
42 Henricus Cornelius Agrippa, *Of the Vanitie and Uncertaintie of Artes and Sciences*, English transl., London, Henry Wykes, 1569, p. 16.
43 Francesco Patrizzi, *De historia*, quoted by J. H. Franklin, *Jean Bodin and the Sixteenth-Century Revolution in the Methodology of Law and History*, New York, Columbia University Press, 1963, pp. 100–101.
44 Sir Philip Sidney, *An Apologie for Poetrie* (1595), ed. E. S. Shuckburgh, Cambridge, Cambridge University Press, 1948, p. 15.
45 See e.g. Montaigne's essay, 'Apology for Raymond Sebond', which clearly shows the influence of the recently rediscovered Sextus Empiricus. D. M. Frame (ed.), *The Complete Works of Montaigne*, London, Stanford University Press, 1958, pp. 318–457.
46 François La Mothe Le Vayer, *Du peu de certitude qu'il y a dans l'Histoire*, in *Deux Discours*, Paris, L. Billaine, 1668, p. 7.
47 Pierre Le Moyne, *Of the Art Both of Writing and Judging of History*, English transl., London, R. Sare & J. Hindmarsh, 1695, p. 76.
48 Le Moyne, *History*, pp. 80–81, 121–122.
49 Bolingbroke, *Letters*, pp. 188, 386, 98–99 (my emphases). It is noteworthy that Bolingbroke refers the prospective historian to 'memorials

. . . collections of public acts and monuments . . . private letters, treaties. All these must come into your plan of study . . . : many not to be re[a]d through, but all to be consulted and compared'. And for recent events, 'even pamphlets, writ on different sides and on different occasions . . . will help you to come at truth', so long as one is on guard against the rhetoric, taking care to 'neglect all declamation, weigh the reasoning, and advert to fact' (pp. 188, 386).

50 Bolingbroke, *Letters*, pp. 107–108, 135–136 (my emphases). Cf. *The Works*, 4 vols, Philadelphia, Carey & Hart, 1841, vol. 2, p. 487: 'The degree of assent, which we give to history, may be settled, in proportion to the number, characters, and circumstances of the original witnesses.'

51 A. Froude, *Short Studies on Great Subjects*, i, 1894, p. 21; Carl Becker, *Atlantic Monthly*, October 1910, p. 528; quoted by Carr, *What Is History?*, pp. 26, 21.

52 Cf. the well-known distinction proposed by C. P. Scott in the context of journalism: 'Facts are sacred, opinion is free.'

53 Quoted by Carr, *What Is History?*, p. 8 (my emphases).

5 INTERNAL CHALLENGES TO THE OLD MODEL: SOME MAJOR FORCES

1 Plato, *Theaetetus* 167, in *The Dialogues*, transl. B. Jowett, 5 vols, Oxford, Clarendon Press, 1875, vol. 4, p. 316.

2 L. Kolakowski, quoted by S. H. Rigby, *Marxism and History: A Critical Introduction*, Manchester, Manchester University Press, 1987, p. 7.

3 *Capital*, quoted by Rigby, *Marxism*, p. 34.

4 This and the following quotation are from Engels's funeral oration (1883).

5 Karl Marx, *Selected Writings*, ed. D. McLellan, Oxford, Oxford University Press, 1977, p. 300.

6 Marx, *Selected Writings*, p. 192; *Critique of Political Economy*, Preface, quoted by D. McLellan, *Marx*, Glasgow, Fontana, 1975, p. 40.

7 Marx's emphasis here was foreshadowed by Giambattista Vico in *The New Science* (1725), transl. T. G. Bergin and M. H. Fisch, Ithaca, Cornell University Press, 1970: 'The whole life of these heroic states centres in the conflict between patricians and plebeians.'

8 Marx and Engels, *The German Ideology*, quoted by A. Giddens, *The Class Structure of the Advanced Societies*, London, Hutchinson, 1981, p. 29.

9 Thomas Babington Macaulay, *Edinburgh Review*, May 1828, reprinted in *Miscellaneous Writings*, ed. T. F. Ellis, 2 vols, London, Longman & Co., 1860, vol. I, p. 277.

10 Jean Jaurès, Introduction to *The Socialist History of the French Revolution*, originally published 1901–1909, reprinted in F. Stern (ed.), *The Varieties of History*, New York, Meridian Books, 1956, pp. 164ff.

11 Quoted by Raphael Samuel (ed.), *People's History and Socialist Theory*, London, Routledge & Kegan Paul, 1981, p. xxxiii.

12 Hélène Cixous, quoted by C. Weedon, *Feminist Practice and Post-structuralist Theory*, Oxford, Blackwell, 1987, p. 67. Chris Weedon's book provides a lucid introduction to many of the issues in this section.
13 See Natalie Z. Davis, 'Gender and genre: women as historical writers, 1400–1820', in P. H. Labalme (ed.), *Beyond Their Sex: Learned Women of the European Past*, New York, New York University Press, 1984, pp. 153–182.
14 Catherine Macaulay, *The History of England*, 8 vols, London, J. Nourse, 1763–1783, vol. 1, pp. viii–x.
15 Robert Pierpoint, '*History*'. *The Marble Statue in the Entrance Hall of Warrington Town Hall*, reprinted for private circulation from *Warrington Guardian*, 25 November, 5 December 1908, p. 3.
16 Alice Stopford Green, Essay of June, 1897, published as *Woman's Place in the World of Letters*, London, Macmillan, 1913, p. 32.
17 Gilles Ménage, *The History of Women Philosophers* (1690), transl. B. H. Zedler, Lanham, University Press of America, 1984; William Alexander, *The History of Women from the Earliest Antiquity to the Present Time*, 2 vols, London, W. Strahan & T. Cadell, 1779; W. E. H. Lecky, *History of European Morals*, 2 vols, London, Longmans, Green & Co., 1869. On the last, see B. C. Southgate, 'W.E.H. Lecky: a mid-nineteenth century contributor to women's history', *History of European Ideas*, 1994, vol. 21, pp. 261–266.
18 Bonnie S. Anderson and Judith P. Zinsser, *A History of Their Own: Women in Europe from Prehistory to the Present*, 2 vols, Harmondsworth, Penguin, 1990, vol. 2, p. xi.
19 Mary Kinnear, *Daughters of Time. Women in the Western Tradition*, Ann Arbor, University of Michigan Press, 1982, p. 6.
20 Anderson and Zinsser, *History*, vol. 2, p. xix (my emphases).
21 Anne Conway, *The Principles of the Most Ancient and Modern Philosophy*, ed. P. Loptson, The Hague, Nijhoff, 1982. Margaret Alic, in *Hypatia's Heritage*, London, Women's Press, 1986, introduces her theme of women in science with an account of Anne Conway; the philosophical assessment is by Richard H. Popkin.
22 Joan Kelly, 'Did Women have a Renaissance?', in *History and Theory: The Essays of Joan Kelly*, Chicago, University of Chicago Press, 1984, pp. 47, 19.
23 Michel Haar, cited by Judith Butler, *Gender Trouble: Feminism and the Subversion of Identity*, London, Routledge, 1990, p. 21.
24 Weedon, *Feminist Practice*, p. 24.
25 Quoted by Weedon, *Feminist Practice*, pp. 66–67.
26 On masculinity, see Michael Roper and John Tosh (eds), *Manful Assertions: Masculinities in Britain since 1800*, London, Routledge, 1991; John Tosh, 'What Should Historians do with Masculinity?', *History Workshop Journal* 38, 1994, pp. 179–202
27 Salman Rushdie, *The Satanic Verses*, quoted by Homi K. Bhabha, *The Location of Culture*, London, Routledge, 1994, p. 6.
28 Ngugi wa Thiong'o, *Decolonising the Mind*, London, James Curry, 1986, p. 94.
29 Quoted by D. R. Kelley, 'Historia Integra: François Baudouin and his

conception of history', *Journal of the History of Ideas*, 1964, vol. 25, p. 53 (my emphasis).

30 Thomas Baker, *Reflections upon Learning*, London, A. Bosvile, 1699, p. 141.

31 Quoted by Brian Easlea, *Witch Hunting, Magic and the New Philosophy*, Brighton, Harvester Press, 1980, p. 140.

32 Quoted by Edward W. Said, *Culture and Imperialism*, London, Chatto & Windus, 1993, p. 327.

33 See Tosh, 'Masculinity', p. 197.

34 Quoted in Said, *Culture and Imperialism*, p. 237

35 Bhabha, *Location*, pp. 70, 44 (citing Frantz Fanon).

36 Frantz Fanon, quoted in P. Williams and L. Chrisman (eds.), *Colonial Discourse and Post-colonial Theory: A Reader*, Hemel Hempstead, Harvester Wheatsheaf, 1994, p. 37.

37 Bernard S. Cohn, 'Representing authority in Victorian India', in E. Hobsbawm and T. Ranger (eds.), *The Invention of Tradition*, Cambridge, Cambridge University Press, 1983, p. 193. Quotation from *Gazette of India*, Extraordinary, 18 August 1876.

38 Lord Lytton, quoted by Cohn in Hobsbawm and Ranger (eds), *Invention*, p. 206; recommendations of a Kenyan Working Committee quoted by Ngugi, *Decolonising*, p. 100.

39 Ngugi, *Decolonising*, p. 3. Cf. p. 91 for his ironic report of recognising 'Jane Austen's characters in the gossiping women of . . . [a] rural African setting'.

40 See newsreport in *The Daily Telegraph*, 2 January 2001.

41 Ashis Nandy, *Traditions, Tyranny, and Utopias*, New Delhi, Oxford University Press, 1987, p. 31.

42 Homi Bhabha, *Location*, pp. 179, 41. Cf. p. 195: 'It is the "rationalism" of these ideologies of progress that increasingly comes to be eroded in the encounter with the contingency of cultural difference.'

43 Cf. Eric Wolf, *Europe and the People without History*, London, University of California Press, 1982.

44 Said, *Culture and Imperialism*, p. 36.

6 WHAT AND WHY? THE FUTURE OF HISTORY

1 Claire Rayner in *The Sunday Times*, 30 May 1993.

2 Michael Keith and Steve Pile (eds), *Place and the Politics of Identity*, London, Routledge, 1993, p. 3.

3 For an account and evaluation of White's thought, see Keith Jenkins, *On 'What is History?' From Carr and Elton to Rorty and White*, London, Routledge, 1995, ch. 5; and *Why History? Ethics and Postmodernity*, London, Routledge, 1999, ch. 5; also Alun Munslow, *Deconstructing History*, London, Routledge, 1997, ch. 8.

4 Hayden White, *Tropics of Discourse: Essays in Cultural Criticism*, Baltimore, Johns Hopkins, 1978, p. 50.

5 Quoted by J. R. Hale (ed.), *The Evolution of British Historiography*, London, Macmillan, 1967, p. 58.

6 Pieter Geyl, *Use and Abuse of History*, New Haven, Yale University Press, 1955, p. 70.
7 Tony Bennett, *Outside Literature*, London, Routledge, 1990, p. 52. Cf. Robert Young: 'Post-modernism can best be defined as European culture's awareness that it is no longer the unquestioned and dominant centre of the world.' *White Mythologies: Writing History and the West*, London, Routledge, 1990, p. 19.
8 F. S. Fussner, *The Historical Revolution: English Historical Writing and Thought, 1580–1640*, London, Routledge & Kegan Paul, 1962.
9 T. S. Eliot, 'Burnt Norton', from 'Four Quartets', in *Collected Poems, 1909–1962*, London, Faber & Faber, 1974, p. 189.
10 Jack Hexter (1954), quoted by Peter Novick, *That Noble Dream: The 'Objectivity Question' and the American Historical Profession*, Cambridge, Cambridge University Press, 1988, p. 375; H. Butterfield, *The Whig Interpretation of History* (1931), Harmondsworth, Penguin, 1973, p. 30.
11 Butterfield, *Whig Interpretation*, pp. 9, 17.
12 H. Butterfield, *The Origins of Modern Science, 1300–1800*, London, G. Bell & Sons, 1949.
13 M. Ruse, quoted by E. Mayr, 'When is historiography Whiggish?', *Journal of the History of Ideas*, 1990, vol. 51, p. 304.
14 Mayr, 'Whiggish', p. 304 (my emphases).
15 Mayr, 'Whiggish', pp. 305–306, 308.
16 Quoted by J. Cottingham, *The Rationalists*, Oxford, Oxford University Press, 1988, p. 108.
17 F. W. Maitland (1895), quoted by P. Geyl, *Use and Abuse of History*, New Haven, Yale University Press, 1955, p. 62.
18 Samuel Gott, *Nova Solyma the Ideal City: or Jerusalem Regained*, London, Typis Joannis Legati, 1648, vol. 1, p. 252 (my emphasis); Homi Bhabha, *The Location of Culture*, London, Routledge, 1994, p. 219 (and cf. p. 253: 'The time-lag of postcolonial modernity moves *forward*, erasing that compliant past tethered to the myth of progress, ordered in the binarisms of its cultural logic: past/present'); John Forrester, *The Seductions of Psychoanalysis: Freud, Lacan and Derrida*, Cambridge, Cambridge University Press, 1990, p. 206.
19 See Elizabeth Deeds Ermarth, *Sequel to History: Postmodernism and the Crisis of Representational Time*, Oxford, Princeton University Press, 1992.
20 Aristotle, *Metaphysics* I, 984a. Cf. *De Anima* A2, 405b1, where Hippo is cited to exemplify 'cruder thinkers'.
21 A. L. Rowse, *Four Caroline Portraits*, London, Duckworth, 1993, Preface.
22 Milan Kundera, *Immortality*, London, Faber, 1992, p. 136.
23 F. Nietzsche, *Untimely Meditations*, transl. R. J. Hollingdale, Cambridge, Cambridge University Press, 1983, pp. 106, 170.
24 See R. V. Sampson, *Equality and Power*, London, Heinemann, 1965, p. 156. The observation is attributed to Lord Morley in 1897, in relation to Machiavelli.

25 Hayden White, *Tropics of Discourse*, London, Johns Hopkins University Press, 1978, p. 126.
26 White, *Tropics*, pp. 142, 33.
27 Martin L. Davies, 'Orpheus or Clio? Reflections on the use of history', *Journal of European Studies*, 1987, vol. 17, pp. 181, 187, 202, 208; 'History as narcissism', *Journal of European Studies*, 1989, vol. 19, esp. pp. 283ff.
28 Francis Bacon, *The New Organon* (1620) I.civ, cxxiv, ed. F. H. Anderson, Indianapolis, Bobbs-Merrill, 1960, pp. 98, 113.
29 W. B. Carpenter, 'Man the interpreter of Nature', Address to the British Association, 1872, in G. Basalla, W. Coleman, and R. H. Kargon (eds), *Victorian Science*, New York, Doubleday, 1970, p. 419 (emphases in original).
30 For such men as J. B. Bury, to call history a 'science' was to emphasise its 'rationality' and so to confer an academic accolade; and Arthur Marwick is still concerned to emphasise the shared '*systematic*' method of science and history – the one being a systematic study of nature, the other a similarly systematic study of the past. (Arthur Marwick, inaugural lecture at the Open University, 5 October 1993.)
31 Quoted by Hale, *Evolution*, p. 36.
32 Thomas Babington Macaulay (Review, 1828), in *Miscellaneous Writings*, ed. T. F. Ellis, 2 vols, London, Longman & Co., 1860, vol. 1, p. 275.
33 Quoted by Hale, *Evolution*, p. 42.
34 Joseph Glanvill, *Scepsis Scientifica* (1665), in Stephen Medcalf (ed.), *The Vanity of Dogmatizing: The Three Versions*, Hove, Harvester Press, 1970, p. 156.
35 Quoted by Hale, *Evolution*, p. 53.
36 Quoted by R. C. Richardson, *The Debate on the English Revolution*, London, Methuen & Co., 1977, p. 81 (my emphases).
37 Clifford Geertz, quoted by G. Spiegel, 'History, historicism, and the social logic of the text in the Middle Ages', *Speculum*, 1990, vol. 65, p. 68.
38 Simon Schama, *Dead Certainties*, London, Granta, 1992, p. 327 (my emphases).
39 Lawrence Stone, referring to *Dead Certainties* in *Past and Present*, 1992, vol. 135, p. 192.
40 See P. Burke (ed.), *New Perspectives on Historical Writing*, Cambridge, Polity Press, 1992, pp. 238–240. Burke's models are respectively Lawrence Durrell, *The Alexandria Quartet* and John Fowles, *The French Lieutenant's Woman*. His approach is paralleled in geography, where postmodernists challenge conventions by 'adopting a fragmentary writing style that is purposefully ambiguous, incomplete and open-ended'. J. Duncan and D. Ley (eds), *Place/Culture/Representation*, London, Routledge, 1993, p. 7.
41 Antony Easthope, 'Romancing the stone: history-writing and rhetoric', *Social History*, 1993, vol. 18, p. 248.
42 T. Zeldin, 'Social and total history', *Journal of Social History*, 1976, vol. 10, p. 243.

43 White, *Tropics*, p. 47; cf. p. 121: 'Although historians and writers of fiction may be interested in differing kinds of events, both the forms of their respective discourses and their aims in writing are often the same.'

44 Thomas Söderqvist, 'Existential projects and existential choice in science: science biography as an edifying genre', in Michael Shortland and Richard Yeo (eds), *Telling Lives in Science: Essays on Scientific Biography*, Cambridge, Cambridge University Press, 1996, pp. 78–79. I am grateful to Thomas Söderqvist for having given me a copy of his interesting paper before publication.

45 Thomas Sprat, *History of the Royal Society* (1667), ed. J. I. Cope & H. W. Jones, London, Routledge & Kegan Paul, 1959, p. 108.

46 At a seminar at the Open University, 6 October 1993.

47 Glenn Burgess, 'On revisionism: an analysis of early Stuart historiography in the 1970s and 1980s', *Historical Journal*, 1990, vol. 33, pp. 622, 623.

48 Mark Cousins, in D. Attridge *et al.* (eds), *Post-structuralism and the Question of History*, Cambridge, Cambridge University Press, 1987, p. 129.

49 Clarendon, *The History of the Rebellion and Civil Wars*, selections, ed. G. Huehns, London, Oxford University Press, 1955, pp. 1–5. Despite his protestations of impartiality, Clarendon's standpoint is indicated by his use of the word 'rebellion' in his title, and is further revealed by the reference on the title-page to 'the happy End, and Conclusion' of the wars 'by the King's blessed Restoration'.

50 Thomas Hobbes, *Behemoth or the Long Parliament* (1682), ed. F. Tonnies, London, Frank Cass & Co., 1969, pp. 2–4. For his earlier political theories, see esp. *Leviathan*, first published in 1651.

51 S. R. Gardiner (ed.), *The Constitutional Documents of the Puritan Revolution, 1625–1660*, Oxford, Clarendon Press, 1906, p. x.

52 Christopher Hill, *The World Turned Upside Down*, London, Temple Smith, 1972, pp. 13, 311.

53 Lawrence Stone, *The Causes of the English Revolution, 1529–1642*, London, Routledge & Kegan Paul, 1972, pp. xi, xiii, 35, 57–58, 146 (my emphasis).

54 Similarly with a supposed entity of 'revolution': 'Does the attempt to impose a common label of "revolution" on many disparate events result in a typology which makes us misunderstand those events by treating them as more generic, and less individual, than they really were?' Conrad Russell, *The Causes of the English Civil War*, Oxford, Clarendon Press, 1990, p. 8.

55 Russell, *Causes*, pp. 13–14, 58, 185, 208. Further page references will be given in the text (with my emphases).

56 One explicit message appears in the concluding chapter, where it is noted among other things that the English 'are still apt to insist (wrongly) that Britain has a single history and a single culture' (p. 214). This is, as we have seen, entirely consistent with a postmodern position.

57 Pierre Droit de Gaillard (1579), quoted by D. R. Kelley, 'Historia

Integra: François Baudouin and his conception of history', *Journal of the History of Ideas*, 1964, vol. 25, p. 35.

58 Martin Davies, 'Narcissism', p. 270, citing Hans Blumenberg.

59 P. Lee, in A. Aldrich (eds.), *History in the National Curriculum*, London, Kogan Page, 1991, pp. 42–46. Within these pages, I have changed the order of some quotations, and in some cases added emphases; but I hope not to have misrepresented Peter Lee's position.

60 Paul Valéry, quoted by White, *Tropics*, p. 36. Because of its infinite potentialities, Valéry concludes that 'history is the most dangerous product evolved from the chemistry of the intellect'.

61 Eric Hobsbawm, *Age of Extremes: The Short Twentieth Century, 1914–1991*, London, Michael Joseph, 1994.

62 Söderqvist, in Shortland and Yeo (eds), *Telling Lives*, p. 47

63 Quoted from Keats's letters by W. Walsh, *The Use of Imagination*, London, Chatto & Windus, 1964, p. 90.

64 Bolingbroke, *Letters on the Study and Use of History* (1752), London, Alexander Murray, 1870, pp. 109–110.

65 F. Nietzsche, *Untimely Meditations*, transl. R. J. Hollingdale, Cambridge, Cambridge University Press, 1983, pp. 144–145 (my emphasis).

66 Alasdair MacIntyre, in R. Rorty, J. B. Schneewind, and Q. Skinner (eds), *Philosophy in History*, Cambridge, Cambridge University Press, 1984, p. 34.

67 Thomas Hobbes, *Body, Man, and Citizen*, ed. R. S. Peters, London, Collier-Macmillan, 1962, p. 51.

68 Antony Easthope, 'Romancing the stone: history-writing and rhetoric', *Social History*, 1993, vol. 18, pp. 248, 246.

POSTSCRIPT

1 G. R. Elton, *Return to Essentials*, Cambridge, Cambridge University Press, 1991, pp. 41, 49, 26.

2 Felipe Fernández-Armesto, *Truth: A History and a Guide for the Perplexed*, London, Bantam, 1997, pp. 7, 8, 162, 226.

3 Richard Evans, *In Defence of History*, London, Granta, 1997.

4 Allan Bloom, *The Closing of the American Mind*, New York, Simon and Schuster, 1987, p. 346.

5 Elizabeth Fox-Genovese and Elisabeth Lasch-Quinn (eds), *Reconstructing History*, London, Routledge, 1999, pp. xvi, xvii, 75.

6 Keith Windschuttle, *The Killing of History: How Literary Critics and Social Theorists are Murdering our Past*, New York, Free Press, 1997, pp. 2, 4, 36.

7 On these developments, see Steven Shapin, *A Social History of Truth. Civility and Science in Seventeenth-Century England*, London, University of Chicago Press, 1994.

8 See also the new genre of 'biofiction', in which distinctions between ('factual') biography and fiction become clouded.

9 Andrew Preston, *The Mail on Sunday*, 7 January 2001.

10 *The Daily Telegraph*, 15 January 2001.

11 *The Daily Telegraph*, 19 June 2000. Subsequent letters to the paper indicate anger at 'the distortion of historical events by Hollywood' and the 'mucking around with our history' (21 June 2000).

12 *The Sunday Telegraph*, 31 December 2000.

13 Brian Edwards, University of the West of England, as reported in *The Metro* (and other sections of the press), 9 January 2001.

14 Jean Hardouin's views are described in *The Gentleman's Magazine*, vol. 4, 1734, pp. 8, 83, 240–241 (a reference for which I am indebted to J. M. Levine, *Dr Woodward's Shield*, p. 328 n. 17). Hardouin's *An Apology for Homer* was published in Paris in 1716, and in English translation one year later. A case of denying more recent history seems to be implied by Nicholas Colson's statement in 1705, that any denier of the Great Fire of London (only some four decades earlier) must be a madman: *A Modest and True Account* . . . , Antwerp, n. p., 1705, p. 21.

15 Relativism and deconstruction have, for example, been described as 'a seedbed for pseudohistory and Holocaust denial' by Michael Shermer and Alex Grobman, *Denying History*, London, University of California Press, 2000, p. 27. And cf. Saul Friedlander: 'The extermination of the Jews of Europe, as the most extreme case of mass criminality, must challenge theoreticians of historical relativism to face up to the corollaries of positions otherwise too easily dealt with on an abstract level.' *Probing the Limits of Representation*, London, Harvard University Press, 1992, p. 2; cf. pp. 4–5. For another discussion, see Alex Callinicos, *Theories and Narratives: Reflections on the Philosophy of History*, Cambridge, Polity, 1995, pp. 65–75.

16 *Denying History*, p. 101. Other definitions refer to the destruction of members of such other minority groups as Gypsies, Jehovah's Witnesses, and homosexuals.

17 Hans Kellner, ' "Never Again" is Now', reprinted in Keith Jenkins (ed.), *The Postmodern History Reader*, London, Routledge, 1997, p. 406 (my emphasis).

18 Quoted by Shermer and Grobman, *Denying History*, p. 110.

19 Richard Evans, as a witness for the Defence, described the trial as 'a victory for historical scholarship' (Lecture at Kingston University, 6 December 2000).

20 David Irving has described himself as 'an historian of worldwide reputation', though referred to by an opponent as exemplifying 'those who murder history'. Shermer and Grobman, *Denying History*, p. 12.

21 Quoted by Anna Green and Kathleen Troup (eds), *The Houses of History: A critical reader in twentieth-century history and theory*, Manchester, Manchester University Press, 1999, p. 230.

22 I rely here on Richard Evans (lecture, 6 December 2000). That Irving was impressed and influenced by personal witnesses concerning Hitler himself, is indicated by his admission, quoted by Shermer and Grobman, *Denying History*, p. 58: 'this was really the seminal point, the seminal experience – to find twenty-five people of education, all of whom privately spoke well of him.'

23 In relation to David Irving's denial of the gas chambers at Auschwitz, the judge referred to 'his dismissal of the eye-witnesses en masse as

liars or as suffering from a mental problem'. As reported in *The Daily Telegraph*, 12 April 2000.

24 The judge concluded that there was 'clear evidence that . . . Irving is anti-Semitic', and that 'he has on many occasions spoken in terms which are plainly racist'. As reported in *The Daily Telegraph*, 12 April 2000.

25 John Keegan in *The Daily Telegraph*, 12 April 2000.

26 In Germany, there is now a law against 'defaming the memory of the dead'. There were calls for David Irving's works to be removed from public libraries in the London borough of Camden in October 2000: *Ham & High*, 20 October.

27 *The Guardian*, 8 January 2000.

28 *The Daily Telegraph*, 12 January 2000 (my emphasis).

29 *The Daily Telegraph*, 27 January 2000.

30 It was only after composing this title that I re-read Geoffrey Elton's *Return to Essentials*, and saw that I had inadvertently appropriated the title of his inaugural lecture of 1968 (which is included in the same volume). I hope that he would not mind this recycling, but fear that he might.

31 Nietzsche, *Untimely Meditations*, transl. R. J. Hollingdale, Cambridge, Cambridge University Press, 1983, p. 66. For my own further views on the purposes for history, see *Why Bother with History?*, Harlow, Longman, 2000.

32 G. R. Elton, *The Practice of History*, London, Fontana, 1969, p. 11.

33 George Eliot, *Middlemarch* (1871–2), London, Oxford University Press, 1947, pp. 12, 218. The assessment of Casaubon is that of the more romantically inclined Will Ladislaw, who decried the historian's 'groping after . . . mouldy futilities' in the archives, in preference to his young bride.

34 I have elsewhere cited, as an example, Annabel Patterson's choice of 'liberalism' as the value to be worked towards through history: see her *Early Modern Liberalism, Cambridge*, Cambridge University Press, 1997.

Further reading

This highly selective list includes books that can be recommended as readable and/or intellectually stimulating on the main issues treated in this book. Most of the cited works include their own bibliographies, and indicate further directions for research.

On the relationships between history, philosophy, and historiography, Michael Bentley, *Modern Historiography: An Introduction*, London, Routledge, 1999, provides a useful introductory survey; Robert Burns and Hugh Rayment-Pickard (eds), *Philosophies of History*, Oxford, Blackwell, 2000, is a wonderful quarry of sources (introduced by the editors) relating to the application of philosophies to history; while for source-material on historians themselves writing about history, see J. R. Hale (ed.), *The Evolution of British Historiography, from Bacon to Namier*, London, Macmillan, 1964; Fritz Stern (ed.), *The Varieties of History from Voltaire to the Present*, 2nd edn, London, Macmillan, 1970; and Donald R. Kelley (ed.), *Versions of History from Antiquity to the Enlightenment*, London, Yale University Press, 1991. In conjunction with the last, and for illuminating commentary, see Donald R. Kelley, *Faces of History: Historical Inquiry from Herodotus to Herder*, London, Yale University Press, 1998; and for one historian's brief survey, with interesting literary and philosophical references, see Pieter Geyl, *Use and Abuse of History*, New Haven, Yale University Press, 1955. On the current challenge of postmodernism in relation to historical study, Keith Jenkins, *Re-Thinking History*, London, Routledge, 1991, provides an exemplary short introduction.

On the nature and purpose of history through the centuries, there are many guides. For the classical period, see Michael Grant, *Greek and Roman Historians: Information and Misinformation*, London, Routledge, 1995; and (still useful) A. J. Toynbee, *Greek Historical Thought*, London, J. M. Dent, 1924. For the early-modern period,

Joseph M. Levine, *Humanism and History: Origins of Modern English Historiography*, Ithaca and London, Cornell University Press, 1987, is a collection of essays concerned with how and why English historiography developed into its modern form; and this can be supplemented by a further collection of Levine's essays in *The Autonomy of History: Truth and Method from Erasmus to Gibbon*, London, University of Chicago Press, 1999; D. R. Woolf, *The Idea of History in Early Stuart England*, London, University of Toronto Press, 1990, is interesting on the political, moral, and educational applications of history at that time. On the development of American historiography, see the detailed and readable account (focused as the subtitle implies) in Peter Novick, *That Noble Dream: The 'Objectivity Question' and the American Historical Profession*, Cambridge, Cambridge University Press, 1988. A sample to bring the story up to date includes J. Appleby, L. Hunt, and M. Jacob, *Telling the Truth about History*, New York, W. W. Norton & Co., 1994; E. H. Carr, *What is History?*, Harmondsworth, Penguin, 1965, which, together with the works of Geoffrey Elton, should be read in conjunction with the critique of Keith Jenkins, *On 'What is History?'*, London, Routledge, 1995; Gordon Connell-Smith and H. A. Lloyd, *The Relevance of History*, London, Heinemann, 1972, includes criticisms of the historical profession which are still relevant, alas; G. R. Elton, *The Practice of History*, London, Fontana, 1967, a classic of the empiricist tradition; G. R. Elton, *Return to Essentials*, Cambridge, Cambridge University Press, 1991, a defence of 'what may appear to be very old-fashioned convictions and practices' (p. 3) against postmodern challenges; Richard J. Evans, *In Defence of History*, London, Granta, 1997, another defence of an essentially modernist position, on which see Keith Jenkins, *Why History?*, listed under 'possible futures', below, ch. 4; Ludmilla Jordanova, *History in Practice*, London, Arnold, 2000, one historian's assessment of the discipline in practice; John Tosh, *The Pursuit of History*, 3rd edn, Harlow, Longman, 2000, a clear exposition concerned with both theory and practice, now usefully updated in the light of postmodernism.

On some interdisciplinary perspectives, R. L. Gregory, *Eye and Brain: The Psychology of Seeing*, 4th edn, London, Weidenfeld and Nicolson, 1990, continues to provide a good, clear introduction to the problems of perception; and still of interest on perception in relation (primarily) to the visual arts is John Berger, *Ways of Seeing*, Harmondsworth, Penguin, 1972, and E. H. Gombrich, *Art and*

Illusion: A Study in the Psychology of Pictorial Representation, London, Phaidon Press, 1962. On language, an account that is both readable and relevant to historians is provided by Walter J. Ong, *Orality and Literacy: The Technologizing of the Word*, London, Routledge, 1982; the braver might try D. Attridge, 'Language as history/history as language', in D. Attridge, G. Bennington and R. Young (eds), *Post-structuralism and the Question of History*, Cambridge, Cambridge University Press, 1987 (a collection that also includes essays on Marxism, Foucault, etc.); on Foucault in this respect see Alec McHoul and Wendy Grace, *A Foucault Primer: Discourse, power and the subject*, London, UCL Press, 1995; and for Foucault in relation specifically to history, Jan Goldstein (ed.), *Foucault and the Writing of History*, Oxford, Blackwell, 1994. For scepticism, the classic is Richard H. Popkin, *The History of Scepticism from Erasmus to Spinoza*, Berkeley and Los Angeles, University of California Press, 1979. See also ch. 4 of Barbara Shapiro, *Probability and Certainty in Seventeenth-Century England*, Princeton, Princeton University Press, 1983; while those interested in getting to the sources should try Sextus Empiricus, *Outlines of Pyrrhonism*, transl. R. G. Bury, London, Heinemann, 1967, and (for the early-modern period) Montaigne's essay 'Apology for Raymond Sebond', in Donald M. Frame (ed.), *The Complete Works of Montaigne*, London, Stanford University Press, 1958, pp. 318–457. The relationship of history with such other disciplines as psychology and sociology is introduced, with actual examples, in Anna Green and Kathleen Troup (eds), *The Houses of History: A critical reader in twentieth-century history and theory*, Manchester, Manchester University Press, 1999 (useful also for introductions on Marxism, feminism, and post-colonialism).

The literature on Marxism, feminism, and post-colonialism is not always marked by its lucidity, but effort can be rewarded by the following: on Marxism, S. H. Rigby, *Marxism and History: A Critical Introduction*, Manchester, Manchester University Press, 1987; Raphael Samuel (ed.), *People's History and Socialist Theory*, London, Routledge, 1981, a collection of essays on such subjects as socialism, oral tradition, African history, feminism, and patriarchy, with a useful theoretical introduction; on feminism, a particularly lucid introduction is provided by Chris Weedon, *Feminist Practice and Poststructuralist Theory*, Oxford, Blackwell, 1987; while the more adventurous could progress to Judith Butler, *Gender Trouble: Feminism and the Subversion of Identity*, London, Routledge, 1990;

Joan Kelly, *Women, History and Theory: The Essays of Joan Kelly*, Chicago, University of Chicago, 1984; Joan Wallach Scott (ed.), *Feminism and History*, Oxford, Oxford University Press, 1996. For a ground-breaking feminist perspective on the early-modern scientific revolution, see Carolyn Merchant, *The Death of Nature: Women, Ecology, and the Scientific Revolution*, San Francisco, HarperCollins, 1980. On post-colonialism, Patrick Williams and Laura Chrisman (eds), *Colonial Discourse and Post-colonial Theory: A Reader*, Hemel Hempstead, Harvester Wheatsheaf, 1993, is an extremely useful collection of texts, with introductions that commendably aim at overall accessibility (and there are links, too, with e.g. Marxism, feminism, Foucault); Edward Said, *Orientalism*, Routledge, 1978, marks a turning- or starting-point for post-colonial studies; and Said's *Culture and Imperialism*, London, Chatto & Windus, 1993, demonstrates, with wide-ranging cultural references, the author's 'attempts at a contrapuntal reading' of history (p. 134). More difficult, but rewarding, are Homi K. Bhabha, *The Location of Culture*, London, Routledge, 1994; and Robert Young, *White Mythologies: Writing History and the West*, London, Routledge, 1990, which includes chapters on Marxism, Foucault, Said, Bhabha, et al.

On possible futures (or not) for history in postmodernity, see Frank Ankersmit and Hans Kellner (eds), *A New Philosophy of History*, London, Reaktion Books, 1995; Alex Callinicos, *Theories and Narratives: Reflections on the Philosophy of History*, Cambridge, Polity, 1995, which includes sections on Fukuyama, Marxism, progress, etc.; Elizabeth Deeds Ermarth, *Sequel to History: Postmodernism and the Crisis of Representational Time*, Princeton, Princeton University Press, 1992, which presents some intellectually exciting ideas on time in postmodernity; Frank Füredi, *Mythical Past, Elusive Future*, London, Pluto, 1992, good on the ideological aspects of history and on future-focus; Keith Jenkins (ed.), The *Postmodern History Reader*, London, Routledge, 1997, an invaluable collection of texts representing the main positions in contemporary debates; Keith Jenkins, *Why History? Ethics and Postmodernity*, London, Routledge, 1999, which includes some helpful introductions to such postmodernists as Derrida, Baudrillard, Lyotard, and Hayden White; Alun Munslow, *Deconstructing History*, London, Routledge, 1997, a clear introduction to current debates; Lutz Niethammer, *Posthistoire: Has History Come to an End?*, transl. Patrick Camiller, London, Verso, 1992; Beverley Southgate,

Why Bother with History?, Harlow, Longman, 2000, which reviews ancient, modern, and postmodern motivations for historical study. The works of Hayden White are central to any consideration of history's relationship with postmodernism: see especially *Metahistory*, Baltimore, Johns Hopkins, 1973; *Tropics of Discourse: Essays in Cultural Criticism*, London, Johns Hopkins, 1978; *The Content of the Form*, Baltimore, Johns Hopkins, 1987.

In relation to pomophobia, for the fear of postmodernism, Keith Windschuttle, *The Killing of History: How Literary Critics and Social Theorists are Murdering our Past*, New York, Free Press, 1997, is an impassioned and highly readable plea to save history (and western culture more generally) from postmodernism; and Elizabeth Fox-Genovese and Elisabeth Lasch-Quinn (eds), *Reconstructing History*, London, Routledge, 1999, represents 'The Emergence of a New Historical Society' in the context of 'the culture wars', and consists of a collection of essays, of varied interest and relevance, but essentially concerned with the maintenance of modernist history.

On Holocaust-denial, literature grows by the day. Deborah Lipstadt, *Denying the Holocaust: The Growing Assault on Truth and Memory*, Harmondsworth, Penguin, 1994, is the work that sparked the David Irving libel trial (on which works will shortly appear); and Michael Shermer and Alex Grobman, *Denying History: Who Says the Holocaust Never Happened and Why Do They Say It?*, London, University of California Press, 2000, tries to understand Holocaust-denial and presents a seemingly unanswerable case against it. At a more theoretical level, Saul Friedlander (ed.), *Probing the Limits of Representation*, London, Harvard University Press, 1992, includes a number of interesting and concerned essays; and Zygmunt Bauman, *Modernity and the Holocaust*, Cambridge, Polity, 1989, should be compulsory reading for anyone concerned with the Holocaust or with our future.

Bibliography

Agrippa, Henricus Cornelius, *Of the Vanitie and Uncertaintie of Artes and Sciences*, English transl., London, Henry Wykes, 1569.

Aldrich, R. (ed.), *History in the National Curriculum*, London, Kogan Page, 1991.

Alexander, William, *The History of Women from the Earliest Antiquity to the Present Time*, 2 vols, London, W. Strahan & T. Cadell, 1779.

Alic, M., *Hypatia's Heritage*, London, Women's Press, 1986.

Anderson, B. S. and Zinsser, J. P., *A History of Their Own: Women in Europe from Prehistory to the Present*, 2 vols, Harmondsworth, Penguin, 1990.

Ankersmit, Frank and Kellner, Hans (eds), *A New Philosophy of History*, London, Reaktion Books, 1995.

Anon., *God's Judgements upon Drunkards, Swearers and Sabbath-Breakers . . .* , London, E. Tyler, 1659.

Appleby, J., Hunt, L., and Jacob, M., *Telling the Truth about History*, New York, W. W. Norton & Co., 1994.

Aristotle, *Metaphysics*, transl. H. Tredennick, London, Harvard University Press, 1933.

Aristotle, *Poetics and Rhetoric*, ed. T. A. Moxon, London, J. M. Dent & Sons, 1953.

Attridge, D., Bennington, G., and Young, R. (eds), *Post-structuralism and the Question of History*, Cambridge, Cambridge University Press, 1987.

Augustine, Saint, *City of God*, transl. John Healey, 2 vols; London, J. M. Dent and Sons, 1945.

Bacon, Francis, *The Advancement of Learning* (1605), London, Oxford University Press, 1951.

Bacon, Francis, *The New Organon* (1620), ed. F. H. Anderson, Indianapolis, Bobbs-Merrill, 1960.

Baker, H., *The Race of Time*, Toronto, University of Toronto Press, 1967.

Baker, Thomas, *Reflections upon Learning*, London, A. Bosvile, 1699.

Basalla, G., Coleman, W., and Kargon, R. H. (eds), *Victorian Science*, New York, Doubleday, 1970.

Bauman, Zygmunt, *Modernity and the Holocaust*, Cambridge, Polity, 1989.

Bayle, Pierre, *An Historical and Critical Dictionary*, English transl., 4 vols, London, C. Harper, 1710.
Becker, C., *The Heavenly City of the Eighteenth-Century Philosophers*, New Haven and London, Yale University Press, 1932.
Bede, *The Ecclesiastical History of the English Nation*, London, J. M. Dent & Sons, 1958.
Bennett, Tony, *Outside Literature*, London, Routledge, 1990.
Bentley, Michael, *Modern Historiography: An Introduction*, London, Routledge, 1999.
Berger, John, *Ways of Seeing*, Harmondsworth, Penguin, 1972.
Beveridge, W. I. B., *The Art of Scientific Investigation*, London, Heinemann, 1957.
Bhabha, Homi K., *The Location of Culture*, London, Routledge, 1994.
Bloom, Allan, *The Closing of the American Mind*, New York, Simon and Schuster, 1987.
Blundevill, Thomas, *The True Order and Methode of Wryting and Reading Hystories . . .*, London, William Seres, 1574.
Bolingbroke, Lord Henry St John, *The Works*, 4 vols, Philadelphia, Carey & Hart, 1841.
Bolingbroke, Lord Henry St John, *Letters on the Study and Use of History* (1752), London, Alexander Murray, 1870.
Boyle, Robert, *The Works*, ed. T. Birch, 6 vols, London, J. & F. Rivington, 1772.
Braithwait, Richard, *A Survey of History*, London, Jasper Amery, 1638.
Burgess, Glenn, 'On revisionism: an analysis of early Stuart historiography in the 1970s and 1980s', *Historical Journal*, 1990, vol. 33, pp. 609–627.
Burke, P. (ed.), *New Perspectives on Historical Writing*, Cambridge, Polity Press, 1992.
Burns, Robert and Rayment-Pickard, Hugh (eds), *Philosophies of History*, Oxford, Blackwell, 2000.
Butler, Judith, *Gender Trouble: Feminism and the Subversion of Identity*, London, Routledge, 1990.
Butterfield, Herbert, *The Origins of Modern Science, 1300–1800*, London, G. Bell & Sons, 1949.
Butterfield, Herbert, *Man on his Past. The Study of the History of Historical Scholarship*, Cambridge, Cambridge University Press, 1955.
Butterfield, Herbert, *The Whig Interpretation of History* (1931), Harmondsworth, Penguin, 1973.
Cahoone, Lawrence (ed.), *From Modernism to Postmodernism: An Anthology*, Oxford, Blackwell, 1996.
Callinicos, Alex, *Theories and Narratives: Reflections on the Philosophy of History*, Cambridge, Polity, 1995.
Camden, William, *Britannia* (1586), English transl., London, George Bishop & John Norton, 1610.
Carlyle, Thomas, *On Heroes, Hero-Worship, and the Heroic in History*, London, Cassell & Co., 1908.
Carr, E. H., *What Is History?*, Harmondsworth, Penguin, 1964.
Charleton, Walter, *Two Discourses, The First, Concerning the Different Wits of Men*, 3rd edn, London, William Whitwood, 1692.

Clarendon, Earl of, *The History of the Rebellion and Civil Wars*, selections, ed. G. Huehns, London, Oxford University Press, 1955.
Collingwood, R. G. (1946) *The Idea of History*, Oxford, Oxford University Press, 1961.
Colson, Nicholas, *A Modest and True Account of the Chief Points in Controversy, Between the Roman Catholicks and the Protestants*, Antwerp, n.p., 1705.
Connell-Smith, Gordon and Lloyd, H. A., *The Relevance of History*, London, Heinemann, 1972.
Conway, Anne, *The Principles of the Most Ancient and Modern Philosophy*, ed. P. Loptson, The Hague, Nijhoff, 1982.
Cottingham, John, *The Rationalists*, Oxford, Oxford University Press, 1988.
Croix, G. E. M. de Ste, *The Class Struggle in the Ancient Greek World*, London, Duckworth, 1981.
Davies, Martin L., 'Orpheus or Clio? Reflections on the use of history', *Journal of European Studies*, 1987, vol. 17, pp. 179–214.
Davies, Martin L., 'History as narcissism', *Journal of European Studies*, 1989, vol. 19, pp. 265–291.
Dion Chrysostom, *Discourses*, transl. J. W. Cohoon, 5 vols, London, Heinemann, 1932.
Douglas, D. C., *English Scholars*, London, Jonathan Cape, 1939.
Duncan, J. and Ley, D. (eds), *Place/Culture/Representation*, London, Routledge, 1993.
Eagleton, Terry, *Literary Theory: An Introduction*, Oxford, Blackwell, 1983.
Easlea, Brian, *Witch Hunting, Magic and the New Philosophy: An Introduction to Debates of the Scientific Revolution, 1450–1750*, Brighton, Harvester Press, 1980.
Easthope, Antony, 'Romancing the stone: history-writing and rhetoric', *Social History*, 1993, vol. 18, pp. 235–249.
Eliot, T. S., *Collected Poems, 1909–1962*, London, Faber & Faber, 1974.
Elton, G. R., *The Practice of History*, London, Fontana, 1969.
Emerson, R. W., *Essays and other Writings*, London, Cassell & Co., 1907.
Ermarth, Elizabeth Deeds, *Sequel to History: Postmodernism and the Crisis of Representational Time*, Princeton, Princeton University Press, 1992.
Evans, Richard J., *In Defence of History*, London, Granta, 1997.
Ferro, Marc, *The Use and Abuse of History, or How the Past Is Taught*, London, Routledge & Kegan Paul, 1984.
Forrester, J., *The Seductions of Psychoanalysis: Freud, Lacan and Derrida*, Cambridge, Cambridge University Press, 1990.
Fox-Genovese, Elizabeth and Lasch-Quinn, Elisabeth (eds), *Reconstructing History*, London, Routledge, 1999.
Foxe, John, *The History of Christian Martyrdom*, ed. J. M. Crombie, London, Gibbings & Co., 1903.
Franklin, J. H., *Jean Bodin and the Sixteenth-Century Revolution in the Methodology of Law and History*, New York, Columbia University Press, 1963.

Friedlander, Saul (ed.), *Probing the Limits of Representation*, London, Harvard University Press, 1992.

Füredi, Frank, *Mythical Past, Elusive Future*, London, Pluto, 1992.

Fussner, F. S., *The Historical Revolution: English Historical Writing and Thought 1580–1640*, London, Routledge & Kegan Paul, 1962.

Galileo, *Dialogue concerning the Two Chief World Systems*, ed. S. Drake, Berkeley, University of California Press, 1970.

Gardiner, S. R. (ed.), *The Constitutional Documents of the Puritan Revolution, 1625–1660*, Oxford, Clarendon Press, 1906.

Geyl, P., *Use and Abuse of History*, New Haven, Yale University Press, 1955.

Gibbon, Edward, *An Essay on the Study of Literature*, London, T. Becket & P. A. De Hondt, 1764.

Giddens, A., *The Class Structure of the Advanced Societies*, London, Hutchinson, 1981.

Glanvill, Joseph, *Scepsis Scientifica* (1665), in Stephen Medcalf (ed.), *The Vanity of Dogmatizing: The Three Versions*, Hove, Harvester Press, 1970.

Goldstein, Jan (ed.), *Foucault and the Writing of History*, Oxford, Blackwell, 1994.

Gombrich, E. H., *Art and Illusion: A Study in the Psychology of Pictorial Representation*, London, Phaidon Press, 1962.

Gott, Samuel, *Nova Solyma the Ideal City: or Jerusalem Regained*, London, Typis Joannis Legati, 1648.

Grafton, A., *Defenders of the Text: The Tradition of Scholarship in an Age of Science, 1450–1800*, Cambridge, Mass. and London, Harvard University Press, 1991.

Grafton, A., *New Worlds, Ancient Texts: The Power of Tradition and the Shock of Discovery*, London, Harvard University Press, 1992.

Gransden, Antonia, *Historical Writing in England, c. 550 to c. 1307*, London, Routledge & Kegan Paul, 1974.

Gransden, Antonia, *Historical Writing in England II, c. 1307 to the Early Sixteenth Century*, London, Routledge & Kegan Paul, 1982.

Grant, Michael, *Greek and Roman Historians: Information and Misinformation*, London, Routledge, 1995.

Green, Alice Stopford, *Woman's Place in the World of Letters*, London, Macmillan, 1913.

Green, Anna and Troup, Kathleen (eds), *The Houses of History: A critical reader in twentieth-century history and theory*, Manchester, Manchester University Press, 1999.

Greenblatt, Stephen, *Learning to Curse: Essays in Early Modern Culture*, London, Routledge, 1990.

Gregory, R. L., *Eye and Brain: The Psychology of Seeing*, 4th edn, London, Weidenfeld & Nicolson, 1990.

Habermas, J., *The New Conservatism: Cultural Criticism and the Historians' Debate*, ed. and transl. S. W. Nicholsen, Cambridge, Polity Press, 1989.

Hale, J. R. (ed.), *The Evolution of British Historiography*, London, Macmillan, 1967.

Hales, John, *Works*, 3 vols, Glasgow, R. & A. Foulis, 1765.

Hanson, N. R., *Patterns of Discovery*, Cambridge, Cambridge University Press, 1961.

Herodotus, *The History*, transl. G. Rawlinson, 2 vols, London, J.M. Dent & Sons, 1910.

Heywoode, Thomas, *Nine Bookes of Various History Concerninge Women*, London, Adam Islip, 1624.

Hill, Christopher, *The World Turned Upside Down*, London, Temple Smith, 1972.

Hobbes, Thomas, translation of Thucydides, *The History of the Grecian War* (1629), 3rd edn, London, D. Brown, 1723.

Hobbes, Thomas, *Body, Man, and Citizen*, ed. R. S. Peters, London, Collier-Macmillan, 1962.

Hobbes, Thomas, *Behemoth, or the Long Parliament* (1682), ed. Ferdinand Tonnies, London, Frank Cass & Co., 1969.

Hobsbawm, Eric, *Age of Extremes: The Short Twentieth Century, 1914–1991*, London, Michael Joseph, 1994.

Hobsbawm, Eric and Ranger, Terry (eds), *The Invention of Tradition*, Cambridge, Cambridge University Press, 1983.

Hope Mason, John, 'Thinking about genius in the eighteenth century', in Paul Mattick (ed.), *Eighteenth-Century Aesthetics and the Reconstruction of Art*, Cambridge, Cambridge University Press, 1993.

Hume, David, *Dialogues concerning Natural Religion*, ed. N. Kemp Smith, Oxford, Clarendon Press, 1935.

Hume, David, 'Of the study of history' (1741), in E. F. Miller (ed.), *David Hume: Essays Moral, Political, and Literary*, Indianapolis, Liberty Classics, 1985.

Jencks, Charles (ed.), *The Post-Modern Reader*, London, Academy Editions, 1992.

Jenkins, Keith, *Re-Thinking History*, London, Routledge, 1991.

Jenkins, Keith, *On 'What is History?'*, London, Routledge, 1995.

Jenkins, Keith, (ed.), *The Postmodern History Reader*, London, Routledge, 1997

Jenkins, Keith, *Why History? Ethics and Postmodernity*, London, Routledge, 1999.

Jones, R. F., *Ancients and Moderns: A Study of the Rise of the Scientific Movement in Seventeenth-Century England*, Berkeley and Los Angeles, University of California Press, 1965.

Jordanova, Ludmilla, *History in Practice*, London, Arnold, 2000.

Josephus, Flavius, *The Wars of the Jews*, transl. W. Whiston, London, J. M. Dent & Sons, 1906.

Karski, Jan, *Story of a Secret State*, London, Hodder & Stoughton, 1945.

Keith, Michael and Pile, Steve (eds), *Place and the Politics of Identity*, London, Routledge, 1993.

Kelley, D. R., 'Historia Integra: François Baudouin and his conception of history', *Journal of the History of Ideas*, 1964, vol. 25, pp. 35–57.

Kelley, D. R. (ed.), *Versions of History from Antiquity to the Enlightenment*, London, Yale University Press, 1991.

Kelley, D., R., *Faces of History: Historical Inquiry from Herodotus to Herder*, London, Yale University Press, 1998.

Kelly, Joan, *Women, History and Theory: The Essays of Joan Kelly*, Chicago, University of Chicago Press, 1984.

Kinnear, Mary, *Daughters of Time. Women in the Western Tradition*, Ann Arbor, University of Michigan Press, 1982.

Kramnick, I. (ed.), *Lord Bolingbroke: Historical Writings*, Chicago, University of Chicago Press, 1972.

Kuhn, T. S., *The Structure of Scientific Revolutions*, Chicago, University of Chicago Press, 1962.

Kundera, Milan, *Immortality*, London, Faber, 1992.

Labalme, P. H. (ed.), *Beyond Their Sex: Learned Women of the European Past*, New York, New York University Press, 1984.

La Mothe Le Vayer, François, *Deux Discours*, Paris, L. Billaine, 1668.

Lecky, W. E. H., *History of European Morals from Augustus to Charlemagne*, 2 vols, London, Longmans, Green & Co., 1869.

Le Moyne, Pierre, *Of the Art Both of Writing and Judging of History*, English transl., London, R. Sare & J. Hindmarsh, 1695.

Levi, Primo, *If This Is a Man*, London, Abacus, 1987.

Levi, Primo, *The Drowned and the Saved*, London, Abacus, 1989.

Levine, J. M., *Humanism and History: Origins of Modern English Historiography*, Ithaca and London, Cornell University Press, 1987.

Levine, J. M., *The Autonomy of History: Truth and Method from Erasmus to Gibbon*, London, University of Chicago Press, 1999.

Lindberg, D. C. and Westman, R. S. (eds), *Reappraisals of the Scientific Revolution*, Cambridge, Cambridge University Press, 1990.

Lipstadt, Deborah, *Denying the Holocaust: The Growing Assault on Truth and Memory*, Harmondsworth, Penguin, 1994.

Livy, Titus, *Roman History*, transl. W. Gordon, Edinburgh, Bell & Bradfute, 1809.

Lowenthal, David, *The Past is a Foreign Country*, Cambridge, Cambridge University Press, 1985.

Macaulay, Catherine Sawbridge, *The History of England*, 8 vols, London, J. Nourse, 1763–1783.

Macaulay, Thomas Babington, *Miscellaneous Writings*, ed. T. F. Ellis, 2 vols, London, Longman & Co., 1860.

Marwick, Arthur, *The Nature of History*, London, Macmillan, 1970.

Marx, Karl, *Selected Writings*, ed. D. McLellan, Oxford, Oxford University Press, 1977.

Mayr, E., 'When is historiography Whiggish?', *Journal of the History of Ideas*, 1990, vol. 51, pp. 301–309.

McHoul, Alec and Grace, Wendy, *A Foucault Primer: Discourse, Power and the Subject*, London, UCL Press, 1995.

McLellan, David, *Marx*, Glasgow, Fontana, 1975.

Megill, Allan, 'The reception of Foucault by historians', *Journal of the History of Ideas*, 1987, vol. 48, pp. 117—141.

Ménage, Gilles, *The History of Women Philosophers* (1690), transl. B. H. Zedler, Lanham, University Press of America, 1984.

Merchant, Carolyn, *The Death of Nature: Women, Ecology, and the Scientific Revolution*, San Francisco, HarperCollins, 1980.

Montaigne, Michel de, 'Apology for Raymond Sebond', in Donald M.

Frame (ed.), *The Complete Works of Montaigne*, London, Stanford University Press, 1958.
Munslow, Alun, *Deconstructing History*, London, Routledge, 1997.
Nandy, Ashis, *Traditions, Tyranny, and Utopias*, Delhi, Oxford University Press, 1987.
Newton, Isaac, *Opticks*, ed. I. B. Cohen, New York, Dover Publications, 1952.
Newton, Isaac, *Principia*, ed. F. Cajori, 2 vols, Berkeley and Los Angeles, University of California Press, 1966.
Ngugi wa Thiong'o, *Decolonising the Mind: The Politics of Language in African Literature*, London, James Curry, 1986.
Niethammer, Lutz, *Posthistoire: Has History Come to an End?*, transl. Patrick Camiller, London, Verso, 1992.
Nietzsche, Friedrich, *On the Advantage and Disadvantage of History for Life*, transl. P. Preuss, Indianapolis, Hackett Publishing Co., 1980.
Nietzsche, Friedrich, *Untimely Meditations*, transl. R. J. Hollingdale, Cambridge, Cambridge University Press, 1983.
Novick, Peter, *That Noble Dream: The 'Objectivity Question' and the American Historical Profession*, Cambridge, Cambridge University Press, 1988.
Oakeshott, M., *On History*, Oxford, Blackwell, 1983.
Orwell, George, *Nineteen Eighty-Four* (1949), Harmondsworth, Penguin, 1987.
Pascal, Blaise, *Pensées*, transl. W. F. Trotter, London, J. M. Dent & Sons, 1931.
Patterson, Annabel, *Early Modern Liberalism*, Cambridge, Cambridge University Press, 1997.
Patrides, C. A., *The Grand Design of God: the lierary forum of the Christian view of history*, London, Routledge & Kegan Paul, 1972.
Plato, *The Dialogues*, transl. B. Jowett, 5 vols, Oxford, Clarendon Press, 1875.
Plumb, J. H., *The Death of the Past*, London, Macmillan, 1969.
Plutarch, *Lives*, transl. J. and W. Langhorne, 6 vols, London, Lackington, Allen & Co., 1803.
Polybius, *The Histories*, transl. E. S. Shuckburgh, with new introduction by F. W. Walbank, 2 vols, Westport, Conn., Greenwood Press, 1974.
Popkin, Richard H., *The History of Scepticism from Erasmus to Spinoza*, Berkeley and Los Angeles, University of California Press, 1979.
Popkin, Richard H., *Isaac La Peyrère (1596–1676). His Life, Work and Influence*, Leiden, E. J. Brill, 1987.
Preston, J. H., 'Was there an Historical Revolution?', *Journal of the History of Ideas*, 1977, vol. 38, pp. 353–364.
Raleigh, Sir Walter, *The History of the World*, London, W. Burre, 1614.
Raleigh, Sir Walter, *The Marrow of History*, abbreviated by Alexander Ross, 2nd edn, London, J. Stephenson, 1662.
Rhys, E. (ed.), *The Growth of Political Liberty: A Source Book of English History*, London, J. M. Dent & Sons, 1921.
Richardson, R. C., *The Debate on the English Revolution*, London, Methuen & Co., 1977.

Rigby, S. H., *Marxism and History: A Critical Introduction*, Manchester, Manchester University Press, 1987.
Rorty, Richard, *Contingency, Irony and Solidarity*, Cambridge, Cambridge University Press, 1989.
Rorty, R., Schneewind, J. B., and Skinner, Q. (eds), *Philosophy in History. Essays on the Historiography of Philosophy*, Cambridge, Cambridge University Press, 1984.
Ross, Alexander, *The History of the World*, London, John Clark, 1652.
Rowse, A. L., *Four Caroline Portraits*, London, Duckworth, 1993.
Russell, Conrad, *The Causes of the English Civil War*, Oxford, Clarendon Press, 1990.
Said, Edward, *Orientalism*, London, Routledge, 1978.
Said, Edward, *Culture and Imperialism*, London, Chatto & Windus, 1993.
Sampson, R. V., *Equality and Power*, London, Heinemann, 1965.
Samuel, Raphael (ed.), *People's History and Socialist Theory*, London, Routledge & Kegan Paul, 1981.
de Saussure, Ferdinand, *Course in General Linguistics* (1916), ed. C. Bally and A. Sechehaye, London, Peter Owen, 1960.
Schama, Simon, *Dead Certainties*, London, Granta, 1992.
Scott, Joan Wallach (ed.), *Feminism and History*, Oxford, Oxford University Press, 1996.
Selden, John, *Historie of Tithes*, London, 1618.
Sextus Empiricus, *Works*, transl. R. G. Bury, London, Heinemann, 1949.
Shapiro, Barbara J., *Probability and Certainty in Seventeenth-Century England*, Princeton, Princeton University Press, 1983.
Shermer, Michael and Grobman, Alex, *Denying History: Who Says the Holocaust Never Happened and Why Do They Say It?*, London, University of California Press, 2000.
Sidney, Sir Philip, *An Apologie for Poetrie* (1595), ed. E. S. Shuckburgh, Cambridge, Cambridge University Press, 1948.
Simon, Richard, *A Critical History of the Old Testament* (1678), English transl., London, Walter Davis, 1682.
Smiles, Samuel, *Self-Help; with Illustrations of Conduct and Perseverance*, London, John Murray, 1890.
Söderqvist, Thomas, 'Existential projects and existential choice in science: science biography as an edifying genre', in M. Shortland and R. Yeo (eds), *Telling Lives in Science: Essays on Scientific Biography*, Cambridge, Cambridge University Press, 1996, pp. 45–84.
Southgate, Beverley, 'W.E.H. Lecky: a mid-nineteenth century contributor to women's history', *History of European Ideas*, 1994, vol. 21, pp. 261–266.
Southgate, Beverley, *Why Bother with History? Ancient, Modern, and Postmodern Motivations*, Harlow, Longman, 2000.
Spiegel, Gabrielle, 'History, historicism, and the social logic of the text in the Middle Ages', *Speculum*, 1990, vol. 65, pp. 59–86.
Spiegel, Gabrielle, 'History and post-modernism', *Past and Present*, 1992, vol. 135, pp. 194–208.
Sprat, Thomas, *History of the Royal Society* (1667), ed. J. I. Cope and H. W. Jones, London, Routledge & Kegan Paul, 1959.

Stephen, Leslie, *The English Utilitarians*, 3 vols, London, Duckworth & Co., 1900.

Stern, F. (ed.), *The Varieties of History from Voltaire to the Present*, New York, Meridian Books, 1956.

Stone, Lawrence, *The Causes of the English Revolution, 1529–1642*, London, Routledge & Kegan Paul, 1972.

Stone, Lawrence, 'History and postmodernism', *Past and Present*, 1992, vol. 135, pp. 189–194.

Thompson, E. P., *The Making of the English Working Class*, Harmondsworth, Penguin, 1968.

Thucydides, *The Peloponnesian War*, transl. R. Crawley, London, J. M. Dent & Sons, 1910.

Toews, J. E., 'Intellectual history after the linguistic turn: the autonomy of meaning and the irreducibility of experience', *American Historical Review*, 1987, vol. 92, pp. 879–907.

Tosh, John, *The Pursuit of History*, 3rd edn, Harlow, Longman, 2000.

Toynbee, A. J., *Greek Historical Thought*, London, J. M. Dent, 1924.

Trevelyan, G. M., *English Social History*, London, Longmans Green & Co., 1944.

Trevor-Roper, Hugh, *The Rise of Christian Europe*, London, Thames & Hudson, 1965.

Vasari, Giorgio, *Lives of the Most Eminent Painters, Sculptors, and Architects* (1550), transl. J. Foster, 5 vols, London, Henry G. Bohn, 1880–1885.

Vico, Giambattista, *The New Science* (1725), transl. T. G. Bergin and M. H. Fisch, Ithaca, Cornell University Press, 1970.

Walsh, W., *The Use of Imagination. Educational Thought and the Literary Mind*, London, Chatto & Windus, 1964.

Walton, Izaak, *The Lives of Dr John Donne; Sir Henry Wotton; Mr Richard Hooker; Mr George Herbert; and Dr Robert Sanderson*, London, Bell & Daldy, 1866.

Weedon, Chris, *Feminist Practice and Poststructuralist Theory*, Oxford, Blackwell, 1987.

Wheare, Degory, *The Method and Order of Reading Both Civil and Ecclesiastical Histories* (1635), transl. E. Bohun, London, Charles Brome, 1685.

White, Hayden, *Metahistory: The Historical Imagination in Nineteenth-Century Europe*, Baltimore, Johns Hopkins University Press, 1973.

White, Hayden, *Tropics of Discourse. Essays in Cultural Criticism*, London, Johns Hopkins University Press, 1978.

White, Hayden, *The Content of the Form*, Baltimore, Johns Hopkins, 1987.

Williams, P. and Chrisman, L. (eds), *Colonial Discourse and Post-colonial Theory: A Reader*, Hemel Hempstead, Harvester Wheatsheaf, 1994.

Windschuttle, Keith, *The Killing of History: How Literary Critics and Social Theorists are Murdering our Past*, New York, Free Press, 1997.

Wolf, Eric R., *Europe and the People without History*, London, University of California Press, 1982.

Woolf, D. R., *The Idea of History in Early Stuart England*, London, University of Toronto Press, 1990.

Young, Robert, *White Mythologies: Writing History and the West*, London, Routledge, 1990.

Zeldin, T., 'Social and total history', *Journal of Social History*, 1976, vol. 10, pp. 237–245.

Index

Aborigines 54, 70–1
Abraham 59
Actium, battle of 58
Acton, Lord 25, 166 n. 61
Adam 75, 85
Africa 7, 54, 112–13; history of 54; South 48, 112–13
Agamemnon 15
Agrippa, Henricus Cornelius 86–7
Alban, Saint 44, 164 n. 35
Alberto 69–70
Albinus, Abbot 43
Alcibiades 16
Alexander the Great 97
Alexander, William 101
Algeria 110
Alphonso, King of Spain 31
Amazons 107, 163 n. 16
America 48, 53–4, 69; Americans 155; government policy 108; historians 101, 118; Historical Association 24; Indians 69, 108–9
Antony, Mark 58
Anytus 125
Aristotle 14–19, 94, 118, 123–5; Aristotelian 58, 128; Aristotelianism 17, 70, 118, 128, 130–1
Ascham, Roger 21
Astell, Mary 101
Athens 20; Athenians 33, 68
Atlantis 69, 97
Attridge, Derek 77
Auden, W. H. 64
Augustine, Saint 42
Augustus, Emperor (previously Octavian) 58
Auschwitz 35, 69, 152, 155, 158, 177 n. 23
Australia 54, 70
Austria 71

Bacon, Francis 8, 17–18, 24, 127–8; Baconianism 18, 24–5, 126–8
Baker, Thomas 107
Ballard, George 101
Bantu 112
Baudouin, François 107
Bayle, Pierre 88
Beauvoir, Simone de 106
Becker, Carl 89
Bede, The Venerable 42–5
Behn, Aphra 102
Bennett, Tony 117–18
Bhaba, Homi 122–3
Bible 46, 49, 75, 84–6, 88, 135, 169 n. 40; Biblical criticism 49, 84–6
biography 39–41, 73, 131, 142
Bismarck, Otto von 51
Blake, William 128
Bloom, Allan 149
Blundevill, Thomas 21
Bolingbroke, Lord Henry St. John 49, 59–60, 86, 88–9, 143, 169–70, nn. 49, 50
Bone, John 42
Boyle, Robert 83, 139
Braithwait, Richard 36–8

Brazil 69
Brecht, Bertolt 97
Brodie, Miss Jean 77
Burckhardt, Jacob 74
Burgess, Glenn 132
Burke, Peter 130
Bury, J. B. 19, 26
Butterfield, Herbert 3, 119, 121

Caesar, Julius 58, 73, 97
Calvin, John 118
Camden, William 21
canon 118, 123–5
Carlyle, Thomas 41, 128–30
Carpenter, William 127
Carr, E. H. 28, 73
Carthaginians 68
categorisation 7, 67–8, 106, 111, 123–31, 137, 140
causes 16, 39, 104, 129, 134–40; causality 121, 132–3; causation 46, 57–8, 80, 89, 129–30, 137–8
Cavendish, Margaret 102–3
chance 57–61, 81, 94
Charlemagne 51
Charles I, King 138
Charles V of France 99
Charleton, Walter 18
Charybdis 84
China, history of 85
Christ, Jesus 42, 122, 125, 153
Christianity 6–7, 39, 42–8, 85–6, 108, 122, 156; Christians 49; 'honorary' Christians 39
Christine de Pisan 99
chronology 118–23, 136, 140; constraints of 103–4, 143
Churchill, Sir Winston 52
Cintho, Giraldo 17
Cixous, Hélène 99, 105
Clarendon, Earl of 134–5
Clark, Sir George 90
Cleopatra 58
Clio (Muse of History) 126, 130, 140, 154
Cohn, Bernard 111
Collingwood, R. G. 42
Collins, Michael 151
Columbus, Christopher 54, 112
Comte, Auguste 24
Condorcet, Antoine Nicolas 23
contingency 57–61, 72, 98, 105–6, 112, 117, 137–8, 172 n. 42
Conway, Anne 103
Copernicus 122; Copernicanism 70, 155
Cousins, Mark 3
Cratylus 75–6
Crusades 49
Cuthbert, Saint 45

Darwin, Charles 24–5, 94; Darwinism 120
data 8, 13, 16, 18–19, 25, 51, 63–72, 78–9, 120, 122, 126–8, 132, 137, 145, 157
Davies, Martin 126–7, 140–1, 144
Derrida, Jacques 5, 160 n. 11
detachment 4, 25–8, 74, 80, 83, 136, 156
Diggers 97, 136
Diocletian, Emperor 44
Diodorus Siculus 107
Dion Chrysostom 50–1, 153
Dionysius of Halicarnassus 35–6, 163 n. 13
'docudrama' 2, 150–1
dogmatism 9, 21, 83–4, 89, 117, 131, 134, 137, 139

Eagleton, Terry 5–6
Eakins, David 54
Easthope, Anthony 80, 130, 144
economics 94–6, 102, 107–8
education 9, 11, 38, 60, 77, 140–7
Egypt 58, 152
Eliot, George 126–7, 130, 159
Eliot, T. S. 118, 121
Elizabeth I, Queen 21, 46, 122; Elizabethan Poor Law 118
Elton, G. R. 3, 26–7, 148, 159, 178 n. 30
Emerson, Ralph Waldo 62, 64
empowerment 10, 57–61, 140–7
Engels, Friedrich 94
England 45, 51, 71–2, 87, 103, 122, 128, 134, 137, 139, 159; history of 43, 52–3, 80, 99;

insularity 136; language of 77; newspapers 48; people 76, 97–8, 107
Enlightenment 4, 22–3, 49, 126, 128
entertainment, history as 30–1
Epicureanism 142
Ermarth, Elizabeth Deeds 123
Europe 7, 22–3, 48, 51, 53, 56, 69, 71, 87, 108, 110–13, 122, 137, 177 n. 15; Eurocentrism 7, 23, 54, 69–70, 107–13; Europeanisation 46; European Union 56
Evans, Sir Arthur 152
Evans, Richard 149, 157, 177 n. 19
examples in history 35–41, 142, 163 nn. 16, 19, 164 n. 25

facts 2–3, 8, 13, 17, 19, 23, 26–8, 62, 66–8, 71–2, 74, 78, 89–90, 126, 143, 149, 156, 167 n. 13, 170 n. 52
Fanon, Frantz 110–11
feminism 11, 91, 99–106, 113–15, 124, 145
Fernández-Armesto, Felipe 148
Ferro, Marc 52
fiction 2, 50, 60, 79, 88, 115–16, 128–31, 150–3, 175 n. 43, 176 n. 8
Fifth Monarchists 136
Fontenelle, Bernard de 19
Forrester, John 123
Foucault, Michel 80–1, 168 n. 33
Foxe, John 45
France 51, 87–9, 97, 110; French language 76
Friedlander, Saul 177 n. 15
Froude, J. A. 89, 129
Fukuyama, Francis 98
Fuller, Thomas 73
Fussner, F. S. 118
future 10, 19–20, 33, 36, 39, 52, 56–61, 80, 92–3, 97–9, 101, 106, 114, 116–23, 134, 136, 140–7, 158–9; future-focus 140–7

Galliard, Pierre Droit de 140–1
Galileo 58, 70, 92
Gardiner, S. R. 27, 136
geography 6–7, 13, 122, 174 n. 40; parameters of 136–7, 140
Germany 35, 52, 73, 151; Germans 48, 51, 73
Geyl, Pieter 52, 117
Gibbon, Edward 1–2, 12, 72–3, 128, 161 n. 11
Gilbert, William 58
Glanvill, Joseph 104–5, 129, 138
God (Christian) 21, 25, 39, 42–9, 75–6, 85–6, 128, 134–5; gods (non-Christian) 20, 44, 48; *see also* Providence
Golden Age 77
Gott, Samuel 122
Greece 36, 82, 113, 152; history of 99; people of 11, 32–3, 40, 50
Green, Alice Stopford 101
Green, J. R. 96
Grobman, Alex 154

Haar, Michel 104
Hale, John 27–8
Hardouin, Jean 153
Harris, 'Bomber' 52
Hegel 3, 167 n.13
Herbert, George 40
'heritage industry' 150–2
Herodotus 17, 32, 35–7, 163 n. 5
heroes 41, 123, 136; German 51
Higden, Ranulphus 32
Hill, Christopher 136
Himmelfarb, Gertrude 149
Hippo 123–4, 173 n. 20
Hippocrates 19–20
history, abuse of 49–54, 60, 110, 154, 177 n. 11; contemporary 11, 88, 143–4; 'old model' 9, 13–29, 99, 115, 134
Hitler, Adolf 51, 156–7
Hobbes, Thomas 6, 33, 135, 144
Hobsbawm, Eric 142, 156
Holocaust 2, 148, 153–8, 177 n. 15
Homer 15, 30, 50–1, 144, 153
hubris 32–3, 59, 75
Hume, David 30, 128–9
hypotheses 8, 10, 19, 23, 68, 83, 117, 131–40, 150, 161 n. 15

ideology 2, 6–8, 50–7, 76, 79–81, 93, 98, 107, 142, 155–6, 160 n. 11
imagination 16–19, 30, 115–17, 123, 125–31, 154
impartiality 27, 88, 175 n. 49
imperialism 7, 33, 48, 54, 107–13
India 97, 111–12
interpretation 8, 66–8, 121–2, 126, 133, 145
Ireland 137, 140, 150–1
Irving, David 153–8, 177–8 nn. 20–4, 26
Israel 69
Italy 51, 87

Jackson, Stonewall 41
James I, King 122, 139
James, William 70–1
Japan 112
Jaurès, Jean 97
Jenkins, Keith 10, 154
Jerome, Saint 86
Jerusalem 7
Jews 67, 71, 154, 177 n. 15; history of 34, 42, 46
Johnson, Dr 62, 101
Josephus, Flavius 34–5, 46
Joyce, James 68, 130
judgement 18, 130; freedom of 88; historical 3, 137; suspension of 83; value- 120

Kant, Immanuel 49
Karski, Jan 35
Keats, John 143
Keegan, John 156
Keith, Michael 115
Kellner, Hans 154
Kelly, Joan 104
Kolakowski, L. 93
Kruschev, President Nikita 52
Kundera, Milan 125

La Mothe Le Vayer, François 87–9
language 5–8, 11, 18, 56, 74–81, 91, 103–6, 115, 133; French 76; private 92
Larkin, Philip 122
Lecky, W. E. H. 101
Lee, Peter 140–1
Leibniz, G. W., Baron von 121
Le Moyne, Pierre 31, 34, 87–9
Leonardo da Vinci 66
Levellers 97, 136
Levi, Primo 35, 67–8, 72
Lévi-Strauss 50
linguistics 5, 62, 74–81, 89, 91; 'linguistic turn' 74, 78
Lipstadt, Deborah 153, 157
literature 79; literary studies 5
Livingstone, David 41
Livy 31, 36, 48, 50
Lucian of Samosata 13, 74
Luther, Martin 52
Luxembourg 56
Lycon 125

Macaulay, Catherine Sawbridge 99–101
Macaulay, Thomas Babington 96, 128–30
Maitland, Frederic 122
Manichaeism 67, 151, 167 n.7
maps 6–7
Marwick, Arthur 3
Marx, Karl 93–8; Marxism 3, 11, 91, 93–9, 102, 113-15, 124, 145
Mary, Queen 45–6
masculinity 106, 110
Masham, Damaris 101
mathematics 4, 22
Mather, Cotton 48
Matisse, Henri 112
Mayr, Ernst 120–1
meaning 5, 34, 50, 63–72, 77–9, 105, 109, 116, 124, 133, 145–7; meaninglessness 116, 121, 145
mechanism: conception of nature 4, 102; method 16, 19, 126; model for explanation 22–7; model for society 80; of perception 63–74
Meletus 125
Melian dialogue 33
Ménage, Gilles 101
Merchant, Carolyn 102
Middle Ages 12, 22, 42–3, 67, 73, 103–4, 153; feudalism 94–6; history 167 n. 15; maps 6–7; world 84

miracles 44–5
modernism 11, 104, 131 148–9, 155; modern world 84
Mommsen, Theodor 72–3, 168 n. 19
Montaigne, Michel de 155
moral teaching 32–48, 140–2
Moses 84–5
Muggletonians 136

narrative 22–3, 97, 106–8, 112–16, 122, 128–31, 134, 136, 146, 154
Nazism 52, 154, 156, 158; concentration camps 67; SS 67
Neale, W. and M. 120
Newton, Isaac 19, 22, 83–4; Newtonian mechanics 13
Ngugi wa Thiong'o 107
Nietzsche, Freidrich 125, 144,158–9
Nicolle, Charles 57
Noah 69
Nothelm 43
Novick, Peter 54

Oakeshott, Michael 72–3
objectivity 3, 7–10, 13, 23–9, 51, 54, 62, 74, 92, 130, 134, 149
Octavian *see* Augustus
Odysseus 144
optimism 5, 13, 23, 25
order 105; in history 139; in nature 4; moral 32–8; world 105
Orpheus 127
Orwell, George 56–7, 60, 158
Oswald, King 44

Paine, Thomas 86
Parker, Samuel 19
Pascal, Blaise 58
Patrizzi, Francesco 87
perception 91, 119–21, 127, 135; alternative 91, 109, 112, 123, 143, 155; theories of 11, 16, 63–74, 77, 115
Persians 32–3, 50–1
pessimism 25, 139
Peyrère, Isaac la 84–5
philosophy 1–5, 13, 35, 42, 62, 82–91, 93, 115, 128; history of 124, 144; and history 1–12; of history 2, 54, 62, 160 n. 11; of science 3
physics 4, 13, 25, 133
Picasso, Pablo 112
Pilate, Pontius 125
Pile Steve 115
Planck, Max 25
Plato 1, 10, 12–13, 30, 39, 60, 63, 75, 91, 106, 146, 150
Plumb, J. H. 14
Plutarch 40
poetry 87, 102, 105, 122; and history 15–19, 87, 125–31, 133, 161 n. 11
politics 2, 50–7, 60–1, 81, 119–20, 126, 140–2, 166 n. 68
pomophobia 148–53
post-colonialism 7, 11, 54, 91, 107–15, 124, 145
postmodernism 4–10, 82, 88–90, 103, 105, 114–59, 173 n. 7
power 8, 60–1, 75, 80–1, 96, 104–6, 110; of ideas 94
Presocratics 82
probability, degrees of 83–4, 89, 150
progress 4–5, 22–7, 42, 101–2, 108, 113, 119, 172 n. 42, 173 n. 18; progressiveness 103–4, 119, 122–3
Providence 20, 25, 39, 42–8, 135
psychology 4, 11, 20, 62–74, 82, 90–1
Puritanism 136
Pyrrho of Elis 83
Pyrrhonism 82–4; Historical 86–90

Raleigh, Sir Walter 46–8, 58, 143
Rampton, Richard 157
Ranke, Leopold von 23–4, 28, 72–3, 155
Rayner, Claire 115, 117, 132, 144, 154
reason 18, 83, 102, 113, 125–31, 143; rationalism 104, 172 n. 42
Reformation 45, 52
reinterpretation 68–72, 98
relativism 6–7, 28, 77, 81, 83, 91–2, 105, 112-13, 145, 177 n. 15

Renaissance 36, 40, 48, 66, 83; feminist analysis of 103–4
revolution 66, 96, 145, 175 n. 54; Copernican 118; English 132, 134–40; French 23, 52, 97, 99; historical 118; intellectual 10, 72, 118; Russian 52; scientific 21–2, 102; theological 84–6
Reynolds, Joshua 41
Richard III, King 73
Riebeek, Jan van 112
Romanticism 128–30
Rome 36, 43, 48, 60, 72; Romans 11, 34, 40, 68; Empire 44, 49, 58, 72, 166 n. 66; history of 31, 40, 99
Rorschach ink-blot test 66, 79, 145
Ross, Alexander 54–6
Rowse, A. L. 124–5
Royal Society 84, 88, 104, 127, 131
Rushdie, Salman 107
Russell, Conrad 137–40

Said, Edward 114
Samuel, Raphael 3
Sartre, Jean-Paul 110
Saussure, Ferdinand de 76
scepticism 8, 11, 82–90, 92, 115, 129, 154; ancient 82–3; early-modern 21, 83–4, 131, 150
Schama, Simon 130
science 4–5, 14–15, 19, 21, 23, 25–6, 42, 70, 83–4, 88, 92, 104, 113, 120, 131, 146; and history 19–29, 155, 174 n. 30; history of 103, 119–21; methods of 19–21, 24–5
scientism 23–4, 26, 127–8; aspirations of 14, 19–27
scientists 27, 88–9, 120, 131, 134, 150
Scotland 137, 140
Scott, Sir Walter 128–30
Scylla 84
secularisation 25, 48–50
Selden, John 58–9, 166 n. 68
selection 8, 25, 28, 63–6, 71–2, 120
self 105, 110; -awareness 1, 10, 12, 59, 146; -consciousness 4, 8, 21, 24, 32, 59, 86, 96–7, 104, 110–11, 138, 142–3; -creation 142, 144–7; -importance 125; -indulgence 117; -knowledge 63, 140, 158; and others 109–12; -reflexivity 2, 10, 141
senses 82–4, 127, 156
Sextus Empiricus 83
Shakespeare, William 129
Shermer, Michael 154
Sidney, Sir Philip 16, 87
Simon, Richard 85–6, 88
Slater, John 14
Smiles, Samuel 41
Smohalla 108
Socrates 8, 39, 125
Söderqvist, Thomas 131, 142
Sophocles 16
space, representation of 6–7; constraints of 76
Spain 51; conquistadors of 107
Spark, Muriel 77
Spartans 33, 68
Spiegel, Gabrielle 79
Spielberg, Steven 151
Sprat, Thomas 84, 88–9, 131, 134
Stalin, Joseph 53, 158, 165 n. 51; Stalinist theme-park 152
Stanley, Sir Henry Morton 165 n. 50
Ste Croix, G. E. M. de 98
Stephen, Leslie 2–3, 124–5
Stephenson, George 41
Stone, Lawrence 80, 136–8
Stubbs, William 2, 117
Switzerland 72

Tacitus 36, 153
Thailand 152
theology 45, 48–9, 59
theory 2, 21–2, 26, 36, 62, 74, 146, 148; literary 5; medical 19–21; political 51–2
Thompson, E. P. 97–8
Thucydides 15, 19–21, 32–3, 35–7, 98, 163 n. 5; 'Dame' 99–100
tithes 59
Tolstoy, Leo 1
Tosh, John 28–9, 54, 110
Trevelyan, G. M. 129–30

Trevor-Roper, Hugh 23
Trimble, David 151
Trotsky, Leon 52, 165 n. 50
truth 5, 8–10, 13–29, 32, 34–5, 38–9, 45–6, 62, 65, 69, 75–84, 88–91, 117, 128–30, 134–5, 138, 143, 148–58

USA *see* America
USSR 73

Vasari, Giorgio 40
Vico, Giambattista 128
Victorian period 41, 122
Vietnam 53–4
Vives, Juan Luis 51, 56
Voltaire 48–50, 126

Walton, Izaak 40–1
war 55–6; American, of Independence 151; English civil 134–40; Peloponnesian 20, 33; Persian 32; Trojan 15, 30, 50; Vietnam 53–4; World I 48, 81; World II 35, 52–3, 64, 154, 156
Wedgewood, Josiah 41
Weedon, Chris 105
Wheare, Degory 38–9
Whiggism 119–20, 125
White, Hayden 115–17, 125, 130–1
Windschuttle, Keith 149
witnesses 13, 20–1, 35, 43, 45, 156–8
Woolf, Virginia 99
Wotton, William 41

Xenophon 163 n. 5
Xerxes 32

York Minster 48

Zaire 165 n. 50
Zeldin, Theodore 130